SOUND AND VISION

The Music Video Reader

Edited by
Simon Frith, Andrew Goodwin
and Lawrence Grossberg

London and New York

First published 1993
by Routledge
11 New Fetter Lane, London EC4P 4EE

Simultaneously published in the USA and Canada
by Routledge Inc.
29 West 35th Street, New York, NY 10001

© 1993 Simon Frith, Andrew Goodwin and Lawrence Grossberg

Typeset in 10 on 12 point Times by
Megaron, Cardiff
Printed in Great Britain by
T J Press (Padstow) Ltd, Padstow, Cornwall

British Library Cataloguing in Publication Data

A catalogue record for this book is available from the British Library

Library of Congress Cataloging in Publication Data

Sound and vision : the music video reader / edited by Simon Frith,
Andrew Goodwin, and Lawrence Grossberg.
p.   cm.
Includes bibliographical references and index.
1. Music videos.   I. Frith, Simon.   II. Goodwin, Andrew
III. Grossberg, Lawrence.
PN1992.8.M87S68   1993
791.45′75--dc20   92-25419

ISBN 0–415–09430–5   ISBN 0–415–09431–3 (pbk)

SOUND AND VISION

Music video is one of the most important emergent cultural forms in contemporary popular culture. It has had a profound impact both on music, fashion and youth culture, and on the codes and forms that operate across television, film and advertising. But until now criticism has denied the specific nature of the form and its cultural history. *Sound and Vision* is the first significant collection of new and classic texts on video and brings together some of the leading international cultural and music critics writing today.

Addressing one of the most controversial forms of popular culture in the contemporary world, the book confronts easy interpretations of music television – as promotional vehicles, filmic images, postmodern culture – to offer a new and bold understanding of its place in pop music, television and the media industries. Moving debates on from such early preoccupations as whether videos are promotions of songs or simply mini-films, or whether they represent the destruction or the salvation of pop music, *Sound and Vision* acknowledges the history of the commercial status of pop music as a whole, as well as its complex relations with other media, to offer a new and refreshing interpretation which takes both terms – music and video – seriously. *Sound and Vision* will be an essential text for students of popular music and popular culture.

The editors: Lawrence Grossberg is Professor of Speech Communications and Criticism and Interpretive Theory at the University of Illinois. Simon Frith is Professor of English at Strathclyde University and co-director of the John Logie Baird Centre. Andrew Goodwin is Associate Professor of Communication Arts at the University of San Francisco.

The contributors: Jody Berland, Mark Fenster, Simon Frith, Andrew Goodwin, Lawrence Grossberg, Lisa Lewis, Kobena Mercer, Leslie Savan, Will Straw, Robert Walser.

CONTENTS

CONTENTS

NOTES ON CONTRIBUTORS

Jody Berland teaches Cultural Studies in the Department of Humanities, Atkinson College, York University, Toronto.

Mark Fenster is a visiting lecturer in Telecommunications at Indiana University.

Simon Frith is Professor of English at Strathclyde University and co-director of the John Logie Baird Centre.

Andrew Goodwin is Associate Professor of Communication Arts at the University of San Francisco.

Lawrence Grossberg is Professor of Speech Communications and Criticism and Interpretive Theory at the University of Illinois.

Lisa A. Lewis is the author of *Gender Politics and MTV: Voicing the Difference* and editor of *The Adoring Audience: Fan Culture and Popular Media* also published by Routledge (1992). She lives in Los Angeles where she is peddling her feature script about the life of nineteenth-century musician, Clara Schumann.

Kobena Mercer is Assistant Professor of Art History at the University of California at Santa Cruz.

Leslie Savan writes the Op-Ad column, a pioneering critique of television advertising for the *Village Voice*.

Will Straw is Program Coordinator of Film Studies in the School for Studies in Art and Culture at Carleton University, Ottawa.

Robert Walser is Associate Professor of Music at Dartmouth College. He holds doctoral degrees in musicology and musical performance from the University of Minnesota, and he has performed professionally on guitar and trumpet in many countries.

ACKNOWLEDGEMENTS

Earlier versions of Jody Berland's article were published in *Parachute* 41 (Montreal, December–January 1985–6) and subsequently in the *Journal of Communication Inquiry*, vol. 10, no. 2, 1986.

Leslie Savan's contribution combines three columns which originally appeared in the *Village Voice*, on 8 September 1987, 22 March 1988 and 14 March 1989, respectively.

Kobena Mercer's essay was first published in *Screen*, vol. 27, no. 1, 1986.

Will Straw and Mark Fenster's articles originally appeared in *Popular Music*, 7/3 (1988), published by Cambridge University Press.

Lisa Lewis's article was first published in *Communication*, vol. 9, 1987.

INTRODUCTION

Andrew Goodwin and Lawrence Grossberg

Music television deserves serious attention from students of popular culture. We attempt to begin that task in this book, by bringing together a variety of approaches (many of them written specifically for this volume) that highlight the necessarily interdisciplinary nature of the work, whilst paying particular attention to the most debilitating neglect in music video research: the absence of attention to the music itself, and its location within the pop music industry.

Thus far, the study of music television has been dominated by research which originates beyond the parameters of popular music studies. Whether in the analysis of individual promotional video clips or in the study of televisual packages, much MTV (Music Television) work in this field has emerged from the disciplines of film studies, mass communications or literary theory, and from theoretical concerns with postmodernism and psychoanalytic theory. This is not the place to rehearse our reservations about much of this work (a critique that is addressed in the following pages by Andrew Goodwin, and – more obliquely – by Will Straw and Robert Walser). We do point out, however, that this collection differs in one central respect from nearly all the work published on music television so far: its concerns originate in the contributors' understanding of the place of music video in the popular music industry, and the social relations of production and consumption that centre on that cultural apparatus.

As Will Straw makes clear in the first chapter of this anthology, music videos and their relation to postmodernism can be explained in terms of an analysis of developments internal to the music and its culture. Straw locates the emergence of MTV in the context of the emergence of a new pop mainstream in the early 1980s. Both of these interdependent changes themselves were shaped by the music industry's attempts to respond to particular problems. These responses, which reshaped the roles of career and biography, celebrity and glamour, allow a more concrete understanding of the apparent proximity of music videos and postmodernist descriptions.

Jody Berland continues the logic of this argument by exploring the paradoxical relationship that exists between the image and the sound in music videos. Focusing on the symbol of the guitar in rock culture, she considers the historically changing relations between image and sound as tropes of new relations within the culture of popular music between music and technology, and community and space.

Andrew Goodwin addresses some of the more general limitations of the cultural studies approach to music television inspired by postmodern theory, and offers in its place a textual reading of the most widely discussed site of video distribution (MTV) that considers its historical development and the possibilities for counter-readings that defy the orthodox academic 'line' on MTV.

Simon Frith's consideration of the marketplace and audience research data on music television in a European context reveals the importance, for the analysis of music video, of the broadcaster's search for new audiences; and the centrality of changing notions of 'youth culture'. Embedded in these processes is an old debate – the question of whether television addresses its audience as citizen or consumer. While critics familiar with MTV and MTV Europe might assume that the latter has long since won out over the former, the British experience does suggest the possibility of alternatives.

Leslie Savan's US-based experience, as a writer for the *Village Voice*, unsurprisingly stresses the commercial basis of rock's new mass-mediated appeals. Here were have collected together three of her *Voice* 'Op Ad' columns, respectively dealing with Laurie Anderson, VH-1 (MTV's sister channel, established in 1985 to reach an older audience) and – inevitably – Madonna. While recent cultural studies' criticism has tended to focus on the transgressive and liberatory features of Madonna's career, Savan's article is a welcome reminder of some of the less empowering aspects of her work.

In Part III of this book, we offer four exemplary attempts to read the music video clips themselves. Kobena Mercer integrates his reading of Michael Jackson's *Thriller* tape into an account of the star-imagery associated with Jackson through his music and public, mass-mediated *persona*. Mark Fenster, on the other hand, looks at a much-neglected form: promotional videos which sell country music.

While Lisa Lewis considers the possibilities for proto-feminist uses of MTV clips, Robert Walser's account of heavy-metal clips offers a similarly complex attempt to refuse simple accounts of 'sexism' in music television. Both chapters wrestle with difficult issues of representation and sexuality, and both authors suggest an approach which transcends the limitations of content analysis studies of 'stereotypes' in music video. While music video's critics have been quick to register complaints about MTV's representations of sexuality, both Lewis and Walser argue that this new form is more complex and nuanced than popular criticism (and some academic scholars) imply. A particular strength of Walser's paper is his grasp of the music itself (he is a guitarist, as well as a scholar) and his ability to demonstrate concrete textual links between sound and vision.

Finally, Lawrence Grossberg returns to the themes raised by Straw, Berland and Goodwin, arguing that the particular forms and power of music video which emerged in the 1980s are icons of a new media economy, of a new ratio between sound and vision, within the disparate spaces of rock culture. This new economy, he argues, can be seen within the visual imagery itself by comparing, for example, different movies oriented to the rock audience. Ultimately, this new economy represents the decline of the ideology of authenticity and the emergence of new forms of relations between fans and their music.

Our aim in this book is thus two-fold: to provide a set of readings that may be used in teaching about music television in a broad and open-ended fashion, and at the same time to collect those analyses which have helped to move the study of music television forward, along with some new pieces which suggest future lines of research.

Part I

THE CONTEXT OF MUSIC VIDEOS

1

POPULAR MUSIC AND POST-MODERNISM IN THE 1980s

Will Straw

One of the striking things about recent writing on music video is its pivotal and symptomatic role within a number of disciplinary and theoretical realignments upon the larger terrain of cultural theory. At one level, music television is the latest in a succession of privileged examples invoked in the elaboration of scenarios about the development of the media and culture within late capitalist societies, joining a long list that has included jazz music and advertising. As well, the particular set of theoretical discourses brought to bear on music video signals new alliances and convergences across and within various disciplinary boundaries. It is to a significant extent within studies of music video that the internal crises and territorial disputes which currently mark film theory, television studies, the debate over postmodernism and the sociology of popular music are being foregrounded. Seen from a somewhat different light, recent treatments of music video represent the entry of post-structuralist thought into the American social sciences, where it has converged with sociological concerns and premisses of long-standing (those having to do with the status of mass culture) around the work and ideas of Baudrillard.[1]

Writing on music video has had two distinctive moments in its brief history. The first wave of treatments tended to come from the culture surrounding rock music and from those who were primarily interested in music video as something which produced effects on that music. Here, two claims were most common, and generally expressed in the terms and the contexts of rock journalism:

1 that music video had made 'image' more important than the experience of music itself, with effects which were to be feared (for example, the potential difficulties for artists with poor 'images', the risk that theatricality and spectacle would take precedence over intrinsically 'musical' values, etc.);
2 that music video would result in a diminishing of the interpretive liberty of the individual music listener, who would now have visual or narrative interpretations of song lyrics imposed on him or her, in what would amount to a semantic and affective impoverishment of the popular music experience.

In retrospect, these fears seem to have been rooted, less in a specific concern about possible new relationships between sound and image, than in a long-standing caution about the relationship between rock music as a culture of presumed resistance and television as the embodiment of mainstream show business and commercial culture. It may be argued, however, that while the debate over celebrity, authenticity and artifice prominent within Anglo-American rock culture in the early 1980s was in part provoked by issues surrounding music video, it was by no means confined to such issues. In particular, the complex of notions and practices which nourished the British 'New Pop' of 1981–3, and which were central to these debates, involved re-readings of popular music's history and relationship to other cultural forms which went far beyond a response to music video exclusively.[2]

The more recent wave of writing on music video has come both from those with more elaborate theoretical interests, and from people whose point of departure is an interest in television. The particular appeal of music video here is the extent to which it appears to magnify the characteristic functioning of television in general, itself now regarded as the medium most typical of postmodern culture. One finds within much of this writing the articulation of two themes with long and notorious histories within sociologies of the media and of culture: on the one hand, a view of television as embodying the very structure of knowledge and perception in the latter part of the twentieth century; on the other, a view of youth culture as either the most debased or most resistant of cultural forms.

What follows is organized around these two sets of concerns: the one having to do with music video's relationship to rock music, and the other addressing treatments of music video within characterizations of postmodern culture.

MUSIC VIDEO AND THE NEW POP MAINSTREAM

The dominant tendency in discussions of music video's impact on rock music is to exaggerate that impact, and to examine it in isolation from other, perhaps equally significant transformations within Anglo-American rock music and rock culture in the early 1980s. Music video was one of a number of innovations producing major structural changes in the music-related industries during that period, but it is unlikely that it was the most important of these, nor that many of them would not have occurred without it.

The most important of these transformations was the constitution of a new pop music mainstream in North America in the years 1982–3. This mainstream represented the convergence of a number of developments (each involving a partial resolution of problems which the recording industry had recognized since the late 1970s): the rebirth of Top 40, singles-based radio, and with it significant shifts in the relative influence of different music audience groups; an increase in the rate of turnover of successful records and artist career spans; the recovery of the record industry after a four-year slump; and the beginning of music video programming on a national scale.

Together, these developments displaced, if only for a time, what was widely regarded as a permanent structural crisis within the recording industry. By the late 1970s, it was apparent that the objectives of radio broadcasters and record companies were in conflict in important ways: advertisers urged radio stations to pursue audiences (those in their late twenties and older) who were not actively engaged in the purchasing of records, though their overall patterns of consumption made them attractive.[3] By the early 1980s, radio stations were dominated by Adult Contemporary (light pop and soul) and country music formats, neither of which had significant reach among those most involved in buying records. At the same time, those stations directed at the core of record-buyers (those in their late teens and early twenties) were increasingly playing music which was not contemporary or in the charts (the 'classic' album-rock of the previous decade), and therefore not contributing to a significant extent to the innovation or turnover of performers, styles and individual records.

The new mainstream of 1982–3 had its roots in two developments on the margins of these overall trends. On the one hand, certain radio stations in highly competitive markets (most notably KROQ-FM in San Diego) found it feasible to target audiences encompassing disproportionate numbers of teens and females, rather than compete for a small segment of the traditionally more attractive audience of young male adults. A combination of the principles of Top 40 radio (reliance on local personalities, a 'heavy' rotation of music and constant innovation) with the specific musical styles of British post-punk music (ranging from the electropop of The Human League to the various revivalisms of The Stray Cats, Dexy's Midnight Runners and so on) proved extremely successful. While this audience was attractive to advertisers only in a highly competitive and fragmented market, it was extremely useful to record companies inasmuch as it responded quickly and enthusiastically to musical innovation and became a significant force in record sales during this period.[4]

The other development, of course, was the emergence of music television. MTV and similar networks were at one level simply the latest in a series of encounters between television and popular music, encounters which had increasingly proved unsuccessful. Historically, the audience group most active in buying new records (males in their late teens and early twenties) is under-represented within television audiences. While, in absolute terms, that audience was of limited appeal to television advertisers, the traditional impossibility of reaching it at all via television and the precision with which music television networks could target this constituency ensured some level of success. (MTV had as its original target audience the 12 – 34 age demographic, which overlapped significantly with that for album-oriented rock radio and included a similarly high proportion of males.[5])

The emergent mainstream of 1982–4 had as its principal original demographic bases a radio audience (that of teenage girls) long regarded

5

within radio broadcasting as insignificant, and a medium (television) which was for the first time able to attract the traditional core audience for rock music. This re-enfranchisement of younger teenagers, and especially adolescent girls, as radio listeners and record buyers should be seen as a crucial factor in the emergence of certain kinds of para-musical practices around the new musical mainstream.[6] An intensification of the discourses of celebrity around pop music, and the proliferation of fan magazines, pin-ups and other forms of merchandise all signalled the renewed involvement of young adolescents within popular music culture.

At the same time, Anglo-American popular music underwent a process of generic stabilization. Certain formal characteristics came to be found in almost all successful examples of that music, and a mainstream with more stylistic coherence than any, perhaps, since the mid–late 1960s, could be seen to have arrived. The most important of these characteristics was no doubt the restriction of almost all musical practice to the format of the 3–5-minute pop song, but the use of dance-related rhythms and some combination of black-and-white rock idioms were almost equally common. Whereas in the early 1980s the pop/rock charts had consisted of heterogeneous, eclectic groupings of styles and forms,[7] by 1983–4 they had come to manifest an almost unprecedented degree of homogeneity.

The most common way in which these developments have been understood is in terms of a narrative of recuperation: the new mainstream is seen to have enacted, for major record companies, the long-desired co-optation of the critical gestures and innovations of punk, its integration within the mechanisms of celebrity turnover and pop-chart homogeneity.[8] The appeal of this narrative lies in its fidelity to the dominant conceptions of rock culture's politics: conceptions positing a dialectic or struggle between margin and mainstream, resistance and complicity.

What this account most obviously overlooks is the extent to which this emergence of a new mainstream had little to do with the life-cycle of punk/new wave, and much to do with certain structural changes within the production of rock music and the mechanisms through which it is disseminated and promoted. While the increased popularity of British acts within the new American mainstream is a significant phenomenon within the recent history of the recorded music industry, it itself may be viewed most profitably in terms of the ongoing negotiation of a relationship between white rock music and black-based dance music. The historically significant tensions and processes of incorporation within American popular music over the last decade, I would argue, are those between an album-based, predominantly white rock music and the idioms and institutional functioning of dance music. It is this relationship which is crucial to a useful historical understanding of the period in which music video came to assume importance, and to an account of change within the functioning of the music-related industries. Within these developments, the trajectories followed by punk music are of secondary

6

importance, despite the extent to which they are privileged within most historical accounts.

The most important of these changes, I would argue, are (a) an increase in the rate of turnover of acts and records, and general intensification of the velocity of rock music and rock culture; (b) the resurgence of the 45-rpm single and the individual song as the basic units within the marketing of rock music; and (c) changes in the function of celebrity and performer identity within rock culture. Within each of these changes, the introduction of music video is one of a number of determinant factors.

Velocity

By the late 1970s, various mechanisms within the music-related industries had slowed down considerably. The elapsed time between albums by major artists was long, resulting in regular complaints about the shortage of new products. The markers of change and development within individual careers were infrequent, as the time spent on the charts by each successful record stretched into one to two years, and sales of several hundred thousand copies became virtually necessary to justify rapidly rising production costs. The time between recording was frequently taken up with lengthy, time-consuming tours, themselves necessary components in the successful promotion of an album.[9] For the album-rock mainstream, neither AOR radio, increasingly reliant on playlists with a high proportion of 'classic' tracks of the decade, nor Top 40, which played singles subsequent to their release on albums, constituted effective channels for innovation.

This slowing down was not limited to certain measurable processes (recording, touring, etc.). Affected as well was the extent to which, for the radio listener or record-buyer, monitoring the turnover of music was useful and significant for the marking of cultural or social distinction. As I have suggested elsewhere, the album-rock culture of the 1970s was one dependent upon a specific relationship to the passage of time: one in which records and songs from the previous ten years accumulated as acceptable musical resources of the present, rather than functioning as 'oldies' with specific reference to a highly calibrated succession of historical moments.[10]

In periods of little or slow innovation, the stratification of audiences according to the extent of their familiarity with new products obviously is limited. This slowing down of the velocity of innovation in the late 1970s accompanied the ageing of the core rock audience and its movement out of the age-ranges in which it is most involved in the purchasing of recorded music and in what might be called emblematic uses of rock music and information about it.[11]

This slowing down applies only to album-rock as it developed throughout the 1970s. Alongside this mainstream, the sorts of functioning associated with

7

disco music represented a much heightened velocity, based on a markedly different set of institutional relationships and audience positions. Whereas the promotional itinerary for album-rock involved the passage from record companies to radio-format consultants and from these to radio stations, that for disco involved much more immediate forms of feedback: more-or-less instantaneous reporting from record pools and retail stores to radio stations. The mechanisms for the promotion of disco by record labels involved a series of successive decisions as to the allocation of resources, each based on rapid information from those monitoring response in clubs or within the retail sector.[12]

The objective of major record companies in the late 1970s was frequently expressed as that of marrying the high rate of turnover and low production costs of disco records with the career stability and longevity of white album-rock.[13] This would require a musical field in which feedback mechanisms (between airplay and retail sales, for example) were quick, but in which performer identities were distinct and marketable (which was considered not to be the case with disco performers). This distinctiveness was seen as necessary if disco's commodity value within the sales of albums and non-current catalogue products was to be enhanced.

When MTV was launched in 1981 in the US, it had as one of its principal goals the breaking of records which were unable to make the playlists of album-rock radio stations, and it expected to serve as a testing ground for records before their possible adoption by radio station playlists.[14] It was one of a number of conduits which record companies would use, not only for alternative forms of promotion, but for what ultimately proved to be more efficient and inexpensive forms. Dance clubs and a variety of new record formats and merchandising tools (mini-LPs, specially-priced 12″ singles, sampler albums, etc.) were among these.[15]

Arguably, one of MTV's most significant innovations was the institutionalization within North America of an equivalent to national network radio. It was not so much the reach of MTV that was important in this respect as the simultaneity of that reach, and subsequent direct measurable impact on sales. While the aggregate audience of the major FM rock stations in the US was likely greater than that for MTV, playlist adoption of a new record by these stations was likely to be staggered and uneven, while exposure on MTV was even across the country. Both MTV and dance clubs preceded radio in their adoption of new records for playlists; the difference between them, obviously, lay in the fact that dance clubs were for the most part inner urban phenomena, while MTV reached suburban and small-town areas. The impact of MTV should be seen as resulting, not simply from the specific repertory which dominated its playlists at the beginning, but from the extent to which, in conjunction with a resurgent Top 40 radio, it increased the velocity of innovation.

Format

This increased velocity was accompanied by the resurgence of the single 45-rpm record as a commodity form and promotional material within rock music. As Top 40, CHR or Hot Hits radio formats and the dance-club circuit became important elements in the sequence through which a record was promoted, the selection of a single from an album as the focus of promotion acquired an importance which it had not had since the early 1970s. Even more significantly, perhaps, there was a return in many cases (usually those of so-called 'New Music' groups) to the release of singles before albums; an album might now, as it had in the 1960s, follow, rather than precede, a string of successful singles.

In this respect, perhaps the most significant development in which music video participated was the institution of the single-song as the crucial factor in the marketing of an album. Inasmuch as one cut must be selected for the production of an initial videoclip, this song becomes the pivot around which promotional strategies are organized. Even when several songs from an album are selected for single and videoclip release, these releases occur in succession and are based on calculations as to the speed of response of particular audience groups. This remains the case despite the slowing down of turnover on the major charts which has occurred since 1985. Increasingly, as specialized radio formats and charts (such as those for so-called Black, Dance and Adult Contemporary musics) have become integrated within the functioning of the mainstream, their distinctiveness is based on the rapidity and intensity with which their particular constituencies respond to innovation rather than on a set of substantive tastes which they manifest.

In this respect, the videoclip is one among a number of permutations of the basic single-song unit which circulate within the field of rock music today; dance mixes, instrumental versions and excerpts used as part of motion-picture soundtracks are other examples of this. As such, it is part of a more general tendency towards the dismantling of the link between song, album and performer-identity, a link and form of coherence which had been crucial to the meaning of rock/pop music in the 1970s.

Performer identity and the construction of celebrity

As suggested earlier, the warnings expressed about music video most often took the form of the claim that secondary aspects of rock music (performer image, visualization of song content) would come to dominate over primary elements (the elusive 'music itself'). The rise of what might be called a new 'pin-up culture' as part of the reconstituted mainstream of 1982–4 seemed to confirm this, inasmuch as rock music became surrounded, to a much more significant extent than in several years, with the accoutrements of celebrity. The renewed participation of adolescents within the audiences for Hollywood films and the mechanisms of fashion turnover is a further index of the revitalization of commodity production directed at this group.

This should, however, be seen as part of a more general process involving the proliferation and intensification of discourse around rock music. Musical styles and periods within the history of popular music may be distinguished according to the quantity and forms of information which surround the playing and consumption of music. This information may be as minimal as the identification of an artist whose record is played on the radio; it may extend to complex and on-going forms of gossip and biography, or to the contextualization of songs within performers' careers by radio announcers playing those songs. In periods marked by a high rate of turnover, information about the position of records relative to each other according to some measure of popularity generally is widely disseminated and monitored, and published sales charts and other means of monitoring relative success and marking change attract a high level of public interest. (A simple but extremely important factor in MTV's impact on sales, one which was part of its strategy from its inception, was the decision to label songs at their beginning and end. The failure of radio disc jockeys to identify records was seen as limiting the sales potential of country and adult contemporary records. Music video programmes, on MTV, Much Music and elsewhere have adopted as well, with few exceptions, the countdown format.)

These forms of discourse and information circulated around the artists active in the post-1982 mainstream to a significant extent. The role of music video in giving a high definition to the individual images of these performers was not negligible, but 'image', in this context, was simply part of the overall semiotic richness and high level of contextualization with which popular music in this period became endowed.

The paradox of popular music in the mid-1980s was this: while there had apparently been no time in recent memory when the institutions of celebrity and glamour seemed so crucial to it, the individual performer's identity was much less important as a guarantee of successful records than at any time in the last decade.[16] The career patterns of Culture Club, The Human League and ABC demonstrate this: initial successful records were followed by clear failures. The explanation that this was due to over-saturation and burnout, and that this was now part of the permanent condition of celebrity in North American societies, missed the underlying structural reason for this phenomenon: that the record industry now functioned on the basis of songs and their turnover rather than an interest in artists and their unfolding biographies or careers.

In the white rock-music mainstream of the 1970s, the individual career and biography provided the dominant grid through which new records were interpreted and marketed. In the mainstream of the mid-1980s, it was rather the case that performer identity and the discourses of celebrity constituted the trappings through which songs acquired the distinctiveness necessary to their success in the turnover of the pop charts. Star performer figures remained at the centre of popular music, but these succeeded each other in rapid sequence, and this succession was a function of the success of individual records rather than of a sustained interest in the artists themselves. The acknowledged advantage for record companies of this mode of functioning was that it meant successful stars were usually in the early (and less remunerative) stages of contracts, and that their potential for success could be tested by the marketing of a single, a video or a mini-album before investment in an album was forthcoming.[17] With some differences, this represented the successful integration of white pop within the institutional processes characteristic of dance music: processes characterized by a reduction of risk in initial stages, a professionalization of craft roles (production, songwriting), an increased tendency to license products of foreign origin, and short-term strategies for success.

Bound up with these shifts were what might be called a disjunction between performer celebrity – and the contexts within which that celebrity circulated (those of gossip columns, fan magazines, and so on) – and the musical recordings themselves. It is important to note that, despite the proliferation of biographical and other information about the performers dominating this new mainstream, there is very little sense that this information was invoked in the interpretation or understanding of the music itself. The importance of performer biography and personal vision in the rock criticism of the 1970s (when it explicitly adopted many of the concerns of auteurist film criticism) has given way to a much greater autonomy of the discourses of celebrity from those of interpretation. In the new mainstream, the performer functions, either as the point of continuity between rather disparate musical and para-musical practices (as was the case, for example, with Culture Club), or as the point of coherence of a number of strategic operations upon the field of popular/musical culture (as with Madonna). There is little of the two-way passage between a performer's worldview and the meaning of his or her recordings which existed a decade previously.[18]

The dominant form through which popular music was heard or understood within this mainstream was that of the song, and its place within a sequence of songs in dance clubs, on Top 40 radio, or on music television. The frequent claim that music video enacts a dispersion of the authorial voice or performer identity needs to be qualified by the recognition that, even in 1987, this voice or identity are not significant points of departure in the experience of mainstream music video or popular music. Madonna's 'Open your heart' video exemplifies this at a number of levels. Clearly, it highlights the dilemma, familiar from film theory but more pronounced in pop songs (which almost always employ first-person narration), of the disjunction between a verbal narration which is first-person and the specularization of that narrator within a particular fictional space. This should be read, however, less in terms of a problematization or splitting of the enunciative voice, than as typical of an operation which

11

displaces and reconstitutes that voice (however phantasmatically) as the point of origin of strategies which the video has deployed. These strategies themselves come to be judged according to the criteria of ingenuity rather than those of truth or affective investment.

MUSIC TELEVISION AND THE POSTMODERN CULTURE[19]

The remarks which follow are concerned with the status of music television within characterizations of postmodern culture. They are organized around a series of hypotheses which together argue against the ways in which notions of the schizophrenic or fragmentary text have come to function within those characterizations. In particular, I want to suggest that discussions of music video in terms of a politics of the signifier frequently conflate a number of premises within recent cultural theory, in ways which might be considered misleading.

In a number of recent treatments of music video, one finds a confusion between two readings of the apparently self-conscious or self-referential quality of music television: a view of the postmodern 'hyper-real', as a cultural terrain which functions primarily in terms of fluctuating intensities, and a characterization based in the post-structuralist valorization of the signifier as negativity and difference (as in the 'open' or 'writerly' text of Barthes or Sollers).

John Fiske's description of music television is in many ways representative of this tendency. MTV's 'foregrounding of the signifier over the signified' is seen to accomplish both the loss of subject identity in the material play of the signifier which was so essential to the project of *Tel Quel*, and, at the same time, the staging of desire in a fetishization of the signifier so valorized within postmodern politics.[20]

What is elided is the very different senses of the term 'signifier' being deployed here: on the one hand, the post-structuralist sense of signifier as simple absence, productive of desire; on the other, a reduction of the signifier to its plastic, sensory base (colour, sound, etc.). Within the latter reduction, this sensory base then becomes installed as the field of a primary pleasure. This elision is one in which the apparently postmodern immersion in sensory intensities is said to manifest the utopian impulse located, by a whole tradition of writing, within the experience of mass culture. At the same time, however, inasmuch as this enacts a suppression of 'meaning', an investment in the signifier itself, it is able to claim for itself the position of negative commitment *vis-à-vis* hegemonic meanings so essential to the dissident modernist project. One experiences the disruptive metonymy of the passage from signifier to signifier, while resting awhile at each one to enjoy the play of cultural reference.

Against this sense of the postmodern text, as characterized by the dispersed fragment, I would suggest that music video, and other contemporary cultural forms, assume this trauma as their point of departure. The operations of rock culture over the last decade have been directed, less at a disruption or opening up of hegemonic forms – following upon the eclecticism of the 1970s, what would these be? – than at elaborating ceremonial forms of grounding or containment. The importance of this grounding is what distinguishes these texts and cultural forms from the collagist practices of modernism. The following characteristics, it will be argued, are distinctive of various textual practices which one might want to call postmodern.

The resettling of cultural forms within traditional boundaries

Thomas Lawson has shown how the various technologically-based utopian scenarios within the North American art world during the late 1960s and 1970s ran aground: particularly, those which assumed that the effects of video, computer storage systems and so on would be one of an absolute destruction of boundaries between artistic forms (and between these and an extra-textual reality).[21] The unexpected event, in many ways, has been the resurgence over the last decade of a wide range of classical formats and boundaries within artistic practice. The recohering of the various multi-media projects of the early 1970s within a revitalized conception of opera,[22] and so-called 'new narrative' within the cinema, are examples of a tendency towards the resurgence of traditional textual formats and limits.

The shifting status of video is illuminating in this respect. Video's only specificity as a medium, as Scarpetta has argued, lies in its ability to record and present sounds and images simultaneously. Under the imperatives of artistic modernism and their valorization of medium-specific practices, video's most appropriate use seemed to be as part of site installation art.[23] What occurred, in fact, over the last decade, was the rise-to-dominance of the 'tape', the transportable and self-contained video text, as the principal form within video art. The passage of discrete textual forms across a variety of channels has become more common – and a distinctively contemporary form of nomadic operation – than the breaking down of boundaries between those channels.

In rock/pop music, the resurgence of the single in the last half-decade is another manifestation of this wider tendency. What was significant, in the years following punk, was not simply a rise in the relative commercial importance of the single record vis-à-vis the long-playing record (in retrospect, shortlived), but the degree to which the individual song became the privileged limit within which artistic strategies were deployed. Virtuosity, and the overcoming of the limits of the pop song, so central to rock's politics in the 1970s, have given way to a situation in which the most important avant-garde strategies are those which involve a reordering of the pop song from within.[24]

There are clearly a variety of reasons for this, and one should not overlook the extent to which the 'classical' formats which are being revived have in most cases been the most efficient commodity forms within each specific domain. At the same time, this tendency was rooted, in many instances, in a theoretical/ political contextualism that insisted on the value of working within and upon the set of cultural terms and codes already available and accessible (evident in the theoretically-informed practice of pop stars such as Scritti Politti). The music video is typical of these trends, both in its formalizing of the word 'video' as a noun designating a discrete package or format (rather than, for example, a process of recording or transmitting), and through its participation in the return of the single, as discussed above.

The combination of stylistic heterogeneity with formal homogeneity

The questions to which aesthetic strategies in contemporary artistic practices have responded have to do with which elements (codes, materials, etc.) will be brought into play within certain prescribed formal limits. Postmodern texts – such as, arguably, music videos – are not simply 'standardized' returns to commercial straitjackets, nor dispersed and fragmentary 'collages'. They represent a specific relationship between the coherence of certain formal structures and the heterogeneity of the various elements refigured within those structures. Across a series of music videos shown on music television, or records occupying the pop charts, a consistency of rhythm and certain formal limits (verse–chorus structures and lengths) is likely to coexist with the invocation or reworking of a variety of historical styles and imageries.

The history of rock music since punk may be seen as an attempt to find new ways of grounding and reconstructing that music, and the recourse to certain rhythmic patterns is a key aspect of this attempt. The widespread turn to funk and dance rhythms after the initial moment of punk had a number of different meanings – it functioned, among other things, as a populist gesture – but it also involved the search for formal discipline or grounding. Important sections of the European post-punk avant-garde have moved from a collagist use of 'found' and electronic sounds to records whose interest is in the way such materials are integrated within the coherent rhythmic structures of dance music.[25]

What has resulted is a proliferation of textual practices in which highly rigid formal structures coexist with a radical pluralism or eclecticism of integrated and appropriated elements. In the case of a post-punk avant-garde, the widespread retention of rhythmic patterns and particular populist formats (the 12″ dance single) must be seen in terms of a particular historical situation – marked by the banality of breaking down those patterns as a political/ aesthetic project – which is not reducible to a strategic contextualism or a complicity with commercial imperatives (though it is often either of these). The current tendency to conceive postmodern texts in spatial terms, as sites for the encounter of codes and fragments, misses what might be called the 'gravitational' function of underlying structures.

14

The palimpsestic quality of postmodern texts[26]

If this relationship of disciplinary structure to those elements which are assembled within it characterizes a number of postmodern cultural practices, then the notion that these practices simply involve the play of surfaces needs rethinking. Music videos have 'depth', but it is not the opacity of earlier forms, in which meaning is limitless because grounded in an infinity (that of human experience or history). Rather, the depth of these practices is that of the relationship between levels: a level of formal structure which limits the play of quoted fragments, and the level of those fragments themselves and their assemblage.

The most useful way of conceiving this relationship is in terms of the 'palimpsestic' text: that is, the text which is written over another. The latter need not necessarily be another single text (though it sometimes will be: Billy Bragg's 'Don't walk away, Renée' provides an example); more often, in popular music of the 1980s, it will be certain formal or generic patterns. Despite the sense that much of the music of the 1980s is revivalist, the number of examples of mainstream music which simply involve pastiches of earlier styles is rather limited. Most involve the embellishment or transformation of historical forms, such that one witnesses the tendency of those forms to act as gravitational forces, limiting the dispersion of intertextual citation. (In quite different ways, the music of Talking Heads and Kid Creole provide useful examples of this).

In the case of music video, this relationship of levels is more crucial. The relationship of song to visuals is obviously not simply one of narrativization or visualization (if it was, the important questions would remain those of fidelity or success), but rather one between the basic demands of form (some elaboration of proposed themes, a movement towards closure) and the heterogeneity of codes and visual materials held in play by that form. The video for The Pretenders' 'Don't get me wrong' is a useful example. Its homage to *The Avengers* television show is organized so as to make the guest appearance of Patrick MacNee an agent of narrative closure, while the intermittent returns to live-performance footage provide an element of the repetition basic to the structure of popular song.

Whereas in modernist collage, intertextual citation functions most often as an agent of disruption, of aperture, or of what Scarpetta calls 'the eruption of the real',[27] the recourse to certain privileged structures in postmodernist texts is often bound up with the search for means of achieving closure. These instruments – basic song structures, classical narrative patterns, etc. – become, however, highly ceremonialized rather than naïvely revived, and the crucial question in analysis becomes that of what might be called the 'modalization' of their use (i.e., the attitude of irony, homage, etc., implicit in the strategy through which they are deployed). This may be observed in various generic exercises within the contemporary American cinema (*After Hours, Blood*

15

Simple, etc.), and in the reworkings of vaudeville and cabaret which have emerged out of performance art.

Textual form as 'grid'

The two preceding sections sought to argue against the characterization of music video as simply decentred and fragmentary, and the claim that these qualities are definitive of the postmodern text. In particular, an opposition between closed or 'organic' and open or 'collagist' texts seems of little use in isolating the specificity of music video or similar cultural forms. As Laurent Jenny has argued, the formulation of modernist strategies in literature and other cultural forms has seen closure as a property of the individual text and aperture ('openness') as a quality of the surrounding social or historical context which must be in some way evoked textually. Within the postmodern text, on the contrary, the space of closure is that of the surrounding cultural context, now reduced to the existing repertory of historical styles and pre-texts which provide, in a sense, the text's horizon. The text itself is open inasmuch as it is dependent upon the surrounding circle of reference to be complete.[28]

The music video, then, like a variety of texts designated as postmodern, involves a particular play of elements within two forces acting to bring about closure: on the one hand, the underlying structure, with its tendency to ground the assemblage of quoted elements, and, on the other, the immediate cultural horizon from which these elements are taken. The Pretenders' video, with its reference to *The Avengers*, unfolds in the space between the ground of a conventional song structure and the horizon of the limited range of iconographies from which it draws.

For the performer–character, this space is neither the determined one of dictated narrative or enunciative positions, nor that of the absolute freedom of schizophrenic nomadism: rather, it might be conceived in the sense of what Douglas Davis has called the 'grid' structure of certain contemporary cultural forms. The performer-figures in most music videos occupy positions between those of the fully-diegetized character in narrative or poetic scenarios and that of the extra-diegetic musician/singer who stands apart from these scenarios. What is common is the construction of a matrix – which may be narrative, situational or both – within which the ambiguity of performer/character identities is left intact.

The video for Talking Heads' 'Wild life' is both a typical and a literal example of this: its premiss is the establishment of a matrix (a speaking/singing position in front of a microphone) which is occupied by a succession of performers/characters. The grid structure is meaningful only in a context of diminished faith in both the suspension of disbelief in narrative worlds and the avant-gardist imperative to unmask the fictionality of such worlds. It is produced by the banality of wishing to break down barriers between spectacle and audience and the impossibility of remaining innocently embedded within that spectacle: rather, the spectacle constructs a space for a certain limited play, and that play may involve the assumption of created or borrowed identities.[29]

The recentring of rock music on its own history

The processes discussed thus far within a variety of artistic forms – the return of classical formats, the recourse to certain forms as 'grounds' and the functioning of an intertextual 'horizon' – have implications for the relationship of these forms to their histories. The overwhelming tendency in writing on music television is to see its appropriation of historical styles and codes as a process of decontextualization, as part of the diminishing of a sense of historical time within an endless present.

There is much that is pertinent in this critique, but it frequently underestimates the extent to which the play of historical reference within music videos is rooted in a particular logic. The preoccupation with a historical past is reducible neither to a generalized psychosocial condition ('nostalgia'), nor to a frivolous introversion within rock culture. It has much to do with shifts in the politics of that culture, and in particular its renegotiation of a relationship with its own history.

It needs to be remembered that a significant component of rock's politics since the late 1960s was the attempt at a flight from any sense that one's significant background and tradition was that of rock/pop music itself. The two dominant trends in white rock music of the 1970s involved roads out of that tradition: either upward, into a realm of pure or 'serious' music (the tradition of progressive rock), or downward, in the name of popular, pre-rock traditions (as in the revivals of blues, country and other forms in the early 1970s). The sense of a specificity to youth culture, or of a tradition that ran through rock music and included its most commercially popular forms, virtually disappeared.

When these notions return, it is primarily as part of the attempt to reconstruct a rock tradition following the withdrawal of the gesture of punk. In Britain, this involved, in its early stages, a quest for privileged images of rebellion and style in the history of youth culture, and a settling on a limited repertory of these (around mod, ska and rockabilly musics). In North America, this project has had less coherence and urgency about it, but its most distinctive component is the redefining of authenticity as, among other things, the connoisseurist consumption of debased forms of popular culture (hence, the initial fixation on those aspects of 1960s culture least associated with rebellion and artistic credibility, as in the music of the B-52s or Devo).

Both of these tendencies involve a recentring of rock music within its own history, and the acknowledgement that it is on the terrain of popular, even commercial, culture that rock music must function. The revival of Top 40 radio and of dance further this tendency; there is the explicit sense that the

17

crucial genealogical continuities are those which run through the history of the pop-musical mainstream, rather than being found outside of this. The interest in other forms is primarily in terms of ways in which these might be recentred within that mainstream (as in Sade's reworking of the torch tradition upon the terrain of light pop), rather than in parallel genealogies which might be inhabited.

The renegotiated relationship with rock's own history brings with it a preoccupation with traumas specific to that history: in particular, a preoccupation with an originary moment – most often figured as the late 1950s or the early 1960s – and with privileged postures of rebellion or style (which may draw on pre-rock forms, as in Stan Ridgeway's film-noirish 'Drive, she said'). The substance of these moments and these postures is likely to change, but they are at any given moment indexes of the state of this negotiated sense of history, and not the random and meaningless juxtaposition of archival fragments.

There is, nevertheless, in rock video's relationship to history, evidence of a predicament common to a variety of cultural forms: the focus on specific historical moments, less for their intrinsic interest, than for the sense they offer of a moment whose historicity saturates its style. That is, in the absence of a style which innocently and fully can be said to express the present, the attractiveness of styles which seem to embody the historical fullness of the past increases. At the same time, it is the plentitude of this embodiment, rather than specific qualities of the historical moment, which threaten to become the important criteria. The appeal of semiotically rich historical styles is evident in videos like those for Sade's various singles or UB-40's 'Red, red wine', but that appeal lies more in the absolute coherence with which these styles saturate the world of these video clips than in the historical resonance of the moment invoked.[30]

THE POLITICS OF POP

Within writing on rock video, the clearest invocation of the heritage of subcultural theory may be found in discussions of 'recontextualization', a term with a complex history. Its sense has undergone at least one significant shift, and that shift is at the heart of problems in conceiving a politics of popular music and popular culture. In the original work of the Birmingham school, 'recontextualization' designated the endowing of cultural artefacts with subversive or oppositional force (primarily, as in the case of skinhead or gay cultures, through an exaggeration of dominant images of these cultures). This conceptualization was one which grounded the transformed sense of an artefact in some property of that artefact and its history: it was because working-class men had figured stereotypically as beast-like brutes that the stylistic operations of skinhead culture involved the play with brutish imagery.

In the subsequent work of both Iain Chambers and Dick Hebdige, one finds a coherent reworking of these issues and politics, and in particular the development of a new sense of 'recontextualization' which will prove highly influential within the ideologies of post-punk culture. 'Recontextualization' now becomes an activity which is subversive, less because of the specific signs involved and shifts in their meanings, than because the very activity of recontextualization opens up a realm of freedom within (and dependent upon) practices of consumption. The history of this concept is in a sense one in which intrinsic aspects of artefacts themselves gradually become less important than the simple gesture of mixing or recontextualizing them.

In recent writing on rock video, these politics persist in claims that the eclectic assembling of random fragments within videos involves a disengagement from hegemonic notions of stable identity structures.[31] These politics, and the claims made for them, proved resonant during a particular moment in the aftermath of punk, when the project of producing disruptions of specific encodings of the dominant order gave way to the transcendent and extravagant demonstration of individual subjectivity (as with the New Romantics or elements of hip-hop). In retrospect, the fragmentation of subcultural theory may be seen to have emerged at this point: one tendency insisting on the oppositional and disruptive transformation of hegemonic codes, reading youth culture backwards through a history of rebellious moments; the other renewing links with the traditions and literature of dandyism and rooting these in a newly theorized experience of metropolitan culture.

There are two senses in which the legitimacy of a politics of recontextualization seem diminished at the present time. First, if the meaning of the politics of cultural bricolage is rooted in the very act of recontextualization, rather than in specific substantive or pragmatic aspects, then the primary criteria by which these acts come to be judged are those of ingenuity and connoisseurship. The argument may be advanced that these qualities are distributed according to the differential possession of cultural capital, and therefore along the lines of existing social structures, with one of two possible implications: either that they reinforce existing social divisions, or that cultivation of these practices becomes an available useful strategy for social mobility. (The first of these seems to have held true in white rock culture in the US; the second is a traditional feature of British youth culture.)

Second, there is a sense in which the disruptive quality of appropriation and bricolage, arguably a genuinely subversive element within post-punk youth culture, has given way to a tribalist pluralism. In this pluralism, any number of historical styles exist for use in the present, but that use is organized across a multiplicity of coherent images or texts, modelled on privileged styles and stances from the cultural past (rather than through the mixing up of these on the terrain of the individual body, musical text or video). The realm of freedom becomes that of the liberty to choose models from among these. The dominant

19

tendency in recent cultural forms and practices (including dressing) is, I would argue, towards this seriality of coherent identities and away from the disruptive tensions seen by many as central to the politics of popular music.

NOTES

1 The most representative collection of these perspectives may be found in the special issue of *Journal of Communication Inquiry*, vol. 10, no. 1 (Winter 1986), to which (with the happy exception of the article by Jody Berland) this paper was originally intended as a response.

2 For one discussion of the New Pop, see Andrew Goodwin, 'From anarchy to chromakey: music, video, media', *OneTwoThreeFour: A Rock'n'Roll Quarterly*, no. 5 (Spring, 1987), pp. 16–32. The best elaboration of New Pop's place within post-punk culture may be found in the various articles by Simon Reynolds published in the British fanzine *Monitor*.

3 The low correlation between record-purchasing and other economically significant consumption practices may be seen as the crucial structural problem for the music-related industries.

4 See 'AOR loses to hit radio', *Billboard*, 21 February 1981.

5 See 'Cable channel seen helping record sales', *Billboard*, 14 March 1981.

6 Both of these were groups whose consumption of music had continued to decline throughout the 1970s. See 'On target: girls returning to record stores', *Billboard*, 19 May 1984.

7 See, for one diagnosis of the eclecticism of this period, and in particular the success of novelty and medley records, 'Left field hits are falling in as labels take them seriously', *Billboard*, 27 February 1982.

8 A central incident in the lore of post-punk culture is the alleged 'invention' by American record companies of New Wave in the late 1970s, as a palatable and marketable variant of punk most successfully accomplished with The Knack. The British invasion of the early 1980s, from this perspective, came to be seen as a more sustained and devious form of co-optation.

9 See, for example, 'Platinum not enough as album sales soar', *Billboard*, 21 May 1977, and 'And all to the good: CBS's Lundvall sees shifting US market', *Billboard*, 18 June 1977.

10 See my 'Characterizing rock music cultures: the case of heavy metal', *Canadian University Music Review*, no. 5 (1984), pp. 104–23.

11 That is, uses whose principal function or effect derives from the way in which possession of music or information about it confers status within peer groups.

12 See 'Club ability to generate sales cited as criterion for service', *Billboard*, 21 October 1978.

13 See 'Disco forum echoes industry's explosion', *Billboard*, 10 March 1979, and 'Disco – dearth of superstars dims industry future: producer rather than artist is star', *Billboard*, 14 July 1977.

14 See 'Cable channel seen helping record sales', *Billboard*, 14 March 1981.

15 See, for example, 'Tightening radio playlists brings new act alternatives', *Billboard*, 22 November 1981, and 'Canada: limited editions aid PolyGram LP sales', *Billboard*, 10 July 1982.

16 This is discussed in 'Slow going for ballads: Top 40 PDs see an uptempo '84', *Billboard*, 7 January 1984.

17 'New acts: labels play it tight', *Billboard*, 8 October 1983.

18 The narratives of repentance and rebirth surrounding recent records by Iggy Pop

or Boy George frame readings of these records only inasmuch as they generate curiosity or interest in the potential success of the comeback enterprise, not because they are seen to have intimate intertextual connections with them.

19 In this section, I draw extensively on ideas developed in relation to the cinema; see my 'The discipline of forms: mannerism in recent cinema', *Cultural Studies*, no. 3 (1987).

20 John Fiske, 'MTV: post-structural post-modern', *Journal of Communication Inquiry*, vol. 10, no. 1 (Winter, 1986), pp. 74–9. See also, in the same issue, Briankle G. Chang, 'A hypothesis on the screen: MTV and/as (postmodern) signs', pp. 70–3, particularly the discussion of Lacanian notions of desire.

21 Thomas Lawson, 'Toward another Laocoon: or, the snake pit', *Artforum*, vol. XXIV, no. 7 (March, 1986), pp. 97–106.

22 See, for a discussion, Robert Ashley and Peter Gena, 'Everything is opera', *Formations*, vol. 2, no. 1 (Spring, 1985), pp. 42–51.

23 Guy Scarpetta (1985), *L'Impureté*, Paris: Grasset, p. 299.

24 Dub-and-scratch mixes are the best examples of these, but there are other variations as well: the reversing of the relationship between foreground and background which occurs within the records of The Jesus and Mary Chain, for example.

25 The various spinoffs from Throbbing Gristle and the transformations in the music of Cabaret Voltaire provide examples of this.

26 In this section, I draw heavily on the work of Gerard Genette, and in particular his book *Palimpsestes*, Paris, 1983.

27 'L'irruption du "réel" ', *L'Impureté*, op. cit., p. 29.

28 Laurent Jenny, 'Sémiotique du collage intertextuel', *Revue d'Esthètique*, nos. 3/4 (1978), p. 179.

29 I borrow these ideas from Douglas Davis, 'Post-performancism', *Artforum*, vol. XX, no. 2 (October, 1981), pp. 31–9, though my use of them may deviate in certain ways from Davis' intended applications.

30 For an interesting discussion of these questions in relation to cinema, see Christian Zimmer (1984), *Le retour de la fiction*, Paris: Les Editions du CERF.

31 See, again, various of the articles in the special issue of *Journal of Communication Inquiry* devoted to MTV.

Part II

MUSIC AND TELEVISION

2

SOUND, IMAGE AND SOCIAL SPACE: MUSIC VIDEO AND MEDIA RECONSTRUCTION

Jody Berland

In watching a video, the visual plane tends to dominate our attention right away, simply by arresting our eyes, by being (on) television. Television seems to absorb the musical matrix effortlessly and irrevocably into its visual field, to confirm the now commonplace knowledge that music television has reshaped the music industry irrevocably. Yet that which video seems so easily to dominate and to transform – the 3-minute musical single – remains the video's *raison d'être*, its unalterable foundation, its one unconditional ingredient. A single can exist (technically, at least) without the video, but the reverse is not the case. As if in evidence of this, music videos, almost without exception, do not make so much as a single incision in the sound or structure of the song. However bizarre or disruptive videos appear, they never challenge or emancipate themselves from their musical foundation, without which their charismatic indulgences would never reach our eyes.

The musical single may still seem more 'real' because it came first, in literal terms, and because we think of it as the commodity advertised by video. Many critics have argued that the song's power to connect us with something (even with itself) is diminished by the rhetoric of the video, which by acting as promotion for a song, suggests that the song is nothing but an object to be promoted. The commercial relation is one obvious reason for the changes brought about by the televisualization of pop music, and for the evolved meta-language of visual plenitude and semantic cynicism which both confirms and disguises that circulation. Yet the commercial circulation of records and tapes tells us everything and nothing about the 'use' of popular songs by television. Everything in the world of pop music is a commodity, whether sound, image, word or act (just as this book is) – that tells us both everything and nothing about how it works.

Music video draws our attention simultaneously to the song and away from it, positing itself in the place of what it represents. As a genre, its formal structure is based on a paradox, which is unravelled here through the trope of the guitar. Tracing this symbol through some of its history, I will show its foundation in new relations between representation and meaning, sound and image, musical community and technological space, which arise from the movement of pop songs to television and from the industrial consolidation of the genre. I begin by tracing the iconographic language of music video to its roots in the historical interaction between musical and visual communication and communication technologies, suggesting some of the ways that this interaction has been shaped technically and culturally by the colonizing institutions and narratives of the visual media. Film and television's appropriation of pop music culture has played a significant role in the international integration, concentration and expansion of the entertainment industry; this process has important consequences for the organization of social space within which music (and everything else) occurs.

THE IMAGE

Try to imagine it. Elvis before Warhol. Or even Elvis before Ed Sullivan. Chuck Berry before the Beatles. Marlon Brando before Marlon Brando. What is it that gives these images such magical coherence? They haunt the topography of our cultural present; but if you really look at them, they're very distant, very *other*. From our vantage point they represent a tradition – a past, a moment of classical attainment, a shared style, an index of chosen identity – which is both necessary to and lacking in the language of pop culture today. They radiate the purity of style of an era when sound and image, desire and refusal, dance, age and the pocketbook appear to be perfectly conjoined. They form the first perfect myth in the cacophonous constellation we now know officially as 'popular culture'. In their original form they remain as mysterious as they are magical. At the same time these images reproduce themselves all around us, as though coming from nowhere, everywhere, a set of moving images empowered by a history which is forgotten, displaced, floating in the Imaginary.

The theme

In 1927, popular record releases mark the end of silent film. The music consecrating this transformation: naturally, a love song. By 1928, the inclusion of 'showstopping popular tunes' (Kreuger 1975) ensures the success of sound film and leads the record industry to paradise. In 1957, rock'n'roll makes it to the movies. The rock star is no longer a mere musician. One image says it all. Its celebration spreads across the globe.

By 1984, music video is included in Video Culture Canada and in Canada's music industry awards. Music video has swept the music world, stamping musical discourse with an endlessly varied/endlessly repeating choreography of sociable paranoia and resolute self-enactment. The Song is seen. The image is irresistible.

The rise of modern media technology has been founded upon the separation of sound (in recording) and image (in the photograph) and in their subsequent reunification through electronic means. The past sixty to eighty years have been propelled by two changing but inseparable processes of technical production: one which increasingly fractures the practices of making/ recording/hearing/watching/visualizing music, and a second which reconstructs their relationship by artificial means. Such audio/visual reconstruction asserts a continuous social and semantic power over our experiences of sound and image, our ways of communicating in time and space, of being gathered and separated, of assessing value in these experiences. This reconstruction of sound and image has been dominated by the economic, technical, narrative and topographical requirements of the visual media of film and television. This has important consequences for understanding film and television's appropriation of popular music and musical cultures, which have constituted (among other things) an essential fuel in their economic and spatial expansion. These integrative methods need to be comprehended in relation to a different kind of history of production, not of things, but of space.[1]

Electronic reproduction makes it possible to fix and move images or sounds across the barriers of physical time or space. Each new medium finds different ways of moving images or sounds into the social spaces of its users, and so places and displaces its listeners differently. The deployment of modern technologies has absorbed music's role in the ritual evocation of place and has thus effected huge changes in musical cultures and in the social location of the bodies which comprise those cultures. Not surprisingly, the contemporary image tends to present itself as representing (imaging, standing (in) for) what it is also displacing: the social context of the music itself. Each new, powerfully iconographic visualization of musical performance presents itself as the most beneficent offering, a triumph for its beneficiaries, as when Elvis makes it to the movies, 'pop promo' producers make it to a video festival, a local band makes it onto MuchMusic TV. But surely this is the beneficence of the Trojan Horse; like the strategists of ancient myth, its inventors researching the best form in which to invade by request of those who are to be conquered, emulating their collective desires as a means to enter their space and to separate them from it, and thereby conceiving a perfect device to override the limits and differences of inhabited space. What better way to talk about television? Through TV the entertainment industry won control of our living rooms, displacing radio, via which, in its new transistorized form, pop music represented a plausible escape. With music video, the now more heavily integrated music/film/ television industry reasserts its global and its domestic powers, above all the power to enter a space, anyone's space, and to separate them from it.

The story

We are concerned here with the history of technology. The song is an early manifestation of a modern 'cultural technology', if we can understand that term to describe a mediation between a mode of address, the occasion of its reception, and its social and material consolidation as a technique (Mercer

1986). The bourgeois epoch gave rise to the song as an ambivalent articulation of individual self-recognition (and self-doubt), manifesting musically the concept of individual expressive communication by remaining perfectly enclosed in its own structure (Marothy 1974).[2]

With the invention of sound recording, the singer is split from the song, and from the listener, whose relation to the singer is mediated by the song. Nostalgia is bound to run rampant; music is by nature phenomenologically social, even when this becomes a semantic quality, a symbol of sociality evoked in the physical absence of others. Thus the poignant quality of much film music, whose narrative separation from the image evokes a sense of three-dimensional absence. The history of communication technology is the history of the increasing separation of singer, sound and image, their fragmentation into raw materials, and the simultaneous history of their reconstructed unity. This technical reconstruction is instrumental in the changing topography of social, cultural and political space (Berland 1988). The photograph catches the image, and moves it away from its origin. The recording catches sound, and it too can move, without listeners ever setting eyes on the source of what they hear. Film promises to restore the abandoned unity of image and sound or, rather, to take its place, to become that unity within its own self-enclosed structure, in relation to which our presence as viewers is both necessary and invisible.

The mass production of restored images – the talkies – permits a potentially infinite expansion of their audiences. This is a great moment for songs: after sound enters film, music publishers can sell 100,000 song scores in a month, where before 10,000 in a year would have been pretty marvellous (Kreuger 1975). The film companies buy out the sheet music publishing houses and take over the financing of sound-technology development. The song-writers move west. Movies become a hazardous architecture of forgettable stories and unforgettable songs. In early films the songs are incidentals to the plot marketed in illustrated sheet music, then through record sales; now, songs may appear in films as opening or closing framing devices conveniently reproduced on video.

The simultaneous rise of talkies and the record industry marks a new stage in industry integration; this was expressed in and facilitated by technical innovation in film itself. The need to have self-enclosed songs whose sound quality guaranteed secondary sales to record buyers contributed to the early tendency to 'dub' sound – to show a popular actress singing while recording the sound of someone else's voice. The real singer (like today's video producer) was rarely acknowledged in the credits; the technique strengthened the reification of the visual image of the actress (like that of today's rock star) and helped both to justify and to facilitate further centralization of the industry. The songs themselves fit the shape of the emergent record industry's technical apparatus and helped to expand its territory, while gaining their desirability from the aura of the screen.

The more films (and then TV) offer themselves as a marketplace for songs, the more they set the tune. There could be – and have been – countless other ways to employ music in film. But the reconstruction of sound and image has been, from the beginning, economically driven, visually weighted, sumptuously engineered. The increasingly sophisticated production values of the entertainment industry make live music (and later recorded music), and then radio, function as underdeveloped relations of the Image. The more this reconstruction of sound and image is so produced, the more mediated is its method. And the more entranced its spectators: oh, we are all happy children now!

1984

That was the year Video Culture Canada (VCC) moved its annual high-tech trade fair to Ontario Place, a Toronto lakeside entertainment 'environment' for high-tech and simulated three-dimensional display, chosen, no doubt, for its perfect adequacy for 1984. VCC is sponsored by Sony, not 'merely as an advertisement for Sony products' but, they claim, as a celebration of video art and technology which would attempt 'to bridge the gap between the "underground" art of the community and a mainstream audience' (*Now*, Toronto, October 1983). VCC was described as 'bringing video culture to the masses'. But clearly by 1984 that was already being done by music television. VCC initiated a panel on music video, with several prominent producers flown in for the occasion, and a substantial collection of rock videos was included in their 'Media Library' for public (private) viewing.

This was also the year that the Juno Awards, sponsored by Canada's music industry, such as it is, were first bestowed on videos. Their influence preceded them (in 1984 MTV claimed 18 million viewers, around three-quarters of the population of Canada). 'Best singer' Bryan Adams was already doing promos for MuchMusic, the Canadian all-video cable TV station. Award-winners were warmed by the array of TV cameras and industry luminaries to thank 'the people behind Champagne Pictures who made it possible to work with artists like Corey Hart' (video producer Rob Quartley who, at VCC, like fellow panellists, hardly spoke of 'art' at all);[3] and 'God for MuchMusic' (Corey Hart, who attributes his musical inspiration to video imagery, and whose popular success has been explained by the appropriateness of his tough/ vulnerable face for the intimacies of the video camera), and 'the industry for voting for me' from Bryan Adams, whose multiple awards inspired much industry self-congratulation for the rising influence of video. It's certainly not just television that music video promises to redeem.

These rapturous displays of gratitude towards 'the industry' for (like God) making art possible would have seemed in poor taste in the discussion by video producers at VCC. The panellists (Rob Quartley, John Scarlett-Davis, John Sanborn, Rob Frescoe) showed selections of their work and shared fraternal confessions concerning the visual clichés with which 'pop promo' producers indulge themselves and their viewers. You know them without hearing their lists: dry ice and back-lighting, characters mysteriously running up or down stairs or along passages or streets, women undulating in synchronized rows, various alluring angles on female skin, car chases, pilgrimages to exotic places, exploding bombs or battles, anguished heroes, curtained windows. . . . The industry, they claimed, has encouraged a shrinking repertoire of visual signs. It was an opportunity to bemoan their awkward position as anonymous mediators between musicians' contradictory ambitions, the seductive possibilities of the video form, and the simple requirements of the industry's captains. According to these producers, the music industry wasn't making art possible – it was ensuring the impossibility of that which the form itself promised.

On the subject of what that was, they were silent.

It took a member of the panel's audience to question what could be termed a crucial cornerstone of these videos. (Not that blatant sexism, commercial utilitarianism, and a halfway-liberated art-historical ecstasy aren't crucial cornerstones of rock video! But I want to situate 'content' in the context of the issues I have raised.) Why, she asked, did music videos always have to show the guitar somewhere, perpetuating that phallic image of the rock musician and forcing us to admire the neck of every thrusting guitar in the western world? Coming out of the session, fans took issue with this critique. Why shouldn't they show guitars, they argued, following the rationale having been proffered within; after all, these clips are advertisements for records, and advertisers have to display their products clearly, don't they? And what has anyone got against looking at guitars if they like the music?

A clear and straightforward defence. Even Scarlett-Davis wouldn't have belied that one, having elegantly argued that pop promos aren't art anyway, they're just a job hired out to a racist–sexist industry, and music videos should all disappear soon anyway and what's the big fuss about them?[4]

Because the presence of the guitar is so clear and straightforward, so apparently obvious and pragmatic, let us problematize it immediately, and place it as a question at the centre of this investigation. I want to think about that guitar. This calls for a retrospective summary of the economic, iconographic and structural issues relevant to the continuous integration of pop music with the powerful visual media. What is at issue here is not the opposition between 'original' and co-optive texts, but the technological mediation of sound in relation to that of images, and the need to understand such mediation as a productive process that constitutes or changes our relations to each other in spatial and temporal as well as symbolic terms.

The history traced through this paradigm draws to our attention a cumulative integration of symbolic machinery within the universe of signs, manifested in a system of imploding intertextuality which is not simply a fusing of art and commerce, an explosive shrinking of narrative repertoires,

30

nor even an increasingly complex web of self-referential quotation but, in conjunction with all of these, a process of increased vertical and horizontal integration in an emergent system of global cultural production. The absorption of pop music by television contributes to spatial processes of displacement and domestication, as well as to the proliferation and centralization of symbols, and offers an ideal apparatus for the international dissemination of mediated consumption and display in which the uneven development of resources – centre and margin, sound and image – is the order of the day.

THE RESURRECTION

The presentation of the newly created Vitaphone in New York City has created a sensation in motion picture circles. The presentation was made by Warner Brothers, in connection with the Western Electric Company and the Bell Telephone Laboratories, with the showing of the new John Barrymore picture, 'Don Juan'.

The Vitaphone is the newest application of sound to motion pictures. Since the beginning of films, various unsuccessful attempts have been made with so-called 'talking pictures'. The Vitaphone, however, is an unusual thing, miles ahead of the famous early Edison talking pictures. Such an authority as Michael I. Pupin, Professor of Electro-Mechanics at Columbia and President of the American Institute of Electrical Engineers, says: 'No closer approach to resurrection has ever been made by science.'

(*Photoplay*, October 1926 (Kreuger 1975))

We are not prepared for television. Cameras and tape recorders don't make television programs. You have to have trained people to do that. What are we getting now? The pop music of Germany, ABBA, Star Parade and so on. People see these things over and over again. But we don't have the money, experience or capacity to put on shows like that. Even if we do put on something national, it can't compete with all the glittering lights and costumes of foreign products. People begin to believe that you have to have that sort of thing. This development could destroy everything that has come down through the ages, everything that we can proudly call national culture.

(Sri Lankan musician W. B. Makulloluwa (Wallis and Malm 1984))

You can't make a hit record, become known, make money on music, cross national borders or be heard across your own, without making a video. This endows television with a new power: power over music, and power over us through music, which it offers to anyone, anywhere there's a TV, to little kids or Africans or nerds or girls without their lipstick. This resource also endows television with a new language, which invites us to embrace every available

31

visual memory: the dreams of twentieth-century art return to haunt us. For this we are grateful. It all begins to come together before us. The nuances of the face, the texture of the rhythm, the elliptical narrative, the fast-moving polyphony of style, the self-reflective humour, the montage of hospitable quotation and re-enactment, the familiarity of references to something still generic, still somebody's, the generosity with which its images join us to our collective history, our imagined collective history, our collective paranoia, favourite symbols, cynicism, hope. . . . Watching this beneficent hospitality, everything is brought home. *Into* our home. We are on an adventure; we seem to have been there all along.

I am still talking about the guitar.

ANOTHER HISTORICAL TROPE: ELVIS, WITH HEGEL

We see images or hear sounds as part of a remembered *series* of images or sounds, a series which gives each individual form its understood significance. At the same time such a series takes its own general meaning – which is never finally closed – from the patterns, contradictions, repetitions of the individual parts. Over time these patterns change, like patterns of musical practices, for instance, to which echoing images refer. The meanings of specific forms then also change, in response to changing structures of performance, reproduction or perception, circling through appropriations by an audience who know and do different things now. Some are used, and re-used, and reimbued with meaning, until a single image flickering before us resonates with a whole cookbook of crystallized uses: a quantity of qualities, an accumulation of quantities into new qualities, none of them the same as what they were. Thus the gesture of the rocker with the guitar. It draws with it a cinemascope of youthful rebellion, announcing itself as the sudden explosion of a biology that must have been there waiting all along. With this image Youth is born. The memory starts to work in mythological form at the moment the biological mystique overruns itself, makes rock stars millionaires, fills commercials and corporate accounts, its mythological profile already in contestation when the mods beat the shit out of the rockers, or vice versa, or someone else, in an attempt to reclaim the territory.

But the struggle for that image had already begun, let's say with Elvis, the truck driver with the pelvic flip, dreaming about making it into the movies.

He did dream about it. And he did make it, as I hardly need to tell you, via the *Ed Sullivan Show*, American variety entertainment *par excellence* (the Beatles, appearing there in 1963, revealed, according to a 1983 *Rolling Stone* anniversary commemoration, their truly American identity); the *Ed Sullivan Show*, where the cameraman filmed Elvis, primordial pelvic performer, from the waist up.

Actually that camera angle is also something of a myth, recurring in various accounts of the rockin' rebel's rise to the top. Elvis did three performances for the *Ed Sullivan Show* in the winter of 1956–7, one of which was filmed from the waist up. He appeared there only months after Sullivan, the 'King of American TV', swore that Elvis, so-called 'King of Western Bop', would never appear on *his* show. Elvis pocketed $50,000 for the appearances his host had sworn would never happen. That kind of victory is part of the aura of the image, the rock rebel, Elvis or whoever, just as the fight for it is. But whose victory was it? According to one source, those shows were watched by an unprecedented 82.6 per cent of the American population. Yep – another coronation. To Greil Marcus, that figure is totally absurd and unbelievable; 82.6 per cent of the American population didn't even know that Eisenhower was their president. But (as Marcus allows himself to wonder) who cares? You don't need to know about Eisenhower to buy Presley records, and wasn't that exactly the point? (Marcus 1982.)

No one explains why it was the last of the three performances that filmed Elvis from the waist up. That was the title of the record released after the show: 'From the waist up'. By this time, the rock'n'rebel hero had found his own place in the movies, a place hospitable enough to display him from head to toe, complete with pelvic thrusts, and the omniscient guitar.

The space for Elvis had been created by rock movies without actual rock stars: movies like James Dean's *Rebel Without a Cause* and *East of Eden* (1955), Brando's *The Wild One* (1953) or even *The Fugitive Kind* (1960), in which Brando plays a guitar-strumming outcast setting fire (literally, more or less) to the 'Steamin' South'. In these movies, the rebel image's power is still tied to – and combusted against – a particular place and time which suffers a geological rupture in the encounter. But it was *Blackboard Jungle* (1955) that made Bill Haley's 'Rock around the clock' an international anthem of teenage rebellion. A new type of interdependence between rebellion and spectacle was born, the boundary between these the more indecipherable the more remote and self-enclosed the space in which they occurred, our potential resentment considerably softened by the unique, unreplaceable, authentic beauty of the images that made this interdependence possible in the first place. That was easy with rock stars. They just played themselves.

It wouldn't be long before Warhol would challenge viewers with rows of such faces, freezing into ambivalence the power of their authentic/two-dimensional appeal. The introduction of rock stars to the movies marked that contradiction with their vocabulary, but it did more than that. The music helped to sell the movies; movies became crucial vehicles for the sale of records, images and styles. The new pop music was disseminated across wider geo-political expanses, edged out of the local radio/DJ community context of the early 1950s to *American Bandstand* to its position of dominance in the national corporate strategies of the music industry, breaking or marginalizing the regional and racial inflections of its sources just as MTV would do in the 1980s. The globe was next: only the most pristine of rebellions would do.

33

British teenagers got their first taste of the exuberance of this new chaos from *Blackboard Jungle*, thus forging ties of musical influence that have made all subsequent pop music history what it is – among other things, an enormous network of unequally productive branch plants. Seat-slashing began with *Blackboard Jungle*; so too did the boundarizing of youth (rather than race, class, ethnic or nationalist) rebellion. With *Blackboard Jungle*, the implicit connections between rock music, small-town culture, teenage rebellion, fun, anger and fashion were made explicit. But thereupon the connections changed. Movie producers knew a good thing when they saw it and made a score of Rock-around-the-clock clone movies that quickly condensed the rebellion into a structure of pleasurable motifs:

> The kids are putting on the Senior's Hop and somehow they get all these great rock'n'roll stars to appear from out of nowhere to play for them for nothing [oh sure, yeah] but the parents and the school committee won't let them put it on because it's bad or something and somehow the big crisis is resolved and near the end Bill Haley or somebody is playing and the kids are all bopping away and the parents are standing around watching, supervising, and the camera shifts to the parents' feet and their toes are tapping, you know, and they're snapping their fingers and their heads are bopping back and forth, looking at each other and saying, 'Gee this music ain't so bad after all is it? Kinda catchy.'
>
> (Mike Daley, cited in Marcus 1976)

Finally, Elvis didn't need to do what those who made a place for him in the movies (including himself) had done – he didn't need to fight much, except maybe to get his dream-girl's father to recognize what a good guy he really was behind that guitar. Did the same hold true for his fans? Meanwhile the articulate guitar – that inescapable symbol of rebellion and honest speaking – allowed the powerful film magnates to invite the rebels in and reward them with fame, on the house. Rock movies did for rock music what, in a different way, rebel movies were doing for film: mapping weekend routes to post-cowboy rebellion. No longer the horse but the gear-shift and the guitar: inmates of restless solitude for everyone to love, icons of that tough/vulnerable all-American masculinity destined to suffer apparently universal and increasingly asocial anguishes of alienation, balanced precariously between social critique and sentimentality on that same tense edge that James Dean suffers on as he rescues post-war liberalism from melodrama and McCarthy. These images inject 1950s' moralism with a strong dose of youthful distress while, incidentally, helping to rescue the film industry from post-war post-TV disaster (much as music video sought to rescue the television industry from the newer post-pop entertainment technologies).[5] And so the film, hallmark of American success, swallows rock'n'roll, and so rock'n'roll swallows rebellion and embraces it to death, if only temporarily, in the doo-wah-diddies of desire.

34

IN AND OUT OF SPACE TOGETHER

Last summer the American trade paper *Daily Variety* cited a survey affirming that 'MTV viewers are more influenced [in their purchase of records] by the cable music channel than by radio, concerts, or commercial TV.' Who would have imagined, five years ago, that television could equal or surpass radio as the principal music medium?

(Hayes 1984)

Most advertising suggests that the product on display will facilitate or ensure the satisfaction of our great psychological and emotional need: the need to belong, to be accepted, desired. This strategy informs the rhetoric of rock videos, too; they create an imaginary community – with an inviting sense of imaginary relationships. The viewer's access to this imaginary community is mediated by music, by rock stars, by the rock video shows. Of course, economic function is performed here in that the viewer's access to the community must be constantly renegotiated; only the viewer's continued consumption of videos and video programs will ensure the extension of that feeling of belonging and community.

(Marion and McLarty 1984)

Modern science suggests that rather than think of space as a container or bodies as 'things' *in* space, we grasp the organism as a center for the production of space around itself – space is not external to the body but generated by it. . . . Such analysis needs to be completed by a rhythm analysis in which time is then grasped in its spatial form. The data of the unconscious are also to be considered in terms of the spatial articulation between objects and desire. Finally, spatial practice is on this level most concretely articulated in the various historical and cultural systems of *gestuality*.

(Lefebvre 1983)

One of the most important defining characteristics of popular music has been its promotion and valorization of social and physical participation by its particular (groups of) fans. Though early rock'n'roll arose in the wake of teenage flight from the family TV and living room, and played, via the new radio/hi-fi technologies, to fans in the crucial sites of car, drive-in, dance-hall, beach and bedroom, modern rock'n'roll doesn't care where you are, so long as your reception technologies are complete. With or without the sponsoring images, music no longer depends on a shared social space. Now it can be heard anywhere, in any context, drawn into any kind of discourse. You can hear music, but see anything: the walls of an empty room, a passing street, a bar, an ad, a remembered image of someone walking, as easily as moving bodies or the visual resonances of making sound. And you don't have to listen to it, exactly; just to live with it.

Each innovation in the technically mediated reproduction of sound or image precipitates new forms of social practice, and changes the division of labour between playing, listening, recording, moving or watching. All of these, located in space and time, produce meaning for the music. While music fills a space and surrounds you in it, functioning as an extension of your body into the social, and vice versa, television attempts to surround itself with you, to draw your eyes to a single spot and to fix the rest of you before it. In the sense that its images transport you (via your eyes) out of the space you are actually in, it does extend your reach in space, as McLuhan (1964) claims all electronic media do. Music television's paradox is that its 'content' belies its televisual form. It accomplishes this extension of our senses by simulating the space – the social context and the sensory plenitude – of pop music as an activity, and by visualizing and centralizing the symbolic codes which transport the viewers into that simulated space. The image of the guitar constitutes a crucial element of these televisual functions.

Music television is constrained by the imperatives of a universal semantic, one which promises discursively as well as technically to reach you wherever you are. As an industry it must produce viewers on a grand scale, seeking more widely available gestures and proximities. Thus MTV, the first cross-country rock'n'roll station, once tried to excuse its omission of black musicians:

> We have to try and do what we think not only New York and Los Angeles will appreciate, but also Poughkeepsie or the Midwest. Pick some town in the Midwest which would be scared to death by Prince, which we're playing, or a string of other black faces, or black music. . . . You have to play music we think an entire country is going to like. . .
>
> (Levy 1983: 37)

Television asserts a colonizing force because it stockpiles signs against the mobility and challenge of meaning production which technological reproduction has made possible and which modern life has made necessary. While sound recording (like photography) yields rich possibilities for creative appropriation in different spaces or contexts, the economic dynamic of the TV/entertainment industry leads it to seek a quantifiable expansion of spaces that can be entered and turned to profit, that are, from a corporate point of view, both accessible and expendable, reducible to backdrops before the camera, or rooms to put a TV in the middle of. The pleasures of reception are thus becoming inseparable from the pleasure of media competence, the instant recognition of the code that is, must be, made for us. The American media, feeding with the teeth of its own vocabulary, gathers to its centres a selection of recurring images whose serialized passage from source to resource endears itself to its audience, simultaneously making welcome its own transnational semiotic centralization. It creates a form of semantic flattery. The reproduction of symbols = the reproduction of competence = dependent pleasure.

36

And some images are particularly potent. The image of the young-male-musician-with-guitar can mean, in a single flash, everything: bobby sox, punching out the boss, hitting the road, opposing the war, an old Chevy, 1958 in Kansas, dancing till dawn, coming on – this condensation of symbols coding the performance of a performer which can speak of each or any of these without speaking at all. With the emergence of rock video, the 'authenticity' of the performer is assured (if not that of the performance, whose sound is still frequently dubbed). Now the singer plays himself, promising a continuity of self with the space beyond the stage. But it takes a rare musician to not look like a video quotation of the image of Musician; the image shimmers at the border of leaving the music behind, while celebrating itself as musically inspired.

Today's pop icons – seen in beer, pop, fashion and car commercials, graphic design, posters, ads and billboards, music promotion and of course videos – have in common with music video one structural feature which goes beyond their common representational vocabulary: the image of musical presence is split from the musical sound, and makes itself more powerful than the sound precisely on the basis of music's contribution. In this way pop iconography follows the formula Barthes (1973) identified in 'Myth today', in which a sign functions as an alibi for a history which has been drained from its signifier. The image consumes the traces of sociality which music still connotes, encloses its meaning, 'but keeps its life, from which the form of the myth will draw its nourishment' (Barthes 1973: 118). The image speaks in two languages at once, first as literal *meaning* (this is the musician who is singing, this is the meaning of the words) and, at the second order, the plane of myth, as *form*, which puts the meaning at a distance so that it can be appropriated into a new situational intentionality (this is television bringing us a selected pop song, whose meaning, creativity and desirability are best indexed and valorized by the dissemination of symbols in flat audio–visual fabrication). As meta-language, myth's meaning is more determined by its intention than by its literal form; in other words, 'Myth is speech stolen and restored. Only, speech which is restored is no longer quite that which was stolen; when it was brought back, it was not put exactly in its place' (Barthes 1973: 125). Music video presents a particular mode of cultural cannibalization, in which the soundtrack has been digested lifetimes ago, in fact consumed by the image, which appears to be singing.

But it is no use taking the televisual myth at its word, so to speak, and confining the concept of meaning to the plane of symbols, or critical analysis to the visual dimension. Television is *not* only a set of images; it is also a powerful instance of what Lefebvre (1983) calls 'a center for the production of space around itself', that is to say a producer of practices which are (re)articulated spatially in both production and reception. Its own 'spatial articulation between objects and desire', its drive to surround itself with us through a visual rhetoric of 'us', accounts for the mythical nature of the music video. Television offers us music that has been 'stolen and restored', that has been (dis)placed, lifted from its history and from its meaning as a particular type of social practice and returned surreptitiously as another type altogether, one that can be produced for and organized around, that can be lived by watching, two-dimensional images.

Video's assertion of economic and symbolic dominance in the music industry marks an attempt to reorganize our playing, listening, recording, moving and watching practices to facilitate greater corporate centralization. Where radio is mainly regional or local, music television is national; it spans the map as if there were no boundaries, no regions, no borders, encouraging us to see music as a transnational product emanating from an abstract space. Its symbolic landscape fills a vacuum that has been left by its own suspending of music from 'real space', which, like real time, is a concept related to the human body. Video frames the song, encloses it in a shared symbolic (but not physical) space, and invites us to enter that space, or rather, to invite it into our own. Then we go out and buy the records.

In bars the video screen is often silent, displaying ghostly musicians performing to the sound of a separate soundtrack, the particling of audio-visual space making the relationship between performance, physical and social location increasingly complex, unless you go to a live concert, which often (not always) means submitting to a formal collective enactment of spontaneity, the performance's power intensified by its familiarity from previous mass reproduction, or unless you watch the music 'live' on TV or film, rarely a satisfactory substitute, where what you are watching is not (ordinarily) musicians making music in the context of where or why they began (as though place could never be anything other than a sentimentality of origin), but images of them having made it, freed from place and from the struggle for it, placed alongside other constructed or found images – musicians having adventures, or dancing, the continent of Africa exploding, or singing, the monsters approaching, the car cruising, the body bruising, the chorus busy at its doo-wop, the rhythm of these images carefully reunited with the sound of their having made it, with or without any relation to the lyrics of the song itself. And the images' rhythm adheres to physical rhythm in the most empirical sense: faster and faster, *now* the image moves fast enough. The audience moves less and less. It is not only the social/spatial dimension of music so transformed: so too is time, real time, collapsed to the time it takes to sing a song, the once again unilateral $3\frac{1}{2}$ minutes of time, whose imagination spirals in an escalating rapidity of moving images.

Because the image subsumes the music, in most instances, the rhythm of visual editing subsumes the larger rhythm of the song. This enables the visual language of the rock video to surpass, in complexity, subtlety and technical sophistication, the language of any other programming available on contemporary commercial television (aside from some (other) advertising). On the other hand, this visual–semantic complexity rarely extends to new

38

types of synchronization between musical and visual form, or allows the s<
to challenge the video's seduction of the viewer.[6] Music videos are, at one a
the same time, the most innovative mode of visual language available on
television; the most popularly accessible inheritance of twentieth-century
visual art; and mere TV commercials for purchasable products. The image of
the guitar anchors this contradiction.

The guitar proposes all of the meanings I have suggested, and more. It
articulates: this performance is real, a physical act in real space and time, an
authentic cultural event, rock is real speech, today's folk culture, today's
resistance, performance art, truth, today's avant-garde, today's lyric poem –
and also: don't take this seriously as art, you understand, or as anything else
either: this is just a commercial.

WATCHING TV

Technically, 'realism' attaches itself most intimately to the fingers on the frets
of the guitar. The further away from the guitar the camera moves, the more
touched by the flashes and fades of fantasy. The singer stands between these
two poles – the real and the imagined – and heroically mediates their tensions.
If he is a man, the camera makes love to his fingers, his face and his body's
bounce. If she is a woman, it is, in the dominant code, her mouth and the
gestures of her neck. The camera watches from the side, or from down below,
making the singer's stance large, potent, symbolic, and drawing us into the
crowd before the stage. The rest is simulated disequilibrium.

The singer mediates then between an attentive camera perched in 'real time'
and a kaleidoscope of visual editing and time disruption. The stage becomes a
narrative centre of gravity around which pulsate the street, the story,
quotations from old films, newsreels, science fiction, surrealism and other
genres, the chaos of war or the exotica of faraway places, sexual manoeuvres
or imaginings. The singer, a lyrical poet despite the coolly thunderous style,
responds to these with (constructed) exemplary sensitivity.

The video, like the song, has its basis in rhythm. Musically the song, as a
singular structure – the structure never contested in the video – embodies the
attitude of the individualized commodity producer speaking on behalf of a
(real or abstract) collectivity. The rhythm is no abstract matter. While the
sequence of images appears to pulsate with the beat of the percussion (i.e. to
respond to the rhythm as a body would) it follows, in fact, with the ingenuity
of a more obedient rapture, the Song as it has become: a convention inspired
by the Romantics, entrenched by recording techniques in the 1920s ($3\frac{1}{2}$
minutes please), spun through a million juke boxes, reinvented in 1955, or
1967. . . . Each time it breaks from the frame (as with the catalyst of FM radio
in the late 1960s) it is brought back again by the economic discipline of
technical advances. The alternation of verse/chorus/instrumental achieves a

naturalness in our collective bodily memory; its basic pattern structures not only music video but other TV advertisements as well.

In the verse the singer describes; in the chorus he expresses; in the instrumental break something happens, illuminates his cause, elaborates his fantasy, opens up, hesitatingly and circularly, to the largeness of the threatening world. The guitar helps him to speak. In this sense the exploding horizon of visual narrative settles into the landscape of the oldest tune in the book: big world, little me. The rhythm of the song, both first and primary, anticipates and then conquers the eye. The images caress the beat; yet they determine the rhythm of the experience just as the musical rhythm determines their effectiveness. The rhythm conquers all; first the real subject (me watching), and then, after some struggle, of course, the fictional object – the girl, the escape, the search, the movement or mediation across space, which we watch, unmoving. The filmed audience is ecstatic. Let free by the instruments, the story takes a vacation from the voice (the fingers still moving across the fret of the guitar); the story is played out, if there is one, the art displayed, the visible collectivity of the band coheres and fades; when we are returned to our hero he is no longer alone, even if there is no one left on camera, since he has spoken, acted, protested, played, yearned, joined, for us.

The guitar returns. With few exceptions, the cameras are not visible.

THE UNEVEN DEVELOPMENT OF THE SIGN

Current TV commercials reproduce an aura of the 1950s as the quintessence of 'real' popular culture. They quote old songs as 'originals' endowed with the same aura of purity and sociability as a good bottle of beer. This approximates what Walter Benjamin or John Berger claimed for the privileging of the original painting, though the songs are often re-written, as if to promote the contemporaneity of the experience. In any case technological reproduction plays a different role for music. Music reproduction technology (including radio) is cheaper and more accessible, of course, as are most of the three-chord wonder techniques for making music. The sonic exchanges between live and recorded music; between composer, performer, engineer, listener; and between pop and avant-garde music, and all the attendant electronic mediations, are often freely interrogative until they are put to the service of images. This adaptability is mediated and constricted (as well as imitated) by the apparatus and conventions of film and television, which such musical exploration threatens, in a constant and tantalizing gesture, to disrupt.

Through the intervention of the technological processes and dominant codes of music television, music's collectivity becomes the subject of its visual representation precisely as it is thereby structurally diminished. The image of the defiant rocker addresses us with all the power and two-dimensionality of any icon. And the image of the guitar, sliced into the complexity of texture/narrative/image/sound generated by music video, brings the discourse to life,

40

and returns it to normal; swallows the hysteria, completes the sentence, confesses its abridgement, reminds us that all this abundance and complexity before us might have no function other than to sell the song, whose category as Song (as product) is sealed by the richly evocative icon of singer-with-guitar, the icon which promises everything, and surreptitiously ensures that nothing escapes the boundaries to which it has so devotedly been assigned.

This is both a symbolic and a topographical mission. But it is not always a successful one. There are escapes all the time. The more the centre centralizes, the more the materials of independence mobilize themselves. The media, according to McLuhan, centralize and decentralize at the same time. These processes of technical innovation always promise us endless possibilities. The whole television/music/studio/instrument/broadcast/performance/communication structure could change. Transforming the mode of production of music and musical images would inevitably transform their language; place could be represented ('representation' now understood as a different kind of process, less 'imaging, taking the place of', more 'defending the interests of') as a site for safe human occupation, rather than as a backdrop, an otherwise uninhabited stage, a dispensable token of interchangeability susceptible to the requirements of commercial exchange. Could the space of the city become something larger, closer, than a frame for the pictorially exotic? Can TV do this? The logic of this optimism seems vulnerable indeed when framed by the larger logic of our present material and psychic economy.

For McLuhan, artists' deployment of new technologies function as a radar system to help us cope with their impact. Rock videos propose a number of trajectories. The majority balance their promise against a complex inventory of paranoia, which is the other source of their emotional effectiveness. They offer us permission to participate by staying at home. Their compelling images of pursuit and repression mobilize a vocabulary within which the bomb, like its counter-image the guitar, evokes a structure of feeling closely identified with technological hostility to the preservation of place, or of difference, or of futures. An increasing abstraction of human and social space is being articulated, reproduced and contained by the processes I have described. What is coming, and are we coping?[7]

NOTES

1 'The past has left its marks, its inscriptions, but space is always a present space, a current totality, with its links and connections to action. In fact, the production and the product [of space] are inseparable sides of one process. . . . Space has its own reality in the current mode of production and society, with the same claims and in the same global process as merchandise, money, and capital.' (Lefebvre 1979.)

2 '[The song's] role has become a central and decisive element in bourgeois music culture. The social need that gave rise to the song is linked, as to content, with the personal lyrical requirements of the isolated individual and, as to form, with the demand for a genre that could be produced by him alone without the necessity of

41

collective participation or even a collective circumstance. . . . *The forms of "music-making" must change into "musical forms" which will comprise an entity independent of performance ways.*' (Marothy 1974: emphasis added.)

3 'You're constantly taking conventions and twisting them. I think of music video as moving stills. I like the glossy look: each frame should be a grabber. If I was to do a real raunchy punk tune, I'd even be slick in the raunchiness. People are used to watching multimillion dollar productions, that's the standard. . . . It's an international business, and the only way to play international ball is with this type of entertainment/promotion. They go hand in hand . . .' (Rob Quartley, Video Culture Canada brochure, 1984.)

4 'I think most pop promos are blatantly sexist, which I find incredibly offensive. They're just masturbation fantasies for middle America. They just sit there with their cans of beer tossing off while all these scantily clad girls do this and that with men with their big electric guitars like prick extensions. Most pop promos are just fifth rate imagery that's copied from someone who's copied from someone who's copied from someone who's read a coffee table book on Magritte and has probably seen a few film noirs.' (John Scarlett-Davis, interview in *Now*, October 1984.)

5 In 1983, MTV executive Bob Pittman listed the 'psychographic' requirements of targeted viewers: 'Young people who had money and the inclination to buy things like records, candy bars, videogames, beer and pimple cream.' (Levy 1983: 34.)

6 'In the past, whenever the arts were drawn together, a fatal mistake was made. It was thought that the total production could be strengthened by having all the arts proceed in parallel motion: that is to say, whatever happened in one art had to be duplicated at the same instant in all the others. But this technique of synchronization results in an art form that crushes more than it exalts, as Andre Gide has aptly noted of Wagner.' (Schafer 1974.) Cf. Sergei Eistenstein, *Film Form* (New York: Oxford 1949): 'Only a contrapuntal use of sound in relation to the visual montage piece will afford a new potentiality of montage development. . . . The first experimental work with sound must be directed along the line of its distinct non-synchronization with the visual images.'

7 This paper was written in 1984–5. It remains a record of that time.

REFERENCES

Barthes, Roland (1973) *Mythologies*, St Albans: Paladin.

Berland, Jody (1988) 'Locating listening: popular music, technological space, Canadian mediations', *Cultural Studies*, vol. 2, no. 3.

Hayes, D. (1984) 'The sight of music', *Saturday Night*, July.

Kreuger, M. (1975) *The Movie Musical from Vitaphone to 42nd Street, as Reported in a Great Fan Magazine*, New York: Dover.

Lefebvre, Henri (1979) 'Space: social product and use value', in *Critical Sociology*, J. W. Freiburg (ed.), New York: Irvington Publishers Inc.

—— (1983) 'The production of space', unpublished ms, Conference on Marxism and the Interpretation of Culture, Urbana.

Levy, Steven (1983) 'Visions of MTV', *Rolling Stone*, no. 410, 8 December.

McLuhan, Marshall (1964) *Understanding Media*, New York: McGraw-Hill.

Marcus, Greil (1976) 'Rock films', in *The Rolling Stone Illustrated History of Rock and Roll*, Jim Miller (ed.), New York: Rolling Stone Press.

—— (1982) *Mystery Train: Images of America in Rock 'n' Roll Music* (revised edition), New York: Dutton.

Marion, Joanne and McLarty, Lianne (1984) 'Rock video's message', *Canadian Forum*, July.

Marothy, Janos (1974) *Music and the Bourgeois, Music and the Proletarian*, Budapest: Akademiai Kiado.

Mercer, Colin (1986) 'Entertainment, or the policing of virtue', *New Formations*, no. 4.

Schafer, Murray R. (1974) 'The theatre of confluence (notes in advance of action)', *The Canada Music Book*, Winter.

Wallis, Roger and Krister, Malm (1984) *Big Sounds from Small Peoples: The Music Industry in Small Countries*, New York: Pendragon Press.

3

FATAL DISTRACTIONS: MTV MEETS POSTMODERN THEORY

Andrew Goodwin

More so than any cultural form developed in the last twenty years, music video clips and distribution systems like MTV have found themselves associated almost exclusively with one cluster of intellectual concerns. This theoretical paradigm is postmodernism, and it has fast become the academic orthodoxy in communications and cultural studies research concerning music television. Postmodern critics see in MTV a mirror-image of the ideal postmodern text: 'Fragmentation, segmentation, superficiality, stylistic jumbling, the blurring of mediation and reality, the collapse of past and future into the moment of the present, the elevation of hedonism, the dominance of the visual over the verbal. . . ' (Tetzlaff 1986). The emergence in August 1988 of a programme entitled *Post Modern MTV* would seem to be the final confirmation of the intimate ties between the text and the theory.

Given the lack of coherence in current usage of the term 'postmodernism', let me say that the use I wish to critique is that employed, for instance, in Fiske (1986), Tetzlaff (1986), Aufderheide (1986), Wollen (1986) and Kaplan (1987), where the term is articulated in relation to MTV in the following ways:

1 MTV is seen to constitute a typically postmodern development, in its fusion of high art and popular cultural discourses (or perhaps more accurately, its refusal to acknowledge such cultural boundaries).
2 The abandonment of grand narrative structures present in postmodern culture is identified both in the non-realist construction of the video clips and in the MTV text itself, which eschews discrete programmes organized around traditional narrative regimes, in favour of continuous, seamless transmission – both factors imply an unstable text, and perhaps the production of an unstable sense of self (Aufderheide; Kaplan).
3 The borrowing from other texts prevalent in MTV's videos and its own programming is viewed as a form of 'intertextuality' typical of postmodern culture, which often finds an outlet in 'pastiche' (i.e., 'blank parody').
4 Intertextuality and pastiche are supposedly used to blur historical/chronological distinctions, so that conventional notions of past, present

45

and future are lost in the pot-pourri of images, all of which are made to seem contemporary.

5 MTV can be considered a 'schizophrenic' abandonment of rational, liberal–humanist, discourse (Kaplan) which creates a nihilistic, amoral universe of representation on a par with other postmodern texts, such as the Bret Easton Ellis novel *Less Than Zero*, or the David Lynch film *Blue Velvet*. It therefore abandons the realm of political and social engagement as they are generally recognized, leading either to a pessimistic diagnosis (Tetzlaff), or to the suggestion that postmodern culture constitutes new forms of political resistance (Fiske, Kaplan).

In this chapter I will take issue with the approach that views music television as quintessentially 'postmodern', in a critique that works on two levels. In some areas I will seek to demonstrate that the postmodern interpretation is simply empirically wrong. Elsewhere, I concede the validity of some aspects of the postmodern interpretation, but try to establish some possible alternative frameworks that have been lost in the effort to buttress postmodern readings.

I will therefore offer some alternative perspectives based on historical and textual studies of MTV. For while there is a good case to be made for seeing some cultural forms in terms of postmodernity (e.g., twentieth-century architecture, post-war literature, 1980s political discourse), the current fashion for conflating the specificities of different media and genre into a rag-bag category of 'postmodernism' does injustice in equal measure to both the conceptual field and the object of study. Television programmes such as *Miami Vice* (Gitlin 1986), *Moonlighting* (Grossberg 1987), and *USA Today: The Television Show* (Glassner 1989) can be analysed in these terms, and there is a good argument for discussing contemporary pop music in terms of new, possibly postmodern, relations between past and present. But music video in general and MTV in particular both represent a poor choice of case study for advocates of postmodern theory.

I have tried elsewhere to demonstrate some of the inadequacies of postmodernism's encounter with music television in particular (Goodwin 1987a, 1987b, 1992), and popular music in general (Goodwin 1988, 1991), and I will partially summarize those arguments below. But the main project of this chapter is to offer a counter-reading of the most developed and frequently-discussed site of music video distribution – MTV.

THE SEDUCTION OF THE VISUAL

One absence in postmodern theorizing about music television lies in the neglect of music. This difficulty operates at a number of levels. For example, the postmodern analysis of the convergence of avant-garde/modernist and popular/realist texts is insufficiently grounded in an understanding of pop music debates. Because their categories of analysis usually derive from film studies, they do not take account of the different ways in which modes of address operate in cinema and pop music. For instance, pop songs are often performed through a direct and/or first-person mode of address, thus breaking with the illusionism of the 'fourth wall' of naturalistic cinema and television. (I will return to this point in relation to MTV later.) Reading the postmodern accounts which celebrate the fragmentary visual discourses of MTV, one might never notice that its soundtrack is organized around regimes of repetition and tonality that are highly ordered and predictable. Both points should lead us to question analyses which focus on the textual disruption and disorder sometimes evident at the visual level only.

In addition, postmodern classifications of pop often work by defying generic categories in ways that are hard to understand either musicologically or sociologically. Like many writers on the topic, Marsha Kinder (1984) analyses music videos exclusively in terms of their visual components, which are assumed to dominate the aural level of the text, thus opening the way for her to draw out some intriguing connections between music television and dreams. Yet the founding assumption of the analysis is certainly open to question: 'Most concert promotions currently being aired on MTV stress the extravagance of the visual spectacle as much as the music – spectacle designed to match what is being seen on television' (Kinder 1987: 232). But visual spectacles (dancing, gesture, the display of virtuosity, lighting, smoke bombs, dry ice, back projection, etc.) have always worked in tandem with the music itself (see Frith 1988; Allan 1990; Goodwin 1992). Performance videos on music television mirror many of these codes and conventions (established in over thirty years of rock and pop concerts), yet academic theorists frequently make the mistake of relating this iconography to filmic, postmodernist and (in Kinder's case) psychoanalytic categories without taking account of its more prosaic intentions – that of evoking the excitement of live pop performance. These discourses will surely merit further study, including perhaps psychoanalytic interpretation, but we cannot understand them if we reverse the actual chronology of rock music and television. In other words, we should not assume that the signs and conventions of live performance are an imitation of television (although this does occasionally occur – in Madonna's concert performances, for instance).

E. Ann Kaplan does something similar, when she writes: 'Most often the rock video world looks like noplace, or like a post-nuclear holocaust place – without boundaries, definition or recognizable location. Figures are often placed in a smoky, hazy environment . . . the sudden, unexplained explosion is a common feature' (Kaplan 1987: 145). Concert-goers will of course recognize each of the 'post-nuclear' features of the rock video as elements in the staging of live rock shows. The 'unexplained' explosions remain unexplained only if your ears are closed – otherwise it will be noticed that they tend to coincide with the pulse of the music and occur at moments of dramatic crescendo.

Elsewhere Kaplan uses film and postmodern theory to arrive at a classification of music video that is as unconvincing as it is original. To cite one example from dozens that might be chosen: she is able to read a self-mocking song about sexual desire (Van Halen's 'Jump') as a nihilistic text in which 'the aim is clearly to shock and to violate accepted social norms' (Kaplan 1987: 103). This extraordinary conclusion (extraordinary at least to anyone who has listened to Van Halen's mild, sometimes comic, rock music) is reached solely by analysing camera angles and edits, with no reference to the song's music, lyrics or performers.

Even extremely basic musicological terms like rhythm and timbre are usually missing from the lexicon of music video analysis. Music itself is rarely discussed, despite the fact that the most elementary understanding of the form requires us to recognize that there is a correlation between sound and image; most obviously, in camera movement and editing techniques, but also in lighting, *mise-en-scène* and gesture. Disregarding these elements, postmodern analysis often looks at music television as if it were a purely visual form. This is of course a dominant *motif* of that paradigm, in which the seduction of the visual is assumed to have taken hold of contemporary culture in new and increasingly powerful ways. There are perhaps areas of culture (billboards, TV news, advertising) where the imperialism of the image has enjoyed this kind of triumph, but it will be surprising if *music* is one of them, and it has yet to be demonstrated (or even *argued*) that this is in fact the case (see Goodwin 1992).

Finally, I want to note that postmodern analyses often present a one-dimensional account of changing notions of history in pop music, tending to use all instances of quoting from pop's past as though they were simple examples of 'pastiche'. The sometimes banal invocation of 'pastiche' is problematic not only in relation to the video clips, but for our understanding of MTV in a more general way. As I will try to establish in the later sections of this chapter, MTV's intertextuality and its articulation of popular cultural history is often anything but blank. This brings me to the empirical weaknesses in the study of music television itself.

DON'T KNOW MUCH ABOUT HISTORY

Thus far the academic literature on MTV is almost pathologically ahistorical. Unlike the journalistic accounts of MTV, academic writing has usually described MTV as though it were an unchanging form, significant only for its synchronic differences with network television. The diachronic development of its schedule (which has been very considerable indeed) has been almost universally neglected by media scholars. This is, of course, thoroughly unmaterialist; for it is clear that changes in the MTV text result from institutional factors such as shifting personnel and changes in ownership patterns; each of which is intimately connected to the economic and social forces at work in the broadcasting, advertising and music industries.

Furthermore, to miss the development of MTV's schedule is to miss a central, Romantic, imperative. For MTV, like pop music, needs to display its creativity, its ability to change, its refusal to stop moving. It isn't just that MTV must be seen as hip and irreverent, but that it must seem always to be hip and irreverent in *new* ways. Former MTV president Robert Pittman has summed up the problem:

> One of the interesting things is that for all the 'issues' that have been raised about MTV, no one has ever touched on the real issue of MTV, which is: How do you keep the creativity going? How do you convince the creative people to give up a great idea and move on to a new idea? If there is one thing we worry about day after day, it is that issue.
>
> (Quoted in Hilburn 1986)

The imperative is not just to change, but to be seen to keep changing. It is an ideology drawn directly from rock culture that persists in defiance of postmodern theory, and which should encourage us to consider the historical development of MTV.

It is possible to identify three stages in MTV's history, each relating to its increasingly successful efforts to ally itself simultaneously with the major record companies and national advertisers. In the first phase of MTV's history (roughly 1981–3) the need for visually evocative clips led to an emphasis on promotional videos made in Britain. The dominant pop form at that time was the 'New Pop' – music whose stress on style and artifice perfectly suited marketing through video (see Goodwin 1987a, and Will Straw's contribution to this book). As a consequence, MTV in this period was identified heavily with the so-called second 'British Invasion' of synth-pop acts (such as Duran Duran, ABC, The Thompson Twins, Culture Club, Wham!, Thomas Dolby and The Human League). Although more conventional forms of AOR (album-oriented rock) were in fact dominant in the playlist at this time,[1] it was the distinctive look of the New Pop that gave MTV its 'cutting edge' kudos and established its visuals as non-narrative, or anti-realist, in the eyes of many cultural critics.

Both AOR music and the New Pop were dominated by white musicians. During these first seventeen months MTV was accused, time and time again, of racism in its programming policy (see, for instance, Levy 1983; Jhally 1990). Stories abound of its apparently peculiar attitude to black music, but the explanation was quite logical, however unfortunate. MTV followed the music industry in defining 'rock' in essentially racist terms, as a form of music that excluded blacks. It based its playlist on the 'narrowcasting' principle of American radio that viewed rock and 'urban contemporary' (i.e., dance music, often produced by black artists) as incompatible. Consequently blacks were largely excluded from its screens (with the exception of black VJ J. J. Jackson) on grounds of music policy. MTV denied racism, on the grounds that it merely followed the rules of the rock business (which were, nonetheless, the consequence of a long history of racism).

49

In its early years MTV was concerned to mark itself out from conventional television. It needed to establish itself as a unique, new cultural service. In September 1981 Robert Pittman, then Vice-President of Programming, put it like this:

> We're now seeing the TV become a component of the stereo system. It's ridiculous to think that you have two forms of entertainment – your stereo and your TV – which have nothing to do with one another. What we're doing is marrying those two forms so that they work together in unison. We're the first channel on cable that pioneers this. . . . I think that what we've been doing up to now in cable has been dealing with forms that have already had some success on TV. MTV is the first attempt to make TV a new form, other than video games and data channels. We're talking about creating a new form using existing technologies.[2]

MTV's only discrete programmes at this time were 'Concert Specials' and other occasional special programming (such as interviews and music-related movies). MTV was, as many commentators have noted, a form of visual radio, using the format of continuous flow associated with all-music radio stations.

This initial phase represents the peak of the postmodern claim on MTV, for two reasons. First, it is the period when the MTV schedule most closely resembled the arguments advanced by academics. There were only a few discrete programmes during this phase of MTV history, and the relatively small number of video clips available led to a high degree of repetition. For that reason, incidentally, MTV was also postmodern in another sense, because the mixing up of clips in continuous 'flow' blurred the categories of art-rock and pop, thus contributing towards a conflation of popular and high cultural discourses that might have been integrated into the argument for MTV-as-postmodern text.

Second, the video clips themselves, generated in large part by the British music industry, tended towards the abandonment of narrative, and the New Pop groups of this era eschewed the bland realism of performance videos (partly because many of them did not perform, in any traditional sense).

However, these points have to be qualified with three observations. In the first place it needs to be said that even in this period, there were separate programme slots (interview-based programming and Concert Specials) that demanded some acknowledgement – something that most scholars failed to do. Second, while the visual aspect of the early videos was often non-narrative and non-realist, a full account of these texts would involve a discussion of the lyrics and music. While narrative and realism might yet appear to be absent at these levels, there are certainly extraordinary degrees of repetition and stability at the aural level. To the best of my knowledge, no one has argued that these videos are as subversive aurally as they are visually. (Instead it is either argued or more often implied that the visual is dominant.) Furthermore, while the impact of British-based New Pop videos is important, MTV even in this innovative period devoted more air-time to the firmly established format of AOR whose videos were often extremely conventional in being either minimal-realist narratives or performance clips.

Third, it must be noted that this initial phase of MTV, which forms the basis of much scholarly writing about music television, was the least significant historically. MTV's impact on the audience and the industry during its opening seventeen months was negligible, and – as Denisoff (1988) reports – many MTV insiders see January 1983 as the true beginning of the new service, partly because this is the point when it became available in the crucial media gate-keeper markets of Manhattan and Los Angeles. In fact the music television service that now most closely resembles the wall-to-wall flow model discussed by so many critics is not MTV at all, but a newer service called the Video Juke Box Network, whose chief executive Les Garland used to work for MTV. The Video Juke Box Network has no formal programming; it simply screens video clips, on request, which are selected (via telephone) by the viewers in each area. The service has no on-screen VJs, preferring to communicate with its audience via a disembodied, robotic voice that does indeed seem to emanate from some kind of postmodern televisual cyberspace. The Video Juke Box Network has been aggressive in campaigning against MTV, in an effort to characterize its rival as old-fashioned and less liberatory than its own audience-programmed format.

Following its 'second launch', the next phase of MTV (1983–5) saw a shift in both music and programming policy which severely undermines postmodern arguments. The New Pop had gone out of fashion; and in any case, as MTV expanded from the main urban centres of the US on the coasts and into the mid-West cities and towns it needed to reach out with music that appealed to the rockist tastes of its new demographics. Furthermore, the network was no longer dependent on a relatively small number of clips originating in Europe. These factors colluded to generate MTV's embrace of heavy-metal music.

In this phase MTV programmed heavy metal with a vengeance and in doing so keyed into one of the evergreen forms of American popular culture. This was a make-or-break phase for MTV, in which it fought off network and cable competitors (including Ted Turner's Cable Music Channel), an anti-trust suit from the Discovery Music Network, and criticism from both liberals (charging sexism and racism) and conservatives (the National Coalition on Television Violence). Most importantly, MTV counter-attacked its rivals economically by signing exclusivity deals with six major record companies (Viera 1987). Programming policy during this period sees the beginnings of a shift towards the abandonment of continuous 'flow', and the use of discrete programme slots (such as *The Basement Tapes* and *MTV Countdown*, which programmed respectively tapes from new, unsigned acts and the Top 20 clips). It is during this period, as MTV began to move beyond 'flow', that many scholars began writing their analyses of MTV.

The most significant developments here, for cultural studies theorists, are the increasing use of discrete programme slots and the ascendancy of the 'performance' clip. The latter was a direct result of the need for heavy-metal acts to establish an 'authentic' (i.e., documentary rather than fictional) set of images and to display musical competence. Thus, 'on the road' pseudo-documentaries and the use of close-ups to emphasize musical virtuosity became the main staple of the promotional clips. Unlike the New Pop artists, metal acts had no interest in playing with artifice or in displaying their ironic modernism. Between the edits of fingers buzzing up and down fretboards, denim-clad musicians getting on and off tour buses, and the fans sweating and swaying in the stadia of North America, anti-narratives and anti-realism quickly faded into MTV history.

In August 1985, the Warner-Amex consortium which created MTV sold off its controlling interest in MTV Networks (MTVN) to Viacom International. This development is absolutely central for any materialist engagement with the MTV text. As Denisoff (1988) reports, chief executive Robert Pittman had attempted a leveraged buyout of MTVN along with some colleagues, and when this effort lost out to Viacom, Pittman's ascendancy at MTV was bound to end. With it went two of MTV's conceptual building blocks – narrowcasting and 'flow'.

MTV's third phase (since 1986) thus represents a widening musical scope and an accelerated movement towards a more traditional televisual schedule. In February 1985 MTV had announced a cut-back in commitment to heavy-metal clips, but this led to a period of falling ratings and crisis at the network, as MTV was viewed by insiders and critics alike as bland and outdated. For a service that was dependent on viewer perception that it was on the 'cutting edge' of pop culture, this was potentially disastrous. The ratings share fell from a peak of 1.2 million in the fourth quarter of 1983 (during the screening of *The Making of Michael Jackson's 'Thriller'*) to a 0.6 million share in that same period of 1985 (Dannen 1987).

The third phase was born out of this crisis; it involved a return to heavy metal (which became especially marked in 1987), the shift of some middle-of-the-road artists to VH-1 (a 24-hour music video station aimed at 25–54-year-olds launched by MTV Networks in January 1985), the departure of chief executive Robert Pittman in August 1986, and two trends associated with his absence: the decline of 'narrowcasting' and the development of more discrete programme slots, many of them abandoning the staple diet of promotional clips.

While heavy-metal acts are still prevalent, MTV now screens a wider variety of rock and pop music than ever before. The question of racism has been resolved by two developments: the emergence of rap crossover music that combines black and white musical forms (the Beastie Boys, Run DMC/Aerosmith's 'Walk this way', Fat Boys/Beach Boys' 'Wipe out') and the success of black heavy-metal act Living Colour, who were featured heavily throughout 1989. (J. J. Jackson left MTV in 1986, but black Briton Julie Brown has been appearing as a VJ since then.) Along with heavy metal, rap music has been the success story in American music in the 1980s, and was thus afforded its own show on MTV – *Yo! MTV Raps*. Other kinds of music were also given distinct slots (*Club MTV, Headbangers' Ball, 120 Minutes* – programming dance music, hard rock and 'alternative' music, respectively). MTV's new traditionalism is displayed in its new use of broadcast television formats, such as its Beatles cartoons (first aired on the networks), *The Tube* (which came from British television) and (more recently) *Saturday Night Live.* (It is not hard to spot the shows that MTV might pick up in the future. There are some obvious sources of 'hip' programming on the Fox network – *The Simpsons, In Living Colour* – and elsewhere in the schedule: perhaps *Twin Peaks* will enjoy its inevitable renaissance here.) MTV increasingly came to rely on non-music programming (comedy, a game show, a phone-in, a movie news/review magazine, interview programming), some of it derived directly from broadcast television (*Monty Python's Flying Circus, The Young Ones*). A key development was the success of its re-runs of *The Monkees*, first begun in February 1986.

The post-Pittman sea-changes have been very successful for MTV – which is one reason (among many) why it is a mistake to conceptualize Robert Pittman as MTV's 'author'. Ratings began to pick up in mid-1986, and by the third quarter of 1988, Viacom was reporting a 44 per cent gain in earnings from MTV Networks (*Billboard*, 19 November 1988), and its Nielsen ratings made it the second-highest rated basic cable service in the USA.

By 1989 the progress was less dramatic, but MTV Networks was nonetheless in an extraordinary period of expansion. In the summer of 1987 it had launched MTV Europe (in association with British Telecom and Robert Maxwell's Mirror Group Newspapers – although the latter partner later withdrew from this arrangement) and was syndicating MTV packages to broadcasting systems in Japan, Mexico and Australia. It has established an MTV Record Club, selling music, videos and merchandising items such as T-shirts. MTVN is extensively involved in concert sponsorship and scored a *coup* in 1989 when it contributed to the sponsorship of the long-awaited 1989–90 Rolling Stones tour of North America. There were plans for a new MTVN service (significantly, a comedy channel) and in September 1989 an MTV comedienne (star of *Just Say Julie!* and also, confusingly, called Julie Brown) debuted on network television with a CBS pilot programme entitled *Julie Brown: The Show* (she also starred in and co-scripted the Julien Temple movie *Earth Girls Are Easy*). That same year, a weekly version of *Remote Control* went into national syndication in the USA.

By its tenth birthday, MTV had won awards for excellence in cable television (for instance, for its 1989 documentary *Decade*), plaudits from some critics and industry insiders for breaking 'alternative' bands (REM being the most spectacular example) and rap acts (via *Yo! MTV Raps*), a mention in a speech by President George Bush (albeit a derogatory one) and an entry in *Webster's* dictionary (for the term 'Veejay'). MTV's tenth anniversary was marked, significantly, by a foray into prime time, when it celebrated with *MTV 10* – a programme screened on the ABC TV network. Around this same time MTV Networks announced an intention to subdivide into three separate services, in 1993. This may herald the beginning of a fourth phase in MTV's history.

In its first decade MTV has thus moved from an almost exclusive focus upon the promotion of specific areas of pop music (New Pop, heavy metal) to a role as an all-encompassing mediator of rock culture – a televisual *Rolling Stone* (or *Q* magazine) that seeks to keep its viewers up to date with all current forms of music, with developments in popular culture generally (TV, cinema, sports, celebrity news) and occasional 'hard news' stories (abortion, the environment, political news). The network has used its involvement in concert sponsorship to gain exclusive rights to announce tour dates and screen brief television premières of live 'in concert' footage. MTV News is reminding its viewers of the costs of *not* watching, when it concludes with the portentous voice-over: 'MTV News – you hear it first'.

Many of these developments certainly cast doubt on the notion that MTV represents a boundary-less break with sequence, flow and order. That was probably never very accurate as an account of how MTV operated, as the network had since its inception run programming that was organized thematically and sequentially. Since then the growth of genre-based slots and new features such as 'Rock Blocks' (four clips from one artist) have further eroded the usefulness of the postmodern account. Furthermore, the use of these slots tends to compartmentalize the 'popular' (*Club MTV, MTV Top 20 Videos*) from rock's 'high cultural' forms (*120 Minutes, Post Modern MTV*), thus preserving a distinction that music television was supposed to destroy. These trends are extraordinarily important, both in terms of the *structure* of MTV's schedule and the *content* of the programming. It is to those questions that I now turn, beginning with some remarks on the role of the VJs who guide us through the MTV schedule.

TALK IS CHEAP

In an important essay on television *sound* that is still too often neglected, Rick Altman (1987) directs our attention to the central importance of this aspect of the television message and develops Raymond Williams's concept of 'flow'. Altman suggests that the sound portion of the television text is designed primarily to interrupt the 'household flow' of everyday life and push our attention towards the television screen. This aspect of MTV remains neglected, after nearly a decade on the air. Clearly it would require an engagement with the music itself; here I am concerned with the other central aspect of MTV's soundtrack – the on-screen VJs and what they say.

The voices of the VJs offer a variety of appeals, from information and gossip concerning the video clips and their stars (VJ Adam Curry and news presenter Kurt Loder), through endorsement of particular acts (China Kantner and Julie Brown), to humorous and sometimes satirical comments on the world of rock culture (of the current MTV VJs, as I write in September 1989, Kevin Seal is the nearest they have to the rock-critic-as-cynic). Both visually and aurally, the VJs thus *anchor* the MTV text using the familiar conventions of the radio DJ and the news presenter. Just as close-ups of rock stars' faces ground the visual component of video clips, so the VJs help to forge a path through the fast pace and sometimes oblique imagery of MTV, undertaking the role identified by Altman – that of linking televisual and household flow. Thus the VJs routinely trail upcoming segments, with comments such as 'coming up in the next hour, Madonna, Michael Jackson and the new video from Aerosmith'.

But the VJs do more than this. They also offer a girl/boy-next-door point of identification for MTV viewers that is mirrored in the gossipy, humorous scripts, in the *mise-en-scène* of the MTV set (an adolescent's 'den', a dance club) and in the VJ's interaction with viewers during phone-ins, contests and outside broadcasts (such as *Amuck in America*, and its Spring Break and Super Bowl specials). The identification-point established by the VJs is, unsurprisingly, a conscious MTV strategy:

> There were no specifics except that we wanted to create a human status for MTV. We wanted those individuals who would get up and wouldn't try to become stars, that wouldn't try to become entertainers. . . . For that reason we didn't look for celebrities, we looked for those people who wouldn't be overbearing or overpowering.
>
> (John Sykes, MTV's Vice-President of Programming, quoted in Denisoff 1988: 47)

Or, as Robert Pittman put it, the VJs should be 'guides who could sublimate their egos, be *human faces you could relate to*' (quoted in Levy 1983, my emphasis).

This anchoring identification-point is one that has generally been missed in accounts of MTV as an unstable text. It has rarely been noted that during the extraordinary amount of time that the camera looks at the VJs, it usually remains stationary, in a mid-to-close-up shot that typifies the framing of television presenters and personalities. Often there will be distracting moving images in the background, but the VJ will usually remain motionless, and generally speaking so does the camera. In contrast, then, to the aurally-motivated camera movement in the video clips, the framing of the VJs gives us a secure point from which to position ourselves.

The account of the VJ's function echoes John Langer's (1981) analysis of television 'personalities', and suggests the operation of a *hierarchy of identification* in MTV (and perhaps in television more generally). The VJs

55

represent the ordinary, where the rock stars in the video clips represent the glamorous. But the hierarchy of identification goes beyond this fairly obvious point, in ways that help to illustrate the stable nature of the MTV text. Langer's opposition of cinema and television works surprisingly well for rock music and television also. For instance, it is noted that while cinema represents a world that is somehow 'out there', television remains intimate, domestic and always available. This is exactly the relation between pop stars and the VJs. The VJs have no media life outside MTV. They are thus (like news anchors and chat show hosts) conduits who give us, the television viewers, access to pop star celebrities who enjoy fame beyond the confines of the small screen.

This anchoring function of the VJs is partly achieved through the appearance of 'live' transmission. This occurs in two ways. First, the pre-recorded VJ introductions are scripted and presented as though the VJs were (like radio DJs) playing the clips to us live from the television studio, in real time. (In fact, the taped VJ segments are being edited live into video clips and advertisements, by an engineer.) Second, the VJs, unlike the pop stars, are actually speaking. Since most of the musicians who appear on MTV are lip-syncing, the VJs inevitably enjoy a more intimate, apparently direct channel of communication. Again this is an important part of the MTV text that has generally gone unnoticed. The contribution of the VJs can be understood better if MTV is compared to those music television services that use disembodied announcers on sound-only (Superstation WTBS's *Night Tracks*, or the Video Juke Box Network, for instance), where their absence blocks the possibility of constructing an ambience linked to a station-identity; or with the use of celebrity guest VJs (on NBC's *Friday Night Videos*, for instance).

Importantly, Robert Pittman was initially anxious about the stiffness of VJ presentation and soon the VJs were encouraged to take a casual attitude to fluffed lines and on-air mistakes, which are often broadcast despite the fact that these segments are recorded and could thus be corrected before transmission. Here, the VJ portion of the MTV text is clearly drawing on rock and roll, rather than televisual, conventions, in which 'feel' is more important than accuracy. There are two correlations here between MTV and rock culture. First, MTV seeks to present itself as a 'rock' alternative to the pre-rock culture of network television: hence the emphasis on the construction of spontaneity, which has primacy over competence – a fundamental tenet of rock musicology. Second, the VJ presentation calls attention to itself (through the inclusion of 'mis-takes', and through the VJ's frequent references to other studio personnel) and thus echoes the non-naturalistic nature of pop performance. Far from being anarchic, VJ-talk is therefore absolutely conventional, when read in the light of a rock aesthetic. Thus, while it is true that music television's mode of representation breaks with the classic realist text of Hollywood cinema, it nonetheless continues to use processes of identification (the rock star and the TV personality) which are fundamental sources of textual stability, not to mention key elements in the aesthetics of pop music.

AND NOW FOR SOMETHING COMPLETELY FAMILIAR

The VJs help us to negotiate a schedule that has become increasingly complex. As MTV has incorporated more non-music programming and established regular slots for different kinds of music, it has moved away from the format of 24-hour all-music radio, with its exclusive dependence on one musical genre, and evolved a schedule that is often extremely traditional.

In 1988 MTV turned to two classic audience-building techniques of broadcast media scheduling: 'dayparting' and 'stripping'. Both are designed to make the schedule more predictable and to encourage consumers to tune in at the same time each day. 'Dayparting' is the practice of scheduling different kinds of music during separate blocks of each day's programming. (It thus represents a formal break with the 'narrowcasting' music policy of MTV's early history.) 'Stripping' is a practice derived from independent (i.e., non-affiliated) TV stations in the US, in which episodes of the same TV series are screened at the same time each day of the week. Thus MTV's 24-hour 'flow' is increasingly punctuated by regular slots organized around a predictable weekly schedule. As the non-music programming increases, it is becoming harder to distinguish MTV from other entertainment-led developments in the US cable industry.

The result is that MTV's schedule on a typical day in August 1991 looked like this:

7 am	*Awake on the Wild Side*
9 am	Music videos (Daisy Fuentes)
12 noon	Music videos (Andrew Daddo)
3 pm	*Spring Break '91*
4 pm	*Yo! MTV Raps*
4.30 pm	*Totally Pauly*
6 pm	*Dial MTV*
7 pm	*MTV's Half Hour Comedy Hour*
7.30 pm	*Hot Seat*
8 pm	*Prime with Martha Quinn*
10 pm	*House of Style*
11.30 pm	*Bootleg MTV*
12 midnight	*120 Minutes*

Other slots not included here are: *The Day in Rock, The Week in Rock, The Big Picture, MTV's Top 20 Video Countdown* and the *MTV Rockumentary*. Set out in a *TV Guide* or daily newspaper grid, MTV often has *more* individual programme slots than the network broadcasters or its cable rivals (CNN, for instance). Of course, we need to take account of the extensive repetition of segments and programmes. This degree of repetition differentiates MTV (and most cable services) from the practices of network television. However, it is now presented in a framework which is very far indeed from seamless, unbounded 'flow'.

This leads me to comment on the supposedly 'timeless' experience of watching MTV. Clearly the passing of time on MTV *does* work differently from the narrative-based practices of network television. In particular, the degree of narrativity in the video clips themselves is fairly limited, and the absence of a simple beginning–middle–end structure of storytelling in pop lyrics is mirrored at the visual level in most video clips. This combines with the fact that musical narratives do not work through the classic realist formula of equilibrium–action–resolution, thus producing a sense of timelessness in the clips. The absence of narrative development is further exaggerated by the degree of repetition involved in both the heavy rotation of the same clips, and the re-broadcast of the same slots. Music television thus mirrors both rock music itself and the broadcasting practices of all-music radio.

However, critics have hitherto missed some extremely important ways in which the passing of time *is* experienced in music television. First, there is the role of both programme-identification and VJ-talk in locating the clips historically. It is not just that some videos are presented as 'oldies' (on *Closet Classic Capsule* or *Classic MTV* for instance), but that some clips are presented as 'new'. Both in the 'Hip clip of the week' and in the pervasive screening of 'MTV exclusives', the viewer is placed in a relation to the clip that implies a sense of time. We are aware (if we follow pop music, as most MTV viewers do) that we are seeing a mix of very new, current, older and 'historic' clips, and this may well temper the apparently timeless nature of the MTV experience.

Indeed, in 1988 MTV became historically self-conscious, airing *Deja Video* (which was soon retitled *Classic MTV*, and then *Prime with Martha Quinn*). This show features video clips from the early 1980s and is hosted by original MTV VJ Martha Quinn. 'Now you can relive those carefree days of youth', says a voice-over on a trailer for this show, as we look at a shot of a baby. In the summer of 1989 MTV frequently screened 'Woodstock Minutes' – segments of footage from the 1969 Woodstock festival, some of it never previously aired (a strategy derived from its sister channel VH-1, which pioneered the use of extremely short 'Milestones' featuring archive documentary footage of political events from the 1960s). Unlike *Deja Video/Classic MTV*, these clips did not explicitly frame the video clips themselves, but they certainly did work (alongside MTV News items about Woodstock) to contextualize the development of rock, and they suggest the possibility of a movement towards a 'classic rock' format for some sections of MTV programming. This all-too-firmly *historicizing* perspective is already in place on VH-1, where 1960s' pop star Peter Noone (of Herman's Hermits) hosts a daily programme entitled *My Generation*.

Second, many MTV slots (such as the *MTV Countdown*) depend on a temporal experience for the delivery of pleasure. The most obvious example is chart-based programming, which utilizes the narrative enigma of 'which clip will be number one this week?' The process of guessing which videos will be on the chart (and therefore which will be screened) exactly mirrors the narrative element of classic broadcast music programming such as *American Bandstand*, and the BBC's *Top of the Pops*.

Third, there are MTV's special broadcasts (often scheduled on weekends), which increasingly mirror the networks' cyclical organization of television 'seasons'. While MTV, in common with much cable and independent television in the USA, has not generally observed the conventions of the TV season, its year-round flow is organized around various annual events, such as the *MTV Video Music Awards* show, the New Year's Eve special, and outside broadcasts built around national rituals such as Spring Break, Super Bowl, Independence Day, Labor Day, and so on. By the autumn of 1989, viewers could watch trailers advertising 'MTV's new Fall season'.

Clearly, these observations raise empirical questions about reports which stress the importance of the lack of boundaries in MTV programming, its timeless, ahistorical, quality and its refusal to offer a fixed point of identification for the viewer. Whether the purpose is to establish a correlation with dreams or aspects of postmodernism, the analysis must be open to question now that the dreamlike or postmodern experience of watching music television is partially dismantled through the move towards the establishment and maintenance of programming boundaries within its overall 'flow'. Kaplan (1987: 29) typifies the postmodern *oeuvre*, when she writes that 'MTV simply takes over the history of rock and roll, flattening out all the distinct types into one continuous present'. Once again, that statement was inaccurate when it was written; ironically enough, it has been made to look less credible with the passing of time.

MTV's increasingly conventional format can be illustrated through a brief consideration of three shows that have now been aired for some years: *Club MTV, Remote Control* and *The Week in Rock*.

Club MTV needs only a brief comment, but it is interesting because it represents a clear reproduction of a format used in network/broadcast television. Using a set which represents a discotheque, the show plays current dance-music hits, and features video clips, lip-syncing and 'live' performances by current hit-makers and a large portion of audience participation – its anchoring shots are those of audience members dancing, and it includes interviews with audience members, some of whom then introduce the clips. *Club MTV* is hosted by the channel's only black VJ, Julie Brown. In other words, *Club MTV* is a straightforward copy of the syndicated television show *Soul Train*, which was first aired in the early 1970s. While *Soul Train* is its most obvious antecedent, *Club MTV* also resembles chart-shows like *American Bandstand*, *Solid Gold* and the BBC's *Top of the Pops*. It is important for my arguments because, like *Monty Python* and many other MTV programmes, *Club MTV* represents a move back to traditional broadcast television formats.

The game show *Remote Control* first aired on MTV in December 1987 and has been its most successful venture into non-music programming. Unlike *Club MTV, Remote Control* combines a broadcast television format (the game show) with MTV's trademark sense of satire and lampoon. The hosts are deliberately obnoxious; the show's segments are punctuated with cheesy organ music that parodies game-show conventions; while the prizes are displayed, an irksome voice-over underscores game-show consumer greed with a sleazy parody of the genre; the questions are universally lacking in substance (dealing almost exclusively in the *minutae* of television trivia); and the contestants are treated with joking scorn – as losing players are eliminated, they are physically thrown from the studio floor, ejected via the back wall of the set while strapped into their seats.

In a typical *Remote Control* exchange, host Ken Ober asks a contestant where he works. The answer, that he is an employee of the greetings card manufacturer Hallmark, provokes this (sarcastic) response: 'Well, that's great, you know, because Hallmark says the things that *I can't say.*' This joke, an improvization on a continuing MTV riff which lampoons aspects of 'straight', parental, culture finds an echo in network television talk-shows like *Late Night with David Letterman* and *The Arsenio Hall Show*.

Remote Control is interesting for two reasons. First, in its title and content the programme reveals the deep-seated alliance that television and pop music culture have consolidated in the years since punk rock. Its assumption is that knowledge of pop music and television go hand-in-hand. Second, *Remote Control's* parodies key into *the promotion of satire* which is a marked feature of MTV in its third phase (when *The Monkees, The Young Ones* and *Monty Python* were first aired). The problem here, for postmodernism, is that parody and satire, unlike pastiche, clearly articulate a point of view. Furthermore, in the case of MTV, that point of view has a very clear generational basis (the class politics of *Monty Python* are probably lost on large portions of the American audience) which suggests not postmodernity so much as a prior discourse of Romantic rebellion.

MTV's programme *The Week in Rock* reveals a concrete connection with its *Rolling Stone*-like ambitions – it is presented by *Rolling Stone* journalist Kurt Loder, who also anchors MTV News bulletins throughout its general programming. It is no surprise to discover, then, that *The Week in Rock* is the MTV show that most clearly displays its commitment to a traditional, Romantic, rock aesthetic. By this I mean the construction of an ideology around rock music which sets itself up in opposition to selected elements in the commercialization of music, which establishes an opposition between youth and parental cultures, and which maintains a vaguely oppositional left/liberal political agenda. (For instance: introducing the clip for Paula Abdul's 'Cold hearted', VJ Adam Curry refers to record executives portrayed in its opening sequence as 'geeks and goons'. He thus emphasizes an us/them paradigm built around musicians and their various gatekeepers that is employed in numerous other clips, such as Neil Young's 'This note's for you',[3] John Mellencamp's 'Pop singer', Richard Marx's 'Don't mean nothing', Depeche Mode's 'Everything counts', Quiet Riot's 'The wild and the young' and The Clash's 'Radio clash'.)

It is certainly arguable that this Romantic agenda is collapsing throughout the field of pop culture, and MTV is an element in that process (as is *Rolling Stone*). Indeed, it is possible to see much postmodernist commentary on MTV as a displaced account of this phenomenon. However, what has generally been neglected is the extent to which MTV insists on *maintaining* elements of this ideology. No doubt this is largely a cynical operation, but it remains a key factor in the production of meaning in rock culture.

For instance, in the edition of *The Week in Rock* broadcast on 8 July 1989, a counter-cultural sense of rock culture was frequently invoked. This edition of *The Week in Rock* begins with an item about the Supreme Court decision to allow states to restrict abortion rights. Like most of MTV's hard-news items, it is presented with the authoritative gestures and intonation of network news. These news items, like MTV's anti-drugs and anti-drunk-driving ads, indicate that it *is* prepared to suggest that some things *are* worth taking seriously. Regardless of their overt politics, they thus represent a break with the nothing-matters-and-what-if-it-does? worldview often attributed to MTV. Furthermore, the coverage of the Supreme Court abortion decision reveals clear liberal intentions, in its 4:1 ratio of interviewees opposed to and in favour of the decision.

The second portion of the show begins with news footage of Oliver North, captioned with the word 'FREE'. As James Brown's song '(I feel like a) sex machine' plays on the soundtrack, Brown's image then appears next to North's (using split screen) and the caption 'NOT FREE' appears under *his* photograph. The references are to the then recent decision in North's trial (acquitting him on all but three charges and forgoing a jail sentence) and to the jailing of James Brown for drugs and assault offences some months earlier, with a sentence that many commentators and activists found overly punitive. This political montage goes without comment when presenter Loder reappears, but the message can hardly be missed.

Formally, this might appear to be a typical case of the primacy of the image – the articulation of political argument via visual snapshots. And yet the sequence defies two of the key elements identified in recent postmodern discussions of the image. First, while it is (like all images) polysemic, its use of montage contains a compelling preferred reading. Second, that reading implies a clear socio-political stance. In other words, in defiance of postmodernity, the segment takes a position (using, incidentally, the classic *modernist* device of *montage*).

61

In other segments of MTV News the cable channel has offered favourable coverage of the Black Rock Coalition (an activist group designed to promote black musicians working in the hard-rock genre), numerous positive accounts of the development of *glasnost* in the Soviet Union during the late 1980s, sympathetic stories on the AIDS crisis and a sardonic, liberal account of the furore over flag-burning that occurred in the US in the summer of 1989.

These are admittedly fairly mild instances of counter-cultural struggle. Judged by the heady days of the 1960s, or the punk era, they may seem feeble indeed. To that extent MTV absolutely typifies the political trajectory of rock and pop in the 1980s. But it is important to stress them, just as it is necessary to emphasize the continuing commitment to some kind of liberal/progressive politics in the music and videos of acts such as Living Colour, U2, Peter Gabriel, Bruce Springsteen, Los Lobos, Public Enemy, KRS-One, Madonna, Lou Reed, REM, Don Henley and Metallica (each of whom were featured heavily in MTV playlists in the late 1980s and early 1990s), in order to redress the imbalance of the postmodern hermeneutic.

MORE THAN ZERO

Postmodern writers have had a field day with the question of MTV's supposedly ahistorical, apolitical, asocial, amoral aesthetic: 'MTV denies the existence of all but the moment, and that moment exists only on the screen. . . . There aren't any problems on MTV', writes David Tetzlaff (1986). John Fiske (1986) concurs: 'The flashing crashing image-sounds *are* energy, speed, illusion, the hyperreal themselves: they simulate nothing, neither the reality nor the social machine.' E. Ann Kaplan (1987: 146) observes that 'MTV is part of a contemporary discourse that has written out history as a possible discourse.' This is a vivid gloss on Baudrillard, but it is difficult to sustain empirically in relation to MTV.

In one of its most unnerving sequences (initially developed by MTV Europe as 'ONE PLANET – ONE MUSIC'), an MTV station ID segment culminates in the legend: 'ONE WORLD, ONE IMAGE, ONE CHANNEL'. But in fact, there are *two* MTVs. One MTV discourse is the nihilistic, pastiching, essentially pointless playfulness that is invoked in postmodernist accounts of MTV. The other is responsible, socially conscious, satire and parody-based, vaguely liberal . . . and almost invisible in academic accounts of MTV.

The MTV logo itself exemplifies the devil-may-care discourse, which is constructed in part in explicit (and quite conscious) opposition to network television, in that the logo is both inconsistent and irreverent – it takes many different forms and is often presented through visual jokes. Many of its slogans clearly promote just the kind of discourse the postmodernists analyse: 'MTV: WE'RE MAKING IT UP AS WE GO ALONG' and 'MTV: BETTER SORRY THAN SAFE' are two such examples. Something similar occurs when the slogan 'THE WHOLE WORLD IS WATCHING' is used in conjunction with images of cows chewing the cud in a field. (Although, given the roots of *that* slogan in the student demonstrations at the 1968 Democratic convention in Chicago, the Frankfurt School notion of 'incorporation' would be every bit as appropriate as postmodern theory here.) Many of the filmed mini-fictions inserted between clips also fall into this category. The sometimes pointless (but extremely funny) humour of Gilbert Godfrey, who performs stand-up comedic blips between videos from time to time, is a good example. Trailing MTV's *Half-Hour Comedy Hour*, Godfrey asks: 'If it's half ours, who does the other half belong to?'

However, there is another cluster of discourses at play within MTV programming and presentation material – a grouping of quasi-political, volunteerist, socially responsible and sometimes counter-cultural riffs that the postmodernists have chosen to ignore. What, for instance, are we to make of this statement, from former MTVN president Robert Pittman? In an interview in *Channels* magazine, Pittman appears to return to a classic Romantic rock ideology when he says, 'You have to be careful that you stay this side of the line of being perceived by the consumer as a sellout' (quoted in Robins 1989). MTV's sales pitch has to be seen in relation to this ideology of rock, as well as postmodernism. The complicating factor here is the transformation, in the 1980s, of rock's counter-cultural ideology into a discourse that combines traditional notions of rebellion and Romantic rejection of everyday life with a new sense of social responsibility and philanthropic concern. Thus, at the same time that MTV has kept its tongue firmly in its cheek, it also had to come to terms with cause–rock events such as Live Aid, Amnesty International's Conspiracy of Hope tour and the Smile Jamaica benefit concert.

MTV has also run frequent promotional clips for the Rock Against Drugs and Make a Difference anti-drugs campaigns, and in June 1989 banned the video clip for NWA's 'Straight outta Compton' on the grounds that it might seem to glorify crime associated with gang membership. Its screening of the anti-apartheid video 'Sun city' was, as George Lipsitz (1987) notes, reverential and serious. During its broadcast of the Make a Difference rock concert in the Soviet Union in August 1989, it repeatedly used the slogan 'COOL MUSIC, NOT COLD WAR'. On a more radical note, in January 1992 MTV screened Public Enemy's video 'By the time I get to Arizona' with the stated intention of foregrounding that group's concerns about Arizona's non-observance of Martin Luther King Jnr's birthday. The clip, which intercut reconstructions of episodes from King's life with fictional footage of Public Enemy and its entourage assassinating white officials from Arizona, was a trenchant statement of black militancy which offended and upset many liberals.

Even MTV's humour sometimes has a point. A July 1989 episode of *Just Say Julie*, which appeared to be a pointless, irreverent look at the portrayal of animals in music video clips, ended with a caption giving the address of the Campaign for the Ethical Treatment of Animals. During the screening of the anti-Soviet ABC mini-series *Amerika* in February 1987, MTV labelled itself 'MTV-ski' (using the slogan: 'MTV: MUSIC TELEVISION FOR THE RE-EDUCATED') and pointedly screened the red-baiting 1956 Department of Defense film *Red Nightmare*.

And this brings me to the question of MTV's political stance. Analysing one area of MTV's non-music programming (its brief, often humorous, fictional clips), Lawrence Grossberg presents a view of postmodernity that has become a standard interpretation:

> MTV offers us a series of ads promoting Randee [the imaginary leader of an imaginary rock group, Randee and the Redwoods], for president. His entire media campaign is composed of clichéd paradoxes: e.g., Randee at a press conference says that he was misunderstood when he said that 'First there is a mountain, then there is no mountain, then there is'. He points out that he did not mean to say that there is no mountain. 'There is one,' he says to thunderous applause. 'And after I'm elected there will be one.' Feeling something, anything, is better than feeling nothing.
>
> (Grossberg 1988: 44)

Grossberg's analysis is worthwhile and suggestive, because he goes on to show that this postmodern structure of feeling is not merely nihilistic. Grossberg's category of 'ironic inauthenticity' is a useful addition to our understanding of the formations of readership that inform the reception of MTV and contemporary pop music. (But even this category is double-edged, for what is the slogan 'ONE WORLD, ONE MUSIC, ONE CHANNEL' but an Orwellian effort to pursue MTV's global intentions and retain counter-cultural credibility by owning up to the intent? In other words, as with Isuzu's infamous 'Joe Isuzu' television commercials, the *incorporation* of ironic inauthenticity.)

However, we can also provide an alternative concluding sentence for this passage. I would like to re-write Grossberg's gloss thus:

> MTV offers us a series of ads promoting Randee [the imaginary leader of an imaginary rock group, Randee and the Redwoods], for president. His entire media campaign is composed of clichéd paradoxes: e.g., Randee at a press conference says that he was misunderstood when he said that 'First there is a mountain, then there is no mountain, then there is'. He points out that he did not mean to say that there is no mountain. 'There is one,' he says to thunderous applause. 'And after I'm elected there will be one.' Thus parody is used to establish a critique of campaigning strategies in the US political system.

This, in my view, is the *other* MTV. It is the MTV that organized voter registration drives in 1984. And it is the MTV that is neglected in nearly all the published research on music television.

If my analysis is correct then the study of MTV can no longer proceed in a state of occupational amnesia that ignores the twenty years of work in media and cultural studies that preceded the emergence of postmodern theory. That is not to deny MTV's innovations, or its potential for a postmodern reading. As Pfeil (1988) and Grossberg (1988) suggest, work on postmodernism as a condition of reception can be extremely fruitful. But in the analysis of music television as a postmodern *text* scholars need to pay much greater heed to the empirical data and to the contradictions within MTV, which cannot be seamlessly reduced to a single aesthetic category.

ACKNOWLEDGEMENTS

Sections of this chapter are drawn from my book, *Dancing in the Distraction Factory: MTV, Music Television and Popular Culture* (University of Minnesota Press, 1992). Reprinted with permission.

A version of this chapter was presented to the Comparative Arts Colloquium at the University of Rochester, and in a seminar at the Eastman School of Music. My thanks to the organizers and participants of both events. Thanks also to Lawrence Grossberg for his comments.

NOTES

1   Denisoff (1988: 84–5) quotes Les Garland, then Vice-President of Programming, talking in August 1982, thus: 'About 30 to 40 per cent of the music we play is not on the typical AOR radio station.' Note, therefore, how much of the playlist *was* AOR! In early 1983, Garland told a reporter: 'We can show REO Speedwagon *and* Duran Duran. We can show Kenny Loggins *and* Haircut One Hundred. We've been able to invent our own format, because we're the only ones doing it.' ('America gets its MTV', *BAM* magazine, 11 February 1983).
2   Quoted in *Videography*, September 1981.
3   Young's song attacks corporate sponsorship and names names (including some MTV advertisers), which resulted in a controversy concerning MTV's failure to screen the video, directed by Julien Temple (see Reed 1988). Typically, MTV then nominated the clip for its 1989 *Video Music Awards* show, where it won the award for best video of the year. Subsequently, MTV chief executive Tom Freston conceded that MTV's decision to ban the clip was a mistake that lost the channel a considerable amount of credibility with the rock audience – see the interview with Freston in *SPIN*, January 1992.

REFERENCES

Allan, B. (1990) 'Musical cinema, music video, music television', *Film Quarterly*, vol. 43, no. 3.
Altman, R. (1987) 'Television sound', in Horace Newcomb (ed.), *Television: The Critical View*, New York: Oxford University Press.
Aufderheide, P. (1986) 'Music videos: the look of the sound', in Todd Gitlin (ed.), *Watching Television*, New York: Pantheon.
Billboard (1988) 'Viacom's earnings fall: MTV up, Showtime down', 19 November.
Dannen, F. (1987) 'MTV's great leap backward', *Channels*, July/August.
Denisoff, S. (1988) *Inside MTV*, New York: Transaction.

Fiske, J. (1986) 'MTV: post-structural post-modern', *Journal of Communication Inquiry*, vol. 10, no. 1 (Winter).

Frith, S. (1988) 'Video pop', in S. Frith (ed.), *Facing the Music*, New York: Pantheon.

Gitlin, T. (1986) 'We build excitement: car commercials and *Miami Vice*' in T. Gitlin (ed.) *Watching Television*, New York: Pantheon.

Glassner, B. (1989) 'The medium must not deconstruct: a postmodern ethnography of *USA Today the Television Show*'. Paper presented to American Sociological Association Conference, San Francisco, July.

Goodwin, A. (1987a) 'From anarchy to chromakey: music, video, media', *OneTwoThreeFour: A Rock'n'Roll Quarterly*, no. 5 (Spring), Los Angeles.

—— (1987b) 'Music video in the (post) modern world', *Screen*, vol. 28, no. 3 (Summer), London: SEFT.

—— (1988) 'Sample and hold: pop music in the digital age of reproduction', *Critical Quarterly*, vol. 30, no. 3.

—— (1991) 'Popular music and postmodern theory', *Cultural Studies*, vol. 5, no. 2.

—— (1992) *Dancing in the Distraction Factory: Music Television and Popular Music*, Minneapolis: University of Minnesota Press.

Grossberg, L. (1987) 'The in-difference of television', *Screen*, vol. 28, no. 2 (Spring), London: SEFT.

—— (1988) *It's A Sin: Postmodernism, Politics & Culture*, with Tony Fry, Ann Curthoys and Paul Patton, Sydney: Power Publications.

Hilburn, R. (1986) 'MTV's creator tackles new goals', in 'Calendar' section, *Los Angeles Times*, 5 September.

Jhally, S. (1990) *The Codes of Advertising: Fetishism and the Political Economy of Meaning in the Consumer Society*, New York: Routledge.

Kaplan, Ann E. (1987) *Rocking Around the Clock: Music Television, Postmodernism and Consumer Culture*, New York: Methuen.

Kinder, M. (1984) 'Music video and the spectator: television, ideology and dream', *Film Quarterly*, vol. 38, no. 1.

—— (1987) 'Music video and the spectator: television, ideology and dream', in Horace Newcomb (ed.), *Television: The Critical View*, New York: Oxford University Press.

Langer, J. (1981) 'Television's "personality system" ', *Media, Culture & Society*, vol. 3, no. 4.

Levy, S. (1983) '*Ad nauseum*: how MTV sells out rock and roll', *Rolling Stone*, 8 December.

Lipsitz, G. (1987) 'A world of confusion: music video as modern myth', *OneTwoThreeFour: A Rock'n'Roll Quarterly*, no. 5.

Pfeil, F. (1988) 'Postmodernism as a "structure of feeling" ', in Cary Nelson and Lawrence Grossberg (eds), *Marxism and the Interpretation of Culture*, London: Macmillan.

Robins, J. (1989) 'Into the groove', *Channels*, May.

Tetzlaff, D. (1986) 'MTV and the politics of postmodern pop', *Journal of Communication Inquiry*, vol. 10, no. 1.

Viera, (1987) 'The institutionalization of music video', *OneTwoThreeFour: A Rock'n'Roll Quarterly*, no. 5.

Wollen, P. (1986) 'Ways of thinking about music video (and post-modernism)', *Critical Quarterly*, vol. 28, nos 1 & 2.

References to follow

4

YOUTH/MUSIC/TELEVISION

Simon Frith

One of the most striking aspects of British media in the 1980s was their self-reflexivity. By the end of the decade every quality newspaper had a media editor and a media page; Channel 4 broadcast the *Media Show*; the BBC had a weekly television programme looking at television and a weekly radio programme about radio. Even the advertising industry got in on the act. Advertising campaigns were treated as art on *The Late Show*; advertising history became a recurring subject for TV documentaries; the annual advertising industry prize-giving took its television place alongside the BAFTA film and TV awards and the publishing industry's Booker Prize. The media's own disputes and debates, its own stars and success stories, had become a matter for public entertainment.

For broadcasters the Big Issue was the remapping of the audio-visual landscape. What would follow from the new teletechnology, the new picture carriers, from cable and satellite, from deregulating state policies? What was the future of European broadcasting?[1] In the media themselves these questions were discussed in familiar enough terms: lines of battle were drawn up between public service and the free market, between creative integrity and consumer choice. The tone of this version of the argument was best caught in the media pages of Rupert Murdoch's *Sunday Times*. Here, for example, is the voice of the broadcasting establishment, in this case Colin MacCabe, giving the annual *South Bank Show* lecture (broadcast on commercial TV in its 52-minute entirety):

> Speaking to a smug and appreciative studio audience largely composed of broadcasters, he warned portentously that 'free-market television would deliver a range of undifferentiated programmes which would leave us, as citizens, considerably impoverished . . . if we have 80 channels which spread existing resources between them, then we will have 80 channels providing a diet of *I Love Lucy* re-runs and the golden hits of the BBC, liberally interspersed with soft porn . . . it would be criminal folly if our resource-rich industry were dismantled in the name of a quite illusory notion of consumer choice'.

67

In response, the voice of consumer choice, in this case Jonathan Miller, then the *Sunday Times*'s media editor but shortly to become the executive in charge of publicity for Murdoch's Sky Television:

> In the 50 per cent of American homes that have cable, viewers can watch more BBC drama in a week than we can. They can watch gavel-to-gavel coverage of both the House of Representatives and the Senate, and in many states, of their own legislatures. They can tune to hundreds of television stations, each providing hours a day of highly localized news programmes of a type wholly absent from British television. And they can choose from specialized channels for news, the arts, sport, children, film, music, current affairs, and science and nature – as well as a wide variety of general entertainment channels available by subscription or supported by advertising.[2]

The questions here – What is choice? What is market choice? – were at the centre of the political agenda in the 1980s, and in this paper I want to explore some of the issues raised by the valorization of the 'consumer' of television. In particular, I am intrigued by the way in which, for a moment, questions about the television audience got entangled with questions about the youth audience. The resulting rhetorical confusion affected both the ways in which leisure entrepreneurs saw the future of television and the ways in which academic entrepreneurs analysed the implications.[3] If, in the end, 'youth' turned out to be a misleading metaphor for change, it still has, nevertheless, a resonance for cultural theory that needs examination.

YOUTH TELEVISION

British media interest in 'youth television' (which was at its most clamorous in 1988) was triggered by the appointment of Janet Street-Porter as youth adviser to the BBC, a role which was quickly redefined as youth editor (her brief was to commission and develop youth programmes), an appointment which coincided with that of Stephen Garrett as (the second) commissioning editor for youth at Channel 4.

The immediate problem, to which Street-Porter's appointment was a response, was the failure of British broadcasters to reach the young audience. Market research suggested that while 16–24-year-olds made up 15 per cent of the population, they only formed 9 per cent of the television audience; if the average viewer watched 27 hours of television per week, 16–24-year-olds watched only 17 hours (senior citizens watched for 37 hours). Two of the most established youth music programmes had been axed: the BBC's veteran *Whistle Test* (its audience now less than 2 million) and, after five series, Channel 4's *The Tube* (its audience now less than 1 million). *The Roxy*, ITV's attempt at a chart-show rival to *Top of the Pops* (which still reached an audience of 10–12 million) flopped and was dropped. It had never got figures of more than 7 million and, as David Liddimont, commissioning executive for entertainment at Granada, explained, 'It can't sustain a large enough audience at peak time and if it is out of peak time there isn't the money to make the show.'[4]

The questions Street-Porter and Garrett faced were fundamental. What did 'youth TV' now mean? Was pop still its programming basis? Was there still a 'mass' youth audience? How should 'specialist' youth interests be met? It is not clear, a few years on, that Garrett, at least, found satisfactory answers to these questions. He has yet to come up with a youth programme either as popular or as stylistically resonant as *The Tube*. His policy has been to go for more 'grown up' rock and pop shows (*Wired*, *Big World Cafe*) on the one hand, and broader cultural coverage (*Club X*, *Halfway to Paradise*, *The Word*), on the other. Garrett remarked that

> The wonderful thing about being Commissioning Editor for Youth Programming is that there's no such thing as youth programming. I don't have this vision of a spotty 19-year-old in Nottingham to whom I'm saying, 'This is a programme for you!'[5]

But he remained committed both to 'representing' young people on television, and to giving them access to the studio, and, in this respect, Janet Street-Porter's *Def 2* programming for BBC2 has, ironically, been more of a departure from public service ideology.[6]

I will return to Street-Porter's policy later. The point I want to make immediately is that the confusion about the future of youth TV was the context in which the concept of 'youth' became pivotal to arguments about broadcasting choice.

This reflected, in part, the empirical situation: the uses of the television screen developed in the 1980s – for computer and video games, for time-shifting and home rentals, for cable and satellite services – were specifically associated with the youth audience. This was most obvious in the case of the games, but PETAR findings in 1988 similarly revealed the 'appeal of new services to young people'. The first systematic measurement of the European cable/satellite audience, the PETAR figures were read closely by Britain's would-be new broadcasters, and more detailed national studies confirmed the Euro-pattern. Swedish research, for example, showed that take-up of both VCRs and cable services were much higher for families with children; that teenagers watched both rented videos and cabled programmes more than any other members of the family; that adolescent Swedes were the most likely to watch satellite shows rather than national programmes. 'Foreign television', in Keith Roe's words, was 'to a large extent young people's television'. Danish research confirmed this suggestion: there too 9–18-year-olds were the biggest users of satellite services. Dutch figures showed that their heaviest satellite users were under 40, that the use of teletext was highest among 19–34-year-olds, that the only marked increase of time spent with electronic media in the 1980s was among people under 20.[7]

The youth connection with the new satellite and cable services both reflected and was reflected by their sales strategies and launch programming – Sky established its initial Euro-name and lead on the basis of the popularity of its music video outlet, *Skytrax*; Super Channel began broadcasting with ten hours of *Music Box* per day. And youth featured heavily in the sales rhetoric. Richard Branson launched *Music Box* with the pitch that it would be 'slicker, brighter and closer targeted onto the young market than any other cable service today'. Mark Booth, of MTV Europe, argued that

> PETAR proves what we have been saying all along: music is the international language of young adults. We believe MTV is the bright new star which will become the media imperative of the '90s.[8]

The BSB advertising campaign laid great stress on *The Power Station*: 'Four ways of persuading your parents to pay for a TV channel they'll hate', ran the headline (over stills from the other BSB services, the *Movie Channel*, the *Sports Channel*, *Now – the Channel for Living*, and *Galaxy – the Entertainment Channel*).[9]

As it turned out, the BSB campaign was a flop. Its attempt to pitch young people *against* their parents was anachronistic in the new world of television in which a key sales strategy was to treat parents *as* youth. The means to this end was (ageless) 'youth music', and even *The Power Station* never expected to have a *teenage* audience.

MUSIC TELEVISION

For the new European television services, youth programming meant music programming from the start, and this equation also reflected the increasing music industry investment in television. Britain's three biggest independent rock labels, Virgin, Island and Chrysalis, were, by the mid-1980s, equally involved in television (Virgin through *Music Box*, Chrysalis through *Max Headroom*, Island through a variety of music specials and documentaries) and, by the end of the decade, pop video-making had become a significant economic basis for more general independent programme production. *Wired*, for example, Channel 4's premier youth programme in 1989, was made by Initial Film and TV, an offshoot of the video production company MGMM. Typical of the new sort of music/TV company was Hadrian Productions, set up to market 'made-for-TV music projects' world-wide by Tyne-Tees Television and Allied TV, a company run by rock concert promoter Harvey Goldsmith and his partner Ed Simon, Queen manager, Jim Beach, and Alan McKeowan of Witzend Productions.[10]

In one respect, the music industry's 1980s interest in television was simply an effect of following new investment and promotional opportunities (here, at last, was an effective alternative to radio).[11] But the mutually beneficial relationship that emerged (music selling new TV services; new TV services selling music) soon developed its own economic momentum, a momentum that was to lead to the current situation in which record companies make more from exploiting secondary rights (licensing their musical properties to the media) than they do from primary rights, from selling their titles to the public, while television companies make cheap, 'exclusive' (and, if necessary 'independent') long-form music documentaries funded and researched by record companies and their artists themselves.

Two interlinked features of this new music/television arrangement need to be stressed: first, its disregard of national boundaries; second, the involvement of a third partner, the advertiser. From a British perspective the reason why the music industry became so important for the development of new TV programmes was that it already had in place a commercial structure for packaging and distributing entertainment internationally. If the UK was already the source of 35 per cent of European music sales, then it made sense to go for the same percentage of European television sales. MTV entered the European market with a similar belief in music as the basis of an international sales strategy. In the words of Brian Diamond, head of programming:

> One of the things we want to offer the record companies, and the artists themselves, is this idea of: you can promote yourselves through this amazing network because we can pull footage back and forth across the world.[12]

And advertisers were the key players in this global music/television partnership – MTV Europe signed a sponsorship deal with Levi-Strauss almost before it was on the air: 'MTV Europe and Levi-Strauss both generate memorable and award-winning visual identities: blue jeans, youth, rock music and videos are synonymous'. Or, as Levi's European marketing director put it, 'MTV Europe represents a youth lifestyle and Levi-Strauss produces the clothing for that lifestyle.'[13]

Advertisers were necessary to fund the new TV services, and the new model of world music promotion was, in turn, defined by advertisers' accounts of consumption. 'Music is one of the best ways of breaking through linguistic and cultural barriers', explained Bill Lynn, Coca-Cola vice-president (and director of Worldwide Media). His immediate example was a Coca-Cola advertisement featuring Aretha Franklin's 'Freeway of love' – 'There are no Japanese, German or Italian language versions, it's not necessary because that song was a worldwide hit – everybody speaks Aretha!' – but his vision was much wider:

> We are all looking for customers, trying to build our businesses and looking to reach out and communicate to the youth of the world. The advent of the global marketplace, together with the deregulation of TV, radio privatization and the introduction of satellite broadcasting in

71

Europe is creating a new game for us all to play. I believe that, over the next decade, corporations, the music industry and broadcasters are going to be working together in ways no one even dreamed of as little as 10 or 20 years ago, probably in ways none of us foresee right now. . . . I'm, talking about sponsored TV programming that gives much-needed exposure to the careers of up-and-coming music talent and sponsorship of artists and tours. If privatization were to progress, to the point the UK is at today, advertising revenue in Europe will increase by 55% from $4.5 billion to $7 billion. By the year 2000 I think we'll see the targeting of brand-specific music artists, matched precisely to products. Music will play a major role in this new commercial reality – the emergence of a global market.[14]

For Lynn, the 'modern' commercial involved not the 'hard sell' but 'the selling of image' in 'the international language of our times – rock and roll'. Selling the image of youth, in other words (and the biggest pan-European advertisers are still youth-oriented – Coca-Cola, Pepsi-Cola, Nestlé, Levi-Strauss).

THE YOUTH AUDIENCE

The question is what 'youth' now means (and whether the pop and TV industries mean the same thing by it). For the mid-1980s' alliance of the new television, the music industry and global advertisers, 'youth' was constituted as a pop audience, a social group with an identity – a lifestyle – expressed through rock sounds and stars and styles. This was the audience which could now be addressed by television, just as it had always been addressed by pop records, pop radio and pop magazines. For anyone wanting to reach this market, the music industry could claim to provide expert guides.

The new TV pursuit of youth had to do with demographics. The new TV companies believed that the youth audience was there to be taken precisely because it was the market segment that watched existing TV least. Teenagers were thus the last commodity left to be sold to advertisers. This, for example, was MTV Europe's sales-pitch:

Finally, advertisers can reach people by television in a way that was only available to them through the print media. Now advertisers can hit the 16–34's with MTV's laser sharp targeting – not scattered buckshot. This audience's discretionary income is not in piggy banks or pension funds. MTV reaches its viewers all over Europe with a consistent clarity: it's about the cars they drive, the clothes they wear, the foods they fuel themselves with.[15]

The availability of the youth audience was primarily an effect of the second television set. The commercial implications of teenage TV were first realized by computer-game companies, but video rental stores were also quick to exploit TV's movement out of the family living room. By 1988 BARB figures showed that nearly half the UK's households were multi-set, and more systematic audience research suggested that in most households the second set was used for a choice of where to watch rather than what to watch (both sets were tuned to the same programme but in different rooms) *except* in the case of teenagers, who had their own, distinctive viewing habits.[16]

The message had already got through to Britain's terrestrial commercial network, which similarly predicated its expansion into newly available television space (late nights, early mornings) on the availability of 'new', young viewers. TV-am's instant move down market was also a move down the age range, as Roland Rat became a star and pop videos were programmed between the news items; London Weekend Television opened up its night hours with the youth-aimed *Night Network*; Channel 4 broadcast *Network 7* at Sunday lunchtime and began packaging late night rock music films together under the title of *The Late Shift*. By the end of the decade, Pete Waterman's inimitable 'live' disco programme, *Hitman and Her*, could be found on different regional outlets at any time between 12.30 and 3.30am.

The other side of the pursuit of youth was the dumping of the old, as advertisers complained that the TV audience was 'ageing'. Greg Dyke, head of programmes at LWT, explained that he had to remove wrestling, darts and bowls from the company's sports coverage:

> The viewing figures are going down and the sports appeal mainly to older viewers. I want to reach a younger audience which in ITV terms means anyone under 45. We're being urged by our advertisers to change our programme mix to attract better-off viewers.[17]

From this perspective too, then, the 'youth' audience was a valuable commodity, in demand by British advertisers, and British television companies began, for the first time, to do systematic market research, to check programmes (like *The Bill* and even *Coronation Street*) for youth appeal. The problem this research immediately ran into was the empirical definition of 'the youth audience'. Did it mean the Coca-Cola market, the world-wide lifestyle of soft-drinks consumers talking rock'n'roll, turning the TV on to see the endless dissolve between pop video and pop ad? Or was there something more concrete, more *measurable* out there?

Pop viewers, TV youth as traditionally defined by the music industry, by *Top of the Pops*, 12–24-year-olds, were certainly not the 'better off' youth British advertisers were now after. Their ideal audience was made up of 18–34-year-olds, and in commercial TV terms the 'crisis' in youth broadcasting in 1988 actually described the attempt to redirect pop programming from the former to the latter.[18]

This was, perhaps, most clearly symbolized by the change of Channel 4's youth time from early evening Friday (the classic youth slot from *Ready Steady Go* to *The Tube*) to late evening Friday, the time for the new 'young adult' shows like *Halfway to Paradise* and *The Word*. But the change in pop targets was equally evident in the sales pitch for BSB's youth service – '*The Power Station* won't just be endless music videos back to back. You've got too much between the ears for that. Eighteen hours a day there'll be a scratch mix of music, fashions, comedy and travel programmes' – and in the rapid development of MTV Europe as a 'general interest' programme, with specialist music slots, movie programmes, game shows, talk shows, documentaries, etc. Brian Diamond, head of programming, explained that 'there is much more to "youth culture" than just music. . . . MTV has moved into other areas by virtue of viewer demand'. A demand not simply for a mix of 'music, information and entertainment' whenever the set is turned on, but also for specific programmes at specific times. Diamond described his viewers as 'wanting to know what they will be watching at 10 on Thursday night'.[19]

For Diamond (an American) this represented a peculiarity of the European audience, and he described MTV's programming – a precise schedule organized around the video flow – as a 'compromise' between American and European ways of doing things, but we could also see this as the difference between public service and commercial definitions of the young.

In public service terms, youth is a material category, a social group with needs and interests derived from its institutional situation. In Britain, as in other European countries, the state's television 'youth service' is therefore much like its other youth services. Pop music is the dominant form of youth entertainment, but a public service station is equally obliged to provide educational programmes, information and opinions on, say, AIDS and drug-use, help with employment, youth-aimed soaps and quiz shows, youth comedy and news and documentary (BBC Radio 1 remains the British model). The public service address to youth is a mix of the youth club leader and the youth group representative.

In commercial terms, by contrast, youth is a market, a group which consumes in distinctive ways, which purchases specific goods – fashion clothes, music, cosmetics, etc. Youth programming is an integration of entertainment and consumer guidance; the mode of address is that of a sales staff. MTV Europe may employ a broad definition of 'youth culture', not unlike that of the BBC, but it still defines youth interests as market interests. Brent Hanson, head of production, explained their film programmes, for instance, in these terms:

> We have scheduled *MTV at the Movies* and *Kino* at convenient times when people traditionally make their decisions to go to, or rent, movies. We believe these programmes will help viewers evaluate their choices for motion picture entertainment.[20]

In 1980s Britain the political valorization of 'the consumer' extended to the young consumer. Angela McRobbie describes, for example, the shift in the world of teenage girls' magazines, as the self replaced the boyfriend as the focus of attention, and romance was displaced from marriage onto shopping:

While the reader is being constructed in these pages as an intelligent and thoughtful being, she is simultaneously being constructed, in a way hitherto unimagined by magazine editors, as a young consumer. The new magazines marketed for 16-year-olds and over, but read by thousands of 12-year-olds up and down the country, carry glossy adverts not just for make-up but also for the NatWest, for the Midland Bank, for Levis, pizzas, films, other magazines, for Barclays, Benetton and beyond. The 12-year-old might not be able to buy the goods but she is very able to consume the images. She is quite familiar with the world of consumer goods which is now addressing her with greater respect from all sides. Indeed, it celebrates her new independence. It openly welcomes her into the world of emancipated women.[21]

In practice, of course, institutional/lifestyle categories have always fed off each other, but one way of reading the problem of youth TV in the late 1980s is as an attempt to develop a sharper lifestyle account of youth, to devise a form of youth programming that could float quite free of any structural base. In this model 'youth' became a category constructed by TV itself, with no other referent: those people of whatever age or circumstance who watched 'youth' programmes became youth, became, that is, *the future of television*.

'Youth', in this account, no longer described a particular type of viewer, who is attracted to a particular type of programme but, rather, describes an attitude, a particular type of *viewing behaviour*. Janet Street-Porter explained her thinking this way:

I don't really think I make youth programmes. I think the word youth has become this ghastly term. I don't know why I call myself 'Head of Youth Programmes'. I wanted to be head of a department because I wanted to have the clout, but I couldn't think of what else to be head of . . . . I'd like to be called head of 'different' programmes or 'youth*ful*' programmes. . . . I suppose the programmes we make are for people who don't have a lot of responsibilities. The minute you have a *lot* of responsibilities, you stop being receptive to new ideas. As soon as you have a really big mortgage or maybe a baby, you probably don't have as much money left to go out and buy records, or perhaps you can't go to clubs as easily, or you go to the cinema less frequently. That's not to say your brain dies, it just gets harder to do a lot of things. So if I was to specify the people that I think watch the programmes, I'd have to say that they're people who probably haven't got a lot of responsibilities![22]

And, from the advertiser's perspective, it is the right type of 'irresponsible' programming which leads to the right sort of 'irresponsible' viewing which leads to the right sort of 'irresponsible' lifestyle, a 'youthful' mode that is inextricable from an ideology of conspicuous consumption.

MODERN VIEWING

Robert Saucier has described what's involved here as a shift from 'ancient' to 'modern' viewing. In the context of the late 1980s TV modern viewing had three components. First, there was an obsession with modernity itself. The conventional sales connection of youth and up-to-datedness was applied to teletechnology itself. Fashion defined what was on the screen, so that what was 'new' on television was seen as an ever-changing presence, rather than in the 'ancient' metaphor of TV 'seasons'. Visually, this meant the ubiquitous use of computer graphics and video techniques, formal qualities which cut across all programmes regardless of their content to make them *look* young. Janet Street-Porter:

> I'm making programmes for a generation who have grown up with TV, with visual images all around them, who are very familiar with computers and video technology. Their response to television is very often 'so what', so my shows have to set out to arrest audiences, to hold them, to play all sorts of tricks to keep them from turning over.[23]

MTV Europe put a similar stress on the modernity of its imagery, on its televisual sophistication. Its identification spots were commissioned 'from the most talented young animators in Europe. . . . These animated idents are one of the most important elements in demonstrating MTV's leading edge in the visual arena.'[24]

'Modern' viewing was, second, a form of 'electronic populism' – as Andrew Ross has suggested, *Max Headroom* was a youth programme not because of who watched it but because of the expectations it had of its viewers. Its appreciation depended on a certain sort of TV sophistication and knowingness, was defined by a particular experience of and education in the medium. In this sort of show (as in much pop video) television itself became the only historical setting; to interpret what was on the screen needed no reference outside it. Television viewing thus involved a deliberate indiscrimination, a celebration of TV abundance for its own sake. The best-selling UK video in the Christmas of 1988 (and a steady seller ever since) was the BBC's package of *Watch With Mother*, a 1950s programme for infants now being bought by people who were too young to remember it, and Jon Savage described the new wave of late 1980s youth programming as the 'infantilization of a generation':

> Like TV-am, *Night Network* spices up what is essentially a cheap, studio-based programme with cheap, bought-in programming. Both use *Batman*; *Night Network* adds cut-up gobbets of *Captain Scarlet*, a Gerry Anderson puppet drama from the early '70s which falls the wrong side of camp. A *new* Gerry Anderson show, *Dick Spanner*, was a regular feature on Channel 4's Sunday morning youth marathon, *Network 7*. A similar Gerry Anderson puppet character is now part of an extended Tennant's

lager ad campaign, just as an adaptation of the *Captain Scarlet* logo forms part of the *Night Network* titles. Another famous mid-'60s series, *The Prisoner*, appears cut-up into an LBC ad shown many times during *Night Network*'s 1–4am run.[25]

Def 2, similarly, ran old episodes of *Mission Impossible* as a key part of its youth service, and one of Street-Porter's more gooey ideas was *Babylon*, a spot in which 'celebrities reminisce about their favourite cult children's TV shows like *Noggin the Nog*, *Whack-O* and *Captain Pugwash*'.[26]

Savage suggested that the formal sources of such youth programming in Britain were Saturday morning children's TV shows, 'where the plugs are indistinguishable from the programming' (and where pop videos were first deployed), but its immediate attraction to programme controllers (besides its cheapness) was its appeal to the desired demographic, to 'young adults':

> Here is the reason for all that late '60s/early '70s kitsch now infesting TV. As Jonathan Ross [Britain's answer to David Letterman] has so winningly demonstrated, youth TV is now not aimed at the classic teenage, 15–24 age group but at 25–40-year-olds – 'our' generation, the *real* consumers. . . . A camp, ironic sense of TV and pop history have combined to create a self-referential, postmodern form where superficial references and nostalgia-triggers disguise its near total lack of content.[27]

But even modern viewers could, third, discriminate by remote control. Their TV pleasure and displeasure could, for the first time, be registered instantly, by zapping, and so their tastes and taste differences had to be registered instantly by programme makers (just as pop record makers had long had to make their sounds instantly attractive to radio button pushers); this is what Janet Street-Porter meant by 'arresting' her audience. What mattered most in this bid for attention was shows' packaging, and by the end of the 1980s all youth programmes were being described as 'magazines', whether in a direct analogy with music magazines (*Wired* as *Q*), or as a way of justifying their incoherence, the emphasis of form over content. Charlie Parsons, Street-Porter's successor as editor of *Network 7*, claimed for instance that everything in the show 'you might expect to read later in a Sunday colour supplement, in the same way you might find famine in Ethiopia next to Dolly Parton'.[28]

I've so far been describing 'modern viewing' in terms of the peculiarities of British youth TV, but, as I have already suggested, the reason why youth TV became the focus of media attention in the late 1980s was because of the use of youth as a metaphor in the much more general attempt to redefine the TV viewer to match the new TV landscape. For the cable and satellite operators it was necessary to present television viewing as a matter of personal consumer choice, and this meant, first, that TV pleasure had to be described in terms of specific programmes, rather than by reference to 'watching television' as a generally pleasurable activity,[29] and, second, that the 'TV object' had to be

77

shown to be more desirable than other leisure goods.[30] Hence the promotion of a new sort of TV fan and collector, the marketing of 'classic' TV in video stores, the almost continuous screen availability of old shows. What this meant was less the historicizing of television than the laying out of all its wares, the drawing of attention to its particular consumer value.

What I'm suggesting here is that the invocation of 'youth' to sell the new TV apparatus in the late 1980s was a way of putting into play new discourses around the TV audience. The most obvious feature of this was the celebration of the individual viewer, as the sales pitch moved from the family audience to the family member, each to be satisfied by their own channel (sports, music, lifestyle), with the children grasping the point (and the second TV set) first. Unfortunately, this raised immediate problems for the actual mechanics of the TV market, the buying and selling of air-time and audiences. In the end, for example, LWT's *Night Network* (which both pioneered and embodied the sort of youth programming I've been describing) had to be dropped because its viewers didn't show up in the audience figures (it was replaced by cheaper programming, old movies and pop concerts). As LWT's sales controller explained:

> Ad agencies . . . need a currency in which to trade, and the *Night Network* audience – young, single, metropolitan, with a particular kind of lifestyle does not turn up in the BARB ratings.[31]

In more abstract terms what was going on here was an attempt to reorganize the public sphere. The 'public' for television would no longer be drawn together as a single viewing nation (it was, after all, the Coronation which gave TV sales their initial British impetus) but would be expressed in a series of market choices. And as demographic targeting got ever more 'laser sharp', so such choices would be increasingly used to *differentiate* 'taste publics'. This is one reason why pop became such a powerful metaphor for TV: by the mid-1980s the fragmentation of the British pop audience into competing brand identities was so complete that advertisers (like Levi's) had to take their soundtracks from pop's past, when music could still symbolize the community.

This TV sales pitch led, in turn, to a new emphasis on the rational viewer, and it is ironic that John Reith's early BBC critique of 'passive listening', his advocacy of careful programme 'selection', should now feature (if with rather different implications) in the world of multiple channel choice, video recording and time shifting. In James Lardner's *Fast Forward*, one of the first US video store owners, Frank Barnako Jr, is quoted as saying:

> I saw what a difference a VCR in my home made for me and my wife. A VCR let us maximize the value of those hours of the day or week that we decided to devote to watching television. I guess that after you get above thirty thousand dollars a year or so, you should operate on the

assumption that time is your most valuable commodity. If you have a certain hourly value to your employer, you should have at least that hourly value to yourself in your off time, and if you choose to segment some of your off time into recreation, and if that recreation has a component of television watching, it shouldn't just be catch as catch can. And I saw that and I said, 'Gee, if I value my own time like that, I'll bet there are others like me!'[32]

There's a shift here in the gender paradigm of the ideal TV viewer, from the female consumer, the object of seduction by salesmen, to the male consumer, controlling the machinery (which may explain the prevalence of TV-as-car metaphors in postmodern US theory as against the old TV-as-drug idea), but the immediate question raised by the advocacy of the 'rational' viewer was what was now meant by television as a commodity, by TV watching as consumption. What was the commodity? What was being consumed?

THE RIGHT TO CHOOSE

In 1988 Carlton Communications, Britain's largest independent televisual services company, took over Modern Video, a Dutch/US tape-copying company. Michael Green, head of Carlton, commented that:

The philosophy that has drawn me is that the television is an underutilized force. Half of Modern Video's output is not theatrical or entertainment, it is useful: how-to-do-it tapes, kid's tapes. Did you know there are more video outlets in Britain than bookshops? It is today's form. I think of television as a manufacturing process. What is the difference between a television programme and this lighter?[33]

Green was interested in the question of price rationality: what is the relationship between the cost of a television service, on the one hand, and a video, on the other, to their sales? In the end, after all, it would be viewers' price rationality that determined the various take-up rates of cable and satellite subscriptions, pay-as-you-watch TV shows, sell-through versus rented videos, etc.[34]

Given that 'watching television' is such a varied activity, what, then, did it mean to 'own' a TV service? In Britain in the 1980s (unlike Britain in the 1950s) it was clear that a TV set no longer had much value in itself (as a piece of furniture, a status symbol, an icon of modernity). It mattered, rather, as the means of access to what was really desired, some sort of audio-visual experience, and, if they were going to use the language of market choice in talking of people's TV habits, the new entrepreneurs needed to clarify what this experience might be.

It was at this point that the simple-mindedness of the TV version of 'market choice' became apparent: the question of *what* TV viewers want has to be answered, at least in part, in terms of *how* they want it. Why do people prefer to rent films and videos rather than either buy them (like books or records) or get them via cable (a clear preference, even in the USA)? Why is so little of the material that is recorded for later use ever watched? Why do television audiences remain so 'irrational' in their habits, watching programmes they don't like, letting their habits still be shaped by the schedulers' arts?

One of the pleasures of television viewing (what makes it importantly different from cinema-going or magazine reading) is that one doesn't have to 'choose' anything at all, doesn't have to take one's TV screen as any sort of sign of one's identity (which is not to say that some programmes don't, like *Star Trek*, have obsessive fan clubs, just that in the video age such programme love is *not* a question of going with the TV flow). And by the end of the 1980s it had become clear that the discourse of 'modern' viewing was unlikely to be lain over 'ancient' ways. The emerging empirical evidence on European viewer habits suggested the ease with which the new services were being absorbed into old structures – domestic viewing, national viewing: in Holland, for example, Europe's most cabled country, the cable share of the TV market had settled at less than 10 per cent. People like to have access to the specialist services, especially sport, but they would usually rather watch the local Dutch 'family' shows.[35]

None of this was surprising (the history of radio provides clear evidence that competing media don't replace each other) but it did raise questions about the revenue base for the new TV services. For example, however efficient their initial sales appeal, none of Europe's original youth music services did well out of advertising. *Music Box* had to be bailed out by Videomusic, a subsidiary of the Italian Betatelevision in November 1988; *Skytrax* did not feature in Rupert Murdoch's 1990 assault on the UK satellite market (his sales message is now much more reminiscent of ITV's competition with the BBC in the 1950s, populist family entertainment versus the stuffy establishment, the language of ancient rather than modern viewing). *The Power Station* was dropped as soon as the BSB/Sky merger was signed. MTV Europe is still adding subscribers but whether its advertising revenue is growing accordingly is less clear.[36]

In 1988, when 'youth' became a resonant term for arguments about the future of television, the implication was that everything in broadcasting was changing, that young people were, somehow, the 'different' viewers of the future. To get youth programming right was, therefore, to provide a blueprint for the general transformation of viewing behaviour. In 1991, after the passing of a British Broadcasting Act which has embedded in it a concern for both the family audience (in the form of the Broadcasting Standards Council) and the national TV public (in the clauses on broadcasting 'balance'), the future of broadcasting in Britain doesn't look so different from its past, and youth TV has ceased to be of much media concern at all. Perhaps, even then, in 1988, what we should have been discussing was not the brave new world of *Night*

Network and Janet Street-Porter but the remarkable youth/music/TV success of Kylie Minogue, a teenybop star plucked (like David McCallum and David Soul before her) from an 'adult' series by the young audience itself. With an even greater bedroom-wall presence than Madonna (but, like her, marking a significant move from the male to the female idol) Kylie Minogue countered every late 1980s media cliché: the death of the single, the end of teenage, the rise of 'modern' television.[37]

NOTES

1 Satellite channels began broadcasting in Europe in 1984, reaching most households via cable connections. Take-up rates varied greatly from country to country (by the end of the decade the most cabled countries were the Netherlands and Belgium) but all European countries experienced big shake-ups in their broadcasting arrangements, the general tendency being a move away from state broadcasting monopolies to mixed commercial/state systems and the rise of new pan-European operators like Belasconi and MTV Europe, a partnership between Mirror Group Newspapers (then Robert Maxwell), British Telecom and MTV's US parent, Viacom International.

2 Jonathan Miller, 'Choice words on the future of TV', *Sunday Times*, 21 February 1988, p. C11. The other foreign TV system then held up for our admiration was Australian; as its brave new channels went bankrupt, one by one, so its value as a broadcasting example shifted – by the end of the decade the Australian case was mentioned only by the defenders of the British status quo.

3 Hence, for example, the remarkable importance of MTV for 1980s' TV theory.

4 Quoted in Anne Caborn, 'Harvest for the world', *The Independent*, 10 March 1989. See also Martin Wroe, 'Aiming for street credibility', *The Independent*, 23 March 1988.

5 Quoted in Andrew Smith, 'Youth programming', *Melody Maker*, 17 June 1989, p. 36.

6 Street-Porter was recruited to the BBC from Channel 4's *Network 7*, a programme that appealed more to broadcasters trying to reconstitute 'young viewers' than to young viewers themselves. See Lloyd Bradley, 'Less hysterical', *Q*, March 1989, pp. 11–12.

7 Swedish findings are summarized in Keith Roe and Ulla Johnson-Smaragdi, 'The Swedish "Mediascape" in the 1980s', *European Journal of Communication*, 2, 1987. Dutch findings in Frank Olderaan and Nick Jankowski, 'In the cockpit of Europe: media diversification and Dutch user response', in C. B. Becker and K. Schönbach (eds), *Audience Response to Media Content Diversification*, Amsterdam, 1988. Danish research was summarized in annual research reports published by Danmarks Radio. Also see Maggie Brown, 'Satellite viewing grows in Europe', *The Independent*, 26 August 1988. My survey of European TV research was generously supported by Channel 4.

8 MTV Press Release, August 1988.

9 For the BSB advertisement see, for example, *The Independent*, 15 September 1989.
   The rhetorical association of the 'new TV' with youth wasn't confined to Europe. MTV played a similar lead role in the spread of cable in the USA, and Rupert Murdoch's 'fourth network', Fox, was clearly programmed for youth appeal.

10 For a general discussion of music industry investments in the 1980s see 'Picking up the pieces' in S. Frith (ed.), *Facing the Music*, Pantheon, 1989.

11   This wasn't just a matter of picking up video play on one of the specialist music channels. Alan Jones, of Gallup, noted that 'Now that BBC1 and BBC2 are being piped to Holland, most people watch a lot of their pop programmes and although we might think there isn't a great deal of music on TV here, there's enough to influence people. This means that when a British record comes out there's a ready market for it because people have been watching it on TV for five or six weeks.' Quoted in Paul Sexton, 'The power and glory of British music', *Music & Media*, 26 March 1988.

12   Quoted in Keith Roe and Roger Wallis, ' "One planet one music": the development of music television in western Europe, a symposium report', *The Nordicom Review of Nordic Mass Communication Research*, 1, 1989, p. 34. MTV also has services in Japan, Australia and Latin America.

13   John Ankeny, quoted in MTV Europe Press Release, August 1988.

14   Quoted in 'Lynn looks forward to global market', *Music & Media*, 21 May 1988, p. 4.

15   MTV Europe Press Release, August 1988.

16   Private communication from the then head of Channel 4 Research, Sue Stoessl.
      This was one reason why the new satellite services sought to reach domestic subscribers via their adolescent offspring – compare the use of children to sell TV sets in the early 1950s.

17   Quoted in Michael Leapman, 'Darts to go as ITV adopts sleeker image', *The Independent*, 6 June 1988.

18   This also involved a change of gender address – from girls to boys.

19   Quoted in Roe and Wallis, op. cit. *Power Station* quotation from *The Independent*, 15 November 1989, p. 17.

20   MTV Europe Press Release, 1988.

21   Angela McRobbie, 'You should be so lucky', *New Statesman*, 9 September 1988, p. 47.

22   Quoted in Andrew Smith, 'Youth programming', *Melody Maker*, 17 June 1989.

23   Quoted in Andy Medhurst, 'Def sentences', *The Listener*, 29 September 1988.

24   Jon Klein, director of on-air presentation, MTV Europe Press Release, April 1988.

25   Jon Savage, 'All this and less', *New Statesman*, 29 January 1988, p. 24.

26   Johnny Black, 'Who the hell does Janet Street-Porter think she is?', *Q*, June 1988, p. 7.
      'Infantilization' may also explain American intellectuals' obsession with Pee Wee Herman at this time.

27   Savage, op. cit.

28   Quoted in Wroe, op. cit.

29   The increasing contribution of the independent sector to terrestrial broadcasting reinforced this rhetoric: independent producers also have to persuade commissioning editors that there are specific markets for specific programmes.

30   Statistics gathered annually by *Social Trends* suggest that in Britain as the number of viewing opportunities rises the number of hours watched declines.

31   Craig Pearman, quoted in Torin Douglas, 'Ratings flaw that led to night starvation', *The Independent*, 15 February 1989.

32   James Lardner (1987) *Fast Forward. Hollywood and the VCR Wars*, New York: W. W. Norton, pp. 180–1.

33   Quoted in Maggie Brown, 'The single-person television station', *The Independent*, 30 March 1988.

34   This is one reason for the markedly different TV landscapes in Europe: the value of a cable service depends on what else is available, which means both existing national broadcasting and what one can get from one's neighbours. In Sweden,

for example, satellite use varies geographically, according to the bordering country.

35 See, for example, Frank Olderaan and Nick Jankowski, op. cit.
36 MTV's financial health has always been a matter of interest. Throughout the 1980s American media commentators questioned the revenue stability of MTV in the USA. It was said to lack a 'broad' appeal (in 1988 'only 37 per cent of high earners in the United States watched MTV even once a week') and therefore to be relatively expensive for local cable networks (see the comments by David Katz, cited in Roe and Wallis, op. cit.). On the other hand, the service survived and remains impressive for its ability to *change* in the pursuit of profit.
37 Earlier versions of this paper were presented at the Milwaukee TV Conference, University of Wisconsin, Milwaukee, April 1988, and the Gothenburg Symposium on Music Television, University of Gothenburg, September 1988. My thanks to their participants and to Rachel Bowlby and Andrew Goodwin for comments and advice.

5

COMMERCIALS GO ROCK

Leslie Savan

I. AVANT-HARD SELL

It's only mildly surprising that Laurie Anderson has made a commercial. Though she scored the music for a spot in Reebok's first TV campaign, there's nothing 8mm, slo-mo, or 'avant-garde' about it. To her dodge-'em car sound effects, people walk as if they're driving – in quick, short steps, a group of black leather types skid on their 'cycles'; a chauffeur-driven 'limo' carries execs chatting on cellular phones. At the end, her familiar cool voice says, to standard voiceover rhythm: 'Reebok walking shoes. Your mileage may vary.'

The ad's friendly, bright and toylike. But Anderson is usually busy refracting consumer culture, creating a sense of people ping-ponged between products, signs and electronic transmissions. Ironic critique, accessible deconstruction – that's Laurie. But she handles this ad straight. What gives in avantland?

'I'm doing it mostly because I'm putting in a new studio – so my initial reason was the money,' Anderson says. 'But I also had fun playing with new equipment. The agency said, "Do whatever you want." '

'Like most people, I have a fairly ambivalent attitude toward consumerism, a love/hate relationship, but I don't want to be so judgemental. There are plenty of ways to participate in the culture and plenty of ways to sell out. I use a state-of-the-art audio studio – that doesn't mean in my next concert I won't be as snide as I always am about technology.'

Ambivalence has grown hand-in-hand with consumerism and American humour. Torn between resenting Mad Ave's attempt to manipulate us and loving the passive pleasures of it, we devise attitudes to live with it: spoofing consumer culture, accepting it only ironically, enjoying it *because* of its contradictions, or swallowing it straight. Anderson's not Warhol – using products so wholeheartedly that he inverted our perception of them – but Warhol made it possible for Anderson to be an ironic accepter. Now, years of rock stars' unquestioning endorsements have made it possible to view Anderson as a straight accepter.

For the agency, Chiat/Day, NY, which first considered using her for a Sara Lee ad, Anderson was fresh. 'We try to avoid *styles* of advertising,' says creative director Bill Hamilton. (Other ads in the Reebok series are designed to push its athletic brands, broadening its image from yup-sneaker supplier.) 'I'm not putting her on for her star value, but for her production value,' says Hamilton, who'd like Anderson to direct future spots. 'Most people outside New York don't even know who she is.'

But as a star, like David Byrne, of the mainstream avant-garde – a growing group of well-heeled artists who are avant without the garde (as opposed to those breaking the borders of what polite society will accept) – Anderson is leading AV's latest dip into mass pop. Already, soundalikes of 'O Superman' have turned up in ads for the cotton industry and Sterling cars; big-suited Byrne-like dancers bop for Orangina. (Anderson's agent is wondering about legal possibilities.)

'The bottom line is it's very hard to be an artist in the United States of America, and if you can find ways to help support yourself, go ahead,' says Anderson. 'It's very easy to say all advertising is bad. That's very simple-minded. I don't have anything against the structure or even the politics of advertising as long as it isn't harmful.'

But when I hear Anderson structuring a tag-line like every tag on TV, it harms the idea that there's something the sponsored world won't touch.

II. THE LIFESTYLE LIFESTYLE

Another perfect 1980s couple – this time exercised beyond couch potatodom to be bedroom french fries – is almost watching TV. He – Nautilus-made abdominals, dark hair slicked back, eyeglasses worn to be passionately whipped off – is on the floor watching TV in silk pyjama bottoms. She – mussed blonde hair, silk teddy, feminine but sexually assertive – snakes across the bed to seduce him. The action is intercut with the somewhat sexy videos of Bill Medley and Jennifer Warnes' 'Time of my life' and Anita Baker's 'Sweet love'. The woman – with surprising ease, despite interruptions from Hall and Oates – lures the man from the tube. 'It's bound to happen,' a throaty male voice-over explains. 'Once in a while we lose a viewer or two. Even though our audience *loves* to watch their music – hit music – they have other things to attend to. We got exactly what you're looking for' – in the cold glow of the TV, the couple kiss (guy on top) – 'even if you're not watching'.

Yes, sex is better than TV, the ad says, and, sure, you have better things to do than watch it – *you* are not bored and lonely. But, face it, TV is still a *partner* to your lifestyle, even when you opt to be intimate. You baby-boomers even have the set turned on when you're turned on. Afterwards, you can pick back up on the show – all the easier with videos, which do not require great attention to plot. TV rays no longer neutralize sex. Your sex life can merge in and out with the flickering screen: videos as the moving-picture equivalent of an overhead mirror. In fact, TV might get you into bed faster – look how well it worked for *them*.

This is VH-1's first ad campaign since it 'refocused' about a year ago. Out with the Julio Iglesias and country crossovers that helped launch the cable channel three years ago; in with more Anita Baker, Kenny G, Billy Joel, Lionel Richie, and other 'adult' rock.

'When the channel first started, we were much more broadbased, and, frankly, it wasn't that successful,' says VH-1's VP of marketing and advertising, Lesley Schaefer. 'You can't watch Julio Iglesias and turn around and watch a George Harrison clip.'

The other reason for VH-1's 'completely new personality' is to further distinguish it from sister cable channel MTV. VH-1 is targeting a 25- to 49-year-old market; MTV, 12 to 34 (somewhat like the difference, you might say, between 7 Days and the Voice). 'We feel we're really on target with the greying of the whole entertainment business,' says Schaefer. 'It's in movies, in records, on TV.' Like thirtysomething, Moonlighting, Kate & Allie. And last year for the first time, adults bought more records than teens.

'We deliver programming that superserves a particular audience.' Superserves? Narrowcasting like only cable can: not just playing the music that appeals to this audience – heavy on the soft rock, repackaged Elvis, and Beatles – but speciality programmes, like Sunday Brunch, tuned to 'a Sunday morning "kick back and relax" lifestyle'.

Lifestyle is at the crux of the new ads, as another spokeswoman explains: 'The ads say, "Look, you don't always have time to watch, but we understand your lifestyle." '

Lifestyle is now a lifestyle. The Lifestyle lifestyle means entertainment-technology/body-technology, at your fingertips. Monitor, computer, remote control; sex and digital and rock'n'roll.

III. DESPERATELY SELLING SODA

There's never been a media buy like it. Madonna, the commercialized girl who's played hard to get for commercials, debuted the title cut from her then still-unreleased album Like a Prayer on – whoa, as – a Pepsi commercial last Thursday [sic]. The ad was seen the same night in forty countries, by 300 million or so people. A teaser spot running the week before and featuring an aborigine traipsing through the Australian outback (actually the California outback) to catch the commercial conveyed the pancultural ambitions of both soda pop and pop star: 'No matter where you are in the world,' the teaser instructed, 'on March 2 get to a TV and see Pepsi present Madonna.'

'We believe this is the single largest one-day media buy in the history of advertising,' says Pepsi spokesman Ken Ross, figuring the two minutes of prime-time planetary fame cost more than $5 million. And this wasn't just a Eurotrash media buy. Fans in Turkey, Indonesia, and even 'war-torn countries like El Salvador' were also able to put aside their low-intensity conflicts to get down. (Despite Pepsi's earlier made-in-Moscow ad, called 'Glasnost', the Russians refused to air the spot.)

Even Michael Jackson didn't hit the cathode universe with such a bang. His Pepsi spots globe-trotted only after they had run in the USA; and his songs were huge hits *before* he used them to sell something he reportedly won't drink. Just a few months ago George Michael, a sort of Madonna with facial hair, almost beat her to it: snatches of sound from *his* unreleased album popped up in a confused matador/superstar spot for Diet Coke. For her efforts – another Pepsi ad later this year [*sic*] and a Pepsi-sponsored tour – Madonna will make 'short of $10 million', says an industry source, some of which will go to covering tour costs.

The faint pang of disgust raised by Neil Young's video parody of Jackson, Whitney Houston, Eric Clapton, and other corp-rock sellouts last year seems to have passed like a kidney stone. The sheer size and glamour of this ad, coupled with the built-in consensus that arty/vulgar Madonna was made for this kind of thing, has left questions of 'artistic integrity' to Massachusetts liberals.

But the ad itself, if viewed as video, is so canny it cooks. It opens with something all us narcissists can relate to: watching home movies of your own childhood. There's Little Madonna at her eighth birthday party (actually filmed circa 1988) being viewed by the big real Madonna, looking peacefully lovely (in part because for once she's the spectator, albeit of herself). The entire spot is as recursive as a Rod Serling plot, which lends it the sentimental fantasy of most music video. Now Little Madonna, cinemagically transported out of vidworld and into full-colour life, watches the famous Madonna on the black-and-white screen. The star goes back to the mid-1960s, singing and dancing on urban, inter-racial streets, where the kids don't moonwalk perfectly. There's Madonna back at her Catholic girls' school, a black-clad sylph with a crucifix in her cleavage towering over the linen-collared uniforms. Everyone marches in timid lockstep until they glimpse an old poster of the bleached superstar – and suddenly the screen is full of flying frocks as they dance with the lapsed brunette in their midst.

The lyrics have power ('Life is a mystery/Everyone must stand alone/I hear you call my name and it feels like home/When you call my name, it's like a little prayer'), and the music's hooky, but it doesn't really swing until Madonna lets the gospel spirit of the Andre Crouch Singers take over. (This is definitely the commercial version; the actual video, which ran on MTV the following day, is a much more daring mix of black soul and Catholic funk. Madonna is kissed by the reliquary of a black saint, gives herself the stigmata, and jitterbugs in front of a row of burning crosses. Madonna is the kind of Catholic girl who forgets to wear a hat in church – or a dress over her slip. RAI TV in Rome, under pressure from Catholic groups, has banned the video.)

At the end, Little Madonna back in the B&W home movie, looks eerily from across time into the eyes of the real Madonna. As the child toasts her with a bottle of Pepsi, Madonna responds in kind with a can: 'Go ahead. Make a wish.' The tagline comes on – 'Pepsi. A generation ahead' – and the loop is made: if Madonna Louise Veronica Ciccone could wish herself into stardom through the magic of video, a little cola consumer in Thailand or Paraguay can be like a star through the magic of advertising.

The ad is like a wet spot where all this season's hot TV topics have condensed: finding yourself by finding your 'inner child'; depending on yourself (and not on men like Sean [Penn]); the nostalgia of baby-boomers for their 8mm wonder years; Catholicism as the fashionable ethnicity to come *from*, because it's new traditionalist yet earthy; inter-racial mixing as a symbol of mature hipness (not unrelated to the way TV white guys establish soul by playing basketball with black guys). In a *Rolling Stone* interview, Madonna said that when she was little, all her girlfriends were black and that she *feels* black.

All those very American themes would seem to make the ad too parochial to have the big, vague vavavavoom required for global marketing. What's a Tasaday in the Philippines to make of St Mary schoolgirls in a chorus line? Actually, global marketing – crafting a commercial so that advertisers can use the same or nearly the same campaign around the planet with little or no adjustments for language – was the big drive a few years ago. But it never really clicked – except with teenagers.

Marketeers believe that modern communications have spawned a 'global teen', kids who have more in common with kids halfway across the earth than they do with other generations in the next room. Their percussive hormones drive them to Levi's and Swatch, Benetton and BIC perfume. Two new 'global TV' shows – *Buzz* on MTV, which previewed Tuesday [*sic*], and Fox network's *Revolution*, premiering in mid-May [1989] – are both rock'n'roll 'lifestyle magazine' programmes that flash at a super-fast pace. And they're both thirsting for Pepsi or Coke as sponsors.

Music is the universal language and all that, but more importantly, cola is the universal solvent. Fit for any lifestyle, its image mutable, cola is truly *fluid*. Aesthetically, at least on American TV, where hard-liquor ads don't run, soda spots are the kickiest, and they've become the alcoholic content of advertising. Cola is the teen caffeine, accounting for 70 per cent of all soft-drink sales. Pepsi, marketed in 150 countries, is still trying to catch up to Coke worldwide (the real thing outsells Pepsi two-and-a-half to one internationally). But their respective corporate cultures share world hegemony, and to these titans, it's no longer enough to be just an American artist. Madonna has sold 75 million records worldwide – according to some, she's the most famous woman in the world. Naturally Pepsi wants to use her to insure its universal solvency.

As Madonna told *Rolling Stone* (long since gone the whole hog for corp-rock with its little mag for advertisers called *Marketing through Music*): 'I like the challenge of merging art and commerce. As far as I'm concerned, making a video is also a commercial. The Pepsi spot is a great and different way to expose

89

the record. Record companies just don't have the money to finance that kind of publicity. As it is, the music will be playing in the background, and the can of Pepsi is positioned very subliminally. The camera pans by it so it's not a hardsell commercial.'

It's the *subtlety* of the sell that corporate-sponsored rock stars are increasingly judged by, not the fact that they're selling at all. For years, Madonna refused to do an ad – except in Japan (for Mitsubishi), like other big stars (David Byrne, Woody Allan, Paul Newman) who feel advertising would be crass here but is okay there, where they don't have relatives. One factor in Madonna's decision to do the Pepsi ad was the guarantee of exposure. 'I wouldn't say [the long list of countries] was a prerequisite,' says an industry source, 'but there was discussion with Madonna's management and Warner Bros about the number of people reached, or GRPs [gross rating points]. There was discussion of media weight.'

The sense that the inevitable destination of all celebrity journeys is a Pepsi commercial validates the Big Shill of celebrity. Only the networks forged by the multinational pop vendors are vast enough to provide a stage for celeb/ aristos like Madonna; only they heft enough media weight. We were always supposed to love Madonna *because* she luxuriates in media hype, writing jingles for teenage abandon. A Pepsi promo video has *Billboard* executive Sam Holdsworth kind of saying it all: 'She's a commercial character. She's changed her persona three or four times in her career already, from the vamp ingenue to the punk to the techno girl to the who knows what, and I think Pepsi's done the same.'

But in the next breath, he inadvertently spells out what's wrong with the sense that corp-rock is inevitable: 'The whole push in promoting artists nowadays is how do you reach people, how do you reach people that either haven't heard of them, or haven't heard a particular album, or whose image hasn't really penetrated. And that's what advertising is and that's what promotion is, and I think that's what artists are really more and more about these days. Because it's an electronic medium, music's not a personal medium, and to be an international artist you really have to fly on that higher media plane.'

In a press release, Pepsi lays bare its plans for world domination: 'The ground-breaking deal is expected to change the way popular tunes from major artists are released in the future. Traditionally, new songs have been made public through heavy radio airplay. In an innovative twist, the Pepsi–Madonna deal uses television to provide unparalleled international exposure for her new single.'

But if that's the way to enter the pantheon, then what does that make Pepsi and Coke? They are the medium through which the word is passed. They are universal, speaking no language and all languages. And each art/ad is like a prayer unto them.

Part III

VIDEO ANALYSIS

6

MONSTER METAPHORS: NOTES ON MICHAEL JACKSON'S *THRILLER*

Kobena Mercer

Michael Jackson, megastar. His LP, *Thriller*, made in 1982, has sold over 35 million copies worldwide and is said to be the biggest selling LP in the history of pop. Jackson is reputed to have amassed a personal fortune of some 75 million dollars at the age of 26. Even more remarkably, he's been a star since he was 11 and sang lead with his brothers in the Jackson Five, the biggest selling group on the Tamla Motown label in the 1970s. The Jackson Five practically invented the genre of 'teeny-bopper' pop cashed in upon by white pop idols like Donny Osmond. While such figures have faded from memory, classic Jackson Five tunes like 'I want you back' and 'ABC' can still evoke the pride and enthusiasm which marked the assertive mood of the 'Black Pride' cultural movement.

After he and his brothers left Motown in the mid-1970s and took more artistic control over their own productions, Jackson developed as a singer, writer and stage performer. His *Off the Wall* LP of 1979, which established him as a solo star, demonstrates the lithe, sensual texture of his voice and its mastery over a diverse range of musical styles and idioms, from romantic ballad to rock. Just what is it that makes this young, black man so different, so appealing?

Undoubtedly, it is the voice which lies at the heart of his appeal. Rooted in the Afro-American tradition of 'soul', Jackson's vocal performance is characterized by breathy gasps, squeaks, sensual sighs and other wordless sounds which have become his stylistic signature. The way in which this style punctuates the emotional resonance and bodily sensuality of the music corresponds to what Roland Barthes (1977: 188) called the 'grain' of the voice – 'the grain is the body in the voice as it sings'. The emotional and erotic expressiveness of the voice is complemented by the sensual grace and sheer excitement of Jackson's dancing style: even as a child, his stage performance provoked comparisons with James Brown and Jackie Wilson.

But there is another element to Jackson's success and popularity – his image. Jackson's individual style fascinates and attracts attention. The ankle-cut jeans, the single-gloved hand and, above all, the wet-look hairstyle which have become his trademarks, have influenced the sartorial repertoires of black and white youth cultures and been incorporated into mainstream fashion.

Most striking is the change in Jackson's looks and physical appearance as he has grown. The cute child dressed in gaudy flower-power gear and sporting a huge 'Afro' hairstyle has become, as a young adult, a paragon of racial and sexual ambiguity. Michael reclines across the gatefold sleeve of the *Thriller* LP, dressed in crisp black and white on a glossy metallic surface against a demure pink background. Look closer – the glossy sheen of his complexion appears lighter in colour than before; the nose seems sharper, more aqualine, less rounded and 'African' and the lips seem tighter, less pronounced. Above all, the large 'Afro' has dissolved into a shock of wet-look permed curls and a new stylistic trademark, the single lock over the forehead, appears.

What makes this reconstruction of Jackson's image more intriguing is the mythology built up around it, in which it is impossible or simply beside the point to distinguish truth from falsehood. It is said that he has undergone cosmetic surgery to adopt a more white, European look, although Jackson denies it (Johnson 1984). But the definite sense of racial ambiguity writ large in his new image is at the same time, and by the same token, the site of a sexual ambiguity bordering on androgyny. He may sing as sweet as Al Green, dance as hard as James Brown, but he looks more like Diana Ross than any black male soul artist. The media have seized upon these ambiguities and have fabricated a 'persona', a private 'self' behind the image, which has become the subject of speculation and rumour. This mythologization has culminated in the construction of a Peter Pan figure. We are told that behind the star's image is a lonely, 'lost boy', whose life is shadowed by morbid obsessions and anxieties. He lives like a recluse and is said to 'come alive' only when he is on stage in front of his fans. The media's exploitation of public fascination with Jackson the celebrity has even reached the point of 'pathologizing' his personality:

> Even Michael Jackson's millions of fans find his lifestyle strange.
> It's just like one of his hit songs, 'Off the wall'. People in the know say –
> His biggest thrill is taking trips to Disneyland.
> His closest friends are zoo animals.
> He talks to tailor's dummies in his lounge.
> He fasts every Sunday and then dances in his bedroom until he drops of
>   exhaustion. So showbusiness folk keep asking the question: 'Is
>   Jacko Wacko?'
> Two top American psychiatrists have spent hours examining a detailed
>   dossier on Jackson. Here is their on-the-couch report.[1]

Jackson's sexuality and sexual preference in particular have been the focus for such public fascination, as a business associate of his, Shirley Brooks, complains:

He doesn't and won't make public statements about his sex life, because he believes – and he is right – that is none of anyone else's business. Michael and I had a long conversation about it, and he felt that anytime you're in the public eye and don't talk to the press, they tend to make up these rumours to fill their pages.[2]

Neither child nor man, not clearly either black or white and with an androgynous image that is neither masculine nor feminine, Jackson's star-image is a 'social hieroglyph', as Marx said of the commodity form which demands, yet defies, decoding. This article offers a reading of the music video *Thriller* from the point of view of the questions raised by the phenomenal popularity of this star, whose image is a spectacle of racial and sexual indeterminacy.

REMAKE, REMODEL: VIDEO IN THE MARKETING OF *THRILLER*

The videos for two songs from the *Thriller* LP, 'Billie Jean' and 'Beat it', stand out in the way they foreground Jackson's new style. 'Billie Jean', directed by Steve Barron, visualizes the 'cinematic' feel of the music track and its narrative of a false paternity claim, by creating through a 'studio-set' scenario, sharp editing and various effects, an ambience that complements rather than illustrates the song. Taking its cue from the LP cover, it stresses Jackson's style in his dress and in his dance. Paving stones light up as Jackson twists, kicks and turns through the performance, invoking the 'magic' of the star. 'Beat it', directed by Bob Giraldi (who made TV adverts for McDonald's hamburgers and Dr Pepper soft drinks) visualizes the anti-macho lyric of the song. Shots alternate between 'juvenile delinquent' gangs about to begin a fight, and Michael, fragile and alone in his bedroom. The singer then disarms the gangs with superior charm and grace as he leads the all-male cast through a dance sequence that synthesizes the cinematic imagery of *The Warriors* and *West Side Story*.

These videos, executed from designs by Jackson himself, and others in which he appears, such as 'Say, say, say' by Paul McCartney and 'Can you feel it?' by the Jacksons, are important aspects of the commercial success of *Thriller* because they breached the boundaries of race on which the music industry has been based. Unlike stars such as Lionel Richie, Jackson has not 'crossed over' from black to white stations to end up in the middle of the road: his success has popularized black music in white rock and pop markets, by actually playing with imagery and style that has always been central to the marketing of pop. In so doing, Jackson has opened up a space in which new stars like Prince are operating, at the interface between the boundaries defined by 'race'.

'Thriller', the LP title track, was released as the third single from the album. The accompanying video went beyond the then-established conventions and limitations of the medium. According to Dave Laing, these conventions have been tied to the economic imperative of music video:

> First, the visuals were subordinated to the soundtrack, which they were there to sell; second, music video as a medium for marketing immediately inherited an aesthetic and a set of techniques from the pre-existing and highly developed form of television commercials.
>
> (Laing 1985: 81)

Thus one convention, that of fast-editing derived from the montage codes of TV advertising, has been overlaid with another: that of an alternation between naturalistic or 'realist' modes of representation (in which the song is performed 'live' or in a studio and mimed to by the singer or group), and 'constructed' or fantastic modes of representation (in which the singer/group acts out imaginary roles implied by the lyrics or by the 'atmosphere' of the music). 'Thriller' incorporates the montage and alternation conventions, but organizes the flow of images by framing it with a powerful *story-telling* or *narrational* direction which provides continuity and closure. Since 'Thriller', this story-telling code has itself become a music video convention: director Julien Temple's 'Undercover of the night' (Rolling Stones, 1983) and 'Jazzin' for blue jeans' (David Bowie, 1984) represent two of the more imaginative examples of this narrativization of the music by the direction of the flow of images. 'Thriller' is distinguished not only by its internal and formal structure, but also by the fact that it is 'detached' from a primary economic imperative or rationale. The LP was already a 'monster' of a commercial success before the title track was released as a single: there was no need for a 'hard sell'. Thus the 'Thriller' video does not so much seek to promote the record as a primary product, but rather *celebrates the success the LP has brought Michael Jackson* by acting as a vehicle to showcase its star. In the absence of a direct economic imperative, the video can indulge Jackson's own interest in acting: its use of cinematic codes and structures provides a framework for Jackson to act as a 'movie-star'. Jackson himself had acted before, in *The Wiz* (1977), an all-black remake of *The Wizard of Oz* in which he played the Scarecrow. He professes a deep fascination with acting:

> I love it so much. It's escape. It's fun. It's just neat to become another thing, another person. Especially when you really believe it and it's not like you're acting. I always hated the word 'acting' – to say, 'I am an actor'. It should be more than that. It should be more like a believer.[3]

In 'Thriller', Jackson acts out a variety of roles as the video engages in a playful parody of the stereotypes, codes and conventions of the 'horror' genre. The inter-textual dialogues between film, dance and music which the video articulates also draw us, the spectators, into the *play* of signs and meanings at work in the 'constructedness' of the star's image. The following reading of the music video considers the specificity of the music track, asks how the video 'visualizes' the music and then goes on to examine the internal structure of the video as an inter-text of sound, image and style.

'THRILLER': A READING

Consider first the specificity of the music track. The title, which gives the LP its title as well, is the name for a particular genre of film – the 'murder–mystery–suspense' film, the detective story, the thriller. But the lyrics of the song are not 'about' film or cinema. The track is a mid-tempo funk number, written by Rod Temperton, and recalls similar numbers written by the author for Michael Jackson such as 'Off the wall'. The lyrics evoke allusions and references to the cinematic culture of 'terror' and 'horror' movies but only to play on the meaning of the word 'thriller'. The lyrics weave a little story, which have been summarized as 'a night of viewing some . . . gruesome horror movies with a lady friend' (George 1984). The lyrics narrate such a fictional-scene by speaking in the first person:

> It's close to midnight and somethin' evil's lurkin' in the dark/ . . . . You try to scream, but terror takes the sound before you make it/You start to freeze, as horror looks you right between the eyes/You're paralysed.

Who is this 'you' being addressed? The answer comes in the semantic turn-around of the third verse and chorus in which the pun on the title is made evident:

> Now is the time for you and I to cuddle close together/All thru' the night, I'll save you from the terror on the screen/I'll make you see, that [Chorus] This is thriller, thriller-night, 'cause I could thrill you more than any ghost would dare to try/Girl, this is thriller . . . so let me hold you tight and share a killer, thriller tonight.

Thus the lyrics play a *double-entendre* on the meaning of 'thrill'.

As Iain Chambers has observed:

> Distilled into the metalanguage of soul and into the clandestine cultural liberation of soul music is the regular employment of a sexual discourse.
> (Chambers 1985: 148)

Along with the emotional complexities of intimate relationships, physical sexuality is perhaps *the* central preoccupation of the soul tradition. But, as Chambers suggests, the power of soul as a cultural form to express sexuality does not so much lie in the literal meanings of the words but in the passion of the singer's voice and vocal performance. The explicit meanings of the lyrics are in this sense secondary to the sensual resonance of the individual character of the voice, its 'grain'. While the 'grain' of the voice encodes the contradictions of sexual relationships, their pleasures and pain, the insistence of the rhythm is an open invitation to the body to dance. Dance, as cultural form, and sexual ritual, is a mode of decoding the sound and meaning articulated in the music. In its incitement of the listener to dance, to become an active participant in the texture of voice, words and rhythm, soul music is not only 'about' sexuality, but is itself a musical means for the eroticization of the body (Chambers 1985: 143–8). In 'Thriller' it is the 'grain' of Jackson's voice that expresses and plays with this sexual sub-text and it is this dimension that transgresses the denotation of the lyrics and escapes analytic reduction. Jackson's interpretation of Temperton's lyric inflects the allusions to cinema to thematize a discourse on sexuality, rather than film, and the 'story' created by the lyrics sets up a reverberation between two semantic poles: the invocation of macabre movies is offset by the call to 'cuddle close together'.

The element of irony set in motion by this semantic polarity is the 'literary' aspect of the sense of parody that pervades the song. Special sound effects – creaking doors and howling dogs – contribute to the pun on the title. Above all, this play of parody spreads out in Vincent Price's rap, which closes the record. The idea of a well-established white movie actor like Price delivering a 'rap', a distinctly black urban cultural form, is funny enough. But the fruity, gurgling tones of the actor's voice, which immediately invoke the semi-comic self-parody of 'horror' he has become, express the affectionate sense of humour that underpins the song:

Darkness falls across the land. The midnight hour is close at hand.
Creatures crawl in search of blood, to terrorise y'awl's neighbourhood.
And whosoever shall be found, without the soul for getting down, must
stand and face the hounds of hell, and rot inside a corpse's shell.

The parody at play here lies in the quotation of soul argot – 'get down', 'midnight hour', 'funk of forty thousand years' – in the completely different context of horror movies. The almost camp quality of refined exaggeration in Price's voice and his 'British' accent is at striking odds with the discourse of black American soul music.

As we 'listen' to the production of meanings in the music track the various 'voices' involved in the production (Temperton, Jackson, Price, Quincy Jones, etc.) are audibly combined into parody. One way of approaching the transition from music to video, then, would be to suggest that John Landis, its director, brings aspects of his own 'voice' as an 'author' of Hollywood films into this dialogue. It seems to me that Landis's voice contributes to the puns and play on the meaning of 'thriller' by drawing on conventions of mainstream horror movies.

STORY, PLOT AND PARODY

Landis introduces two important elements from film into the medium of music video: a narrative direction of the flow of images and special-effects techniques associated with the pleasures of the horror film. These effects are used in the two scenes that show the metamorphosis of Michael into, first, a werewolf, and then a zombie. The use of these cinematic technologies to create the metamorphoses is clearly what distinguishes 'Thriller' from other music video. 'Thriller' gives the video audience *real thrills* – the 'thrill' of tension, anxiety and fear associated with the pleasure offered by the horror genre. The spectacle of the visceral transformation of cute, lovable Michael Jackson into a howlin' wolf of a monster is disturbing, because it seems so convincing, 'real' and fascinating. As Philip Brophy (1988) remarks:

> The pleasure of the [horror] text is, in fact, getting the shit scared out of you – and loving it: an exchange mediated by adrenalin.

Both special effects and narrative return us to the direction of John Landis, who also directed *An American Werewolf in London* (1979). *American Werewolf* is a horror comedy; it retells the traditional werewolf myth, setting its protagonists as tourists in England attacked by a strange animal, into which one of them then turns during the full moon. The film employs pop tunes to exacerbate its underlying parody of this mythology – 'Moondance' (Van Morrison), 'Bad moon rising' (Creedence Clearwater Revival) and 'Blue moon' (Frankie Lymon and the Teenagers). And this humour is combined with special-effects and make-up techniques which show the bodily metamorphosis of man to wolf in 'real time', as opposed to less credible 'time-lapse' techniques. The 'Thriller' video not only refers to this film, but to other generic predecessors, including *Night of the Living Dead* (1968) by George Romero and *Halloween* (1978) by John Carpenter. Indeed, the video is strewn with allusions to horror films. As Brophy (1988) observes:

> It is a genre which mimics itself mercilessly – because its statement is coded in its very mimicry. . . . It is not so much that the modern horror film refutes or ignores the conventions of genre, but it is involved in a violent awareness of itself as a saturated genre.

Thus cinematic horror seems impelled towards parody of its own codes and conventions. With hindsight it is tempting to suggest that 'Thriller's' music track was almost made to be filmed, as it seems to cue these cinematic references. Certain points within the video appear to be straightforward transpositions from the song: 'They're out to get you, there's demons closin' in on ev'ry side/ . . . Night creatures call and the dead start to walk in their masquerade', and so on. But it is at the level of its *narrative structure* that the video engages in an inter-textual dialogue with the music track.[4]

Unlike most pop videos, 'Thriller' does not begin with the first notes of the song, but with a long panning shot and the 'cinematic' sound of recorded silence. This master-shot, establishing the all-seeing but invisible 'eye' of the camera, is comparable to the discursive function of third-person narration. The shot/reverse-shot series which frames the dialogue between the two protagonists in the opening sequence establishes 'point-of-view' camera angles, analogues to 'subjective', first-person modes of enunciation. It is the use of these specific cinematic codes of narration that structures the entire flow of images and gives the video a beginning, a middle and an end. 'Thriller' incorporates the pop video convention of switching from 'realist' to 'fantastic' modes of representation, but binds this into continuity and closure through its narrative. The two metamorphosis sequences are of crucial importance to this narrative structure; the first disrupts the 'equilibrium' of the opening sequence, and the second repeats but differs from the first in order to bring the flow of images to its end and re-establish equilibrium. Within the story-telling conventions of the horror genre the very appearance of the monster/werewolf/ vampire/alien signals the violation of equilibrium: the presence of the monster activates the narrative dynamic whose goal or end is achieved by an act of counter-violence that eliminates it (Neale 1980).

In the opening sequence of 'Thriller' the dialogue and exchange of glances between Michael and the girl as the male and female protagonists of the story establish 'romance' as the narrative pre-text. The girl's look at Michael as the car stops hints at a question, answered by the expression of bemused incredulity on his face. Did he stop the car on purpose? Was it a romantic ruse, to lure her into a trap? The girl's cocquettish response to Michael's defence ('Honestly, we're out of gas') lingers sensually on the syllables, '*So* . . . what are we going to do now?' Her question, and his smile in return, hint at and exacerbate the underlying erotic tension of romantic intrigue between the two characters. Michael's dialogue gives a minimal 'character' to his role as the boyfriend: he appears a somewhat shy, very proper and polite 'boy next door'. The girl, on the other hand, is not so much a 'character' as the 'girlfriend' type. At another level, their clothes – a pastiche 1950s retro style – connote youthful innocence, the couple as archetypical teen lovers. But this innocent representation is unsettled by Michael's statement: 'I'm not like other guys.' The statement implies a question posed on the terrain of gender, and masculinity in particular: why is he different from 'other guys'?

The sequence provides an answer in the boyfriend's transformation into a monster. But, although the metamorphosis resolves the question, it is at the cost of disrupting the equilibrium of 'romance' between the two protagonists, which is now converted into a relation of terror between monster and victim. The chase through the woods is the final sequence of this 'beginning' of the narrative. The subsequent scene, returning to Michael and the girl as a couple in a cinema, re-establishes the equation of 'romance' and repositions the protagonists as girlfriend and boyfriend, but at another level of representation.

In structural terms this shift in modes of representation, from a fantastic level (in which the metamorphosis and chase take place) to a realist level (in which the song is performed) is important because it retrospectively implies that the entire opening sequence was a film within a film, or rather, a film within the video. More to the point, the 'beginning' is thus revealed to be *a parody of 1950s B-movie horror.* This has been signalled in the self-conscious 'acting' mannerisms Jackson employs and by the pastiche of 1950s teenager styles. The shift from a parody of a 1950s horror movie to the cinema audience watching the film and the long shot of the cinema showing the film, visually acknowledge this 'violent awareness of itself as saturated genre'.

> While Hammer were reviving the Universal monsters . . . American International Pictures began a cycle whose appreciation was almost entirely tongue-in-cheek – a perfect example of 'camp' manufacture and reception of the iconography of terror.
>
> The first film in this series bore the (now notorious) title *I was a Teenage Werewolf* (1957). . . . The absurdity of the plot and acting, and the relentless pop music that filled the soundtrack, gave various kinds of pleasure to young audiences and encouraged the film-makers to follow this pilot movie with *I was a Teenage Frankenstein* and with *Teenage Monster* and *Teenage Zombie*, creations that were as awful to listen to as they were to see.
>
> (Prawer 1980: 15)

Parody depends on an explicit self-consciousness: in 'Thriller' this informs the dialogue, dress-style and acting in the opening sequence. In its parody of a parody it also acknowledges that there is no 'plot' as such: the narrative code that structures the video has no story to tell. Rather it creates a simulacrum of a story, a parody of a story, in its stylistic send-up of genre conventions. But it is precisely at the level of its self-consciousness that 'Thriller's' mimicry of the *gender roles* of the horror genre provides an anchor for the way it visualizes the sexual discourse, the play on the meaning of the word 'thriller' on the music track.

GENRE AND GENDER: 'THRILLER'S' SEXUAL SUBTEXT

As the video switches from fantastic to realist modes of representation, the roles played by the two protagonists shift accordingly. The fictional film within the video, with its narrative pretext of 'romance', positions Michael and the girl as boyfriend and girlfriend, and within this the fantastic metamorphosis transforms the relation into one of terror between monster and victim. If we go back to Michael's statement made in this scene, 'I'm not like other guys', we can detect a confusion about the role he is playing.

The girl's initial reply, 'Of course not. That's why I love you', implies that it is obvious that he is 'different' because he is the real Michael Jackson. When, in her pleasure at his proposal, she calls him by his proper name she interpellates him in two roles at once – as fictional boyfriend and real superstar. This ambiguity of reference acknowledges Jackson's self-conscious acting style: we, the video audience, get the impression he is playing at playing a role and we 'know' that Jackson, the singer, the star, is playing at the role of a 'movie-star'.

In 'Thriller', Michael's outfit and its stylistic features – the wet-look hairstyle, the ankle-cut jeans and the letter 'M' emblazoned on his jacket – reinforce this meta-textual superimposition of roles. If Michael, as the male protagonist, is both boyfriend and star, his female counterpart in the equation of 'romance' is both the girlfriend and at this meta-textual level, the fan. The girl is in two places at once: on screen and in the audience. As spectator of the film within the video she is horrified by the image on the screen and gets up to leave. 'Fooled' by the violent spectacle of the metamorphosis, she mistakes the fantastic for the real, she forgets that 'it's only a movie'. The girl's positions in the fictional and realist scenes mirror those of the video spectator – the effects which generate thrills for the audience are the events, in the story-world, that generate terror for the girl.

The girl occupies a mediated position between the audience and the image which offers a clue to the way the video visualizes the music track. In the middle section, as the couple walk away from the cinema and Michael begins the song, the narrative roles of boyfriend and girlfriend are re-established, but now subordinated to the song's performance. This continuity of narrative function is underlined by the differentiation of costume style: Michael now wears a flashy red-and-black leather jacket cut in a 'futuristic' style and her ensemble is also contemporary – T-shirt, bomber jacket and head of curls like Michael's own. This imagery echoes publicity images of Jackson the stage performer. As the song gets under way Jackson becomes 'himself', the star. The girl becomes the 'you' in the refrain 'Girl, I could thrill you more than any ghost would dare to try'.

On the music track, the 'you' could be the listener, since the personal and direct mode of enunciation creates a space for the listener to enter and take part in the production of meanings. In the video, it is the girl who takes this place and, as the addressee of the sexual discourse enunciated in the song, her positions in the video-text create possibilities for spectatorial identification. These lines of identification are hinted at in the opening scene in which the girl's response to Michael's wooing enacts the 'fantasy of being a pop star's girlfriend', a fantasy which is realized in this section of the video.[5]

BEAUTY AND THE BEAST: MASKS, MONSTERS AND MASCULINITY

The conventions of horror inscribe a fascination with sexuality, with gender identity codified in terms that revolve around the symbolic presence of the monster. Women are invariably the victims of the acts of terror unleashed by the werewolf/vampire/alien/'thing': the monster as non-human Other. The destruction of the monster establishes male protagonists as heroes, whose object and prize is of course the woman. But as the predatory force against which the hero has to compete, the monster itself occupies a 'masculine' position in relation to the female victim.

'Thriller's' rhetoric of parody presupposes a degree of self-consciousness on the part of the spectator, giving rise to a supplementary commentary on the sexuality and sexual identity of its star, Michael Jackson. Thus, the warning 'I'm not like other guys' can be read by the audience as a reference to Jackson's sexuality. Inasmuch as the video audience is conscious of the gossip which circulates around the star, the statement of difference provokes other meanings: is he homosexual, transsexual or somehow presexual?

In the first metamorphosis Michael becomes a werewolf. As the recent *Company of Wolves* (directed by Neil Jordan, 1984) demonstrates, werewolf mythology – lycanthropy – concerns the representation of male sexuality as 'naturally' bestial, predatory, aggressive, violent – in a word, 'monstrous'. Like 'Thriller', *Company of Wolves* employs similar special effects to show the metamorphosis of man to wolf in 'real time'. And like the Angela Carter story on which it is based, the film can be read to rewrite the European folktale of 'Little Red Riding Hood' to reveal its concerns with subjects of menstruation, the moon and the nature of male sexuality. In the fictional opening scene of 'Thriller' the connotation of innocence around the girl likens her to Red Riding Hood. But is Michael a big, bad wolf?

In the culmination of the chase sequence through the woods, the girl takes the role of victim. Here, the disposition of point-of-view angles between the monster's dominant position and the supine position of the victim suggests rape, fusing the underlying sexual relation of 'romance' with terror and violence. As the monster, Michael's transformation might suggest that beneath the boy-next-door image there is a 'real' man waiting to break out, a man whose masculinity is measured by a rapacious sexual appetite, 'hungry like the wolf'. But such an interpretation is undermined and subverted by the final shot of the metamorphosis. Michael-as-werewolf lets out a blood-curdling howl, but this is in hilarious counterpoint to the collegiate 'M' on his jacket. What does it stand for? Michael? Monster? Macho Man? More like Mickey Mouse. The incongruity between the manifest signifier and the symbolic meaning of the Monster opens up a gap in the text, to be filled with laughter.

Animals are regularly used to signify human attributes, with the wolf, lion, snake and eagle all understood as signs of male sexuality. Jackson's subversion to this symbolism is writ large on the *Thriller* LP cover. Across the star's knee lies a young tiger cub, a brilliant little metaphor for the ambiguity of Jackson's image as a black male pop star. This plays on the star's 'man–child' image and suggests a domesticated animality, hinting at menace beneath the cute and cuddly surface. Jackson's sexual ambiguity makes a mockery out of the menagerie of received images of masculinity.[6]

In the second metamorphosis Michael becomes a zombie. Less dramatic and 'horrifying' than the first, this transformation cues the spectacular dance sequence that frames the chorus of the song. While the dance, choreographed by Michael Peters, makes visual one of the lines from the lyric, 'Night creatures crawl and the dead start to walk in their masquerade', it foregrounds Jackson-the-dancer and his performance breaks loose from the video. As the ghouls begin to dance, the sequence elicits the same kind of parodic humour provoked by Vincent Price's rap on the music track. There humour lay in the incongruity between Price's voice and the argot of black soul culture. Here a visual equivalent of this incongruity is created by the spectacle of the living dead performing with Jackson a funky dance routine. The sense of parody is intensified by the macabre make-up of the ghouls, bile dripping from their mouths. Jackson's make-up, casting a ghostly pallor over his skin and emphasizing the contour of the skull, alludes to one of the paradigmatic 'masks' of the horror genre, that of Lon Chaney in *The Phantom of the Opera* (1925).

Unlike the werewolf, the figure of the zombie, the undead corpse, does not represent sexuality so much as asexuality or anti-sexuality, suggesting the sense of *neutral eroticism* in Jackson's style as dancer. As has been observed:

> The movie star Michael most resembles is Fred Astaire – that *paragon of sexual vagueness*. Astaire never fit a type, hardly ever played a traditional romantic lead. He created his own niche by the sheer force of his tremendous talent.
>
> (George 1984: 83–4)

The dance sequence can be read as cryptic writing on this 'sexual vagueness' of Jackson's body in movement, in counterpoint to the androgyny of his image. The dance breaks loose from the narrative and Michael's body comes alive in movement, a rave from the grave: the scene can thus be seen as a commentary on the notion that as star Jackson only 'comes alive' when he is on stage performing. The living dead invoke an existential liminality which corresponds to both the sexual indeterminancy of Jackson's dance and the somewhat morbid lifestyle that reportedly governs his offscreen existence. Both meanings are buried in the video 'cryptogram'.[7]

METAPHOR-MORPHOSIS

Finally, I feel compelled to return to the scene of the first metamorphosis. It enthrals and captivates, luring the spectator's gaze and petrifying it in wonder. This sense of both fear and fascination is engineered by the video's special effects. By showing the metamorphosis in 'real time' the spectacle violently distorts the features of Jackson's face. The horror-effect of the monster's appearance depends on the 'suspension of disbelief': we know that the monster is a fiction, literally a mask created by mechanical techniques, but repress or disavow this knowledge to participate in the 'thrills', the pleasures expected from the horror-text. Yet in this splitting of belief which the horror film presupposes, it is the credibility of the techniques themselves that is at stake in making the 'otherness' of the monster believable (Neale 1980: 45).

The Making of Michael Jackson's Thriller (1984) demonstrates the special effects used in the video. We see make-up artists in the process of applying the 'mask' that will give Jackson the appearance of the monster. Of particular interest is the make-up artists' explanation of how the werewolf mask was designed and constructed: a series of transparent cells, each with details of the animal features of the mask, are gradually superimposed on a publicity image of Jackson from the cover of *Rolling Stone* magazine. It is this superimpositon of fantastic and real upon Jackson's face that offers clues as to why the metamorphosis is so effective. Like the opening parody of the 1950s horror movie and its confusion of roles that Jackson is playing (boyfriend/star), there is a slippage between different levels of belief on the part of the spectator.

The metamorphosis achieves a horrifying effect because the monster does not just mutilate the appearance of the boyfriend, but plays on the audience's awareness of Jackson's double role; thus, the credibility of the special effects violates the image of the star himself. At this meta-textual level, the drama of the transformation is heightened by other performance-signs that foreground Jackson as star. The squeaks, cries and other wordless sounds which emanate from his throat as he grips his stomach grotesquely mimic the sounds which are the stylistic trademark of Jackson's voice and thus reinforce the impression that it is the 'real' Michael Jackson undergoing this mutation. Above all, the very first shots of the video highlight the make-up on the star's face (particularly the eyes and lips), the pallor of his complexion, revealing the eerie sight of his skull beneath the wet-look curls. The very appearance of Jackson draws attention to the artificiality of his own image. As the monstrous mask is, literally, a construction made out of make-up and cosmetic 'work', the fictional world of the horror film merely appropriates what is already an artifice. I suggest that the metamorphosis be seen as *a metaphor for the aesthetic reconstruction of Michael Jackson's face.*

The literal construction of the fantastic monster-mask refers to other images of the star: the referent of the mask, as a sign in its own right, is a commonplace publicity image taken from the cover of a magazine. In this sense the mask refers not to the real person or private 'self' but to Michael Jackson-as-an-image. The metamorphosis could thus be seen as an accelerated allegory of the morphological development of Jackson's facial features: from child to adult, from boyfriend to monster, from star to superstar – the sense of wonder generated by the video's special effects forms an allegory for the fascination with which the world beholds this star-as-image.

In 1983, Jackson took part in a two-hour TV special to celebrate Motown's twenty-fifth anniversary, in which vintage footage was intercut with each act's performance; the film was then edited and used as a 'support' act on Motown artists' tours in England. This is how the reception of the film was described:

> The audience almost visibly tensed as Michael's voice . . . took complete
> control, attacking the songs with that increased repertoire of whoops,

hiccups and gasps, with which he punctuates the lyric to such stylish, relaxing effect. And then he danced. The cocky strut of a super-confident child had been replaced by a lithe, menacing grace, and his impossibly lean frame, still boyishly gangly, when galvanized by the music, assumed a hypnotic, androgynous sexuality. Certainly, it was the first time in a long, long time I'd heard girls scream at a film screen.

(Brown 1984)

Amid all the screaming elicited by 'Thriller' it is possible to hear a parody of those fans' response. As a pop idol Michael Jackson has been the object of such screaming since he was 11 years old.

In 'The face of Garbo' Barthes sought to explore the almost universal appeal of film stars like Chaplin, Hepburn and Garbo by describing their faces as *masks*: aesthetic surfaces on which a society writes large its own preoccupations (see Barthes 1973). Jackson's face can also be seen as such a mask, for his image has attracted and maintained the kind of cultural fascination that makes him more like a movie star than a modern rhythm-and-blues artist. The sexual and racial ambiguity of his image can be seen as pointing to a range of questions about images of sex and race in popular culture and popular music. If we regard his face, not as the manifestation of personality traits but as a surface of artistic and social inscription, the ambiguities of Jackson's image call into question received ideas about what black male artists in popular music should look like. Seen from this angle his experimentation with imagery represents a creative incursion upon a terrain in pop culture more visibly mapped out by white male stars like Mick Jagger, David Bowie and Boy George. At best, these stars have used androgyny and sexual ambiguity as part of their 'style' in ways which question prevailing definitions of male sexuality and sexual identity. Key songs on *Thriller* highlight this problematization of masculinity: on 'Wanna be startin' somethin' ' the narrator replies to rumour and speculation about his sexuality, on 'Billie Jean' – a story about a fan who claims he is the father of her son – he refuses the paternal model of masculinity, and on 'Beat it' – 'Don't wanna see no blood, Don't be a macho man' – he explicitly refuses a bellicose model of manliness.

What makes Jackson's use of androgyny more compelling is that his work is located entirely in the Afro-American tradition of popular music and thus must be seen in the context of imagery of black men and black male sexuality. Jackson not only questions dominant stereotypes of black masculinity, but also gracefully steps outside the existing range of 'types' of black men. In so doing his style reminds us how some black men in the soul tradition such as Little Richard used 'camp', in the sense that Susan Sontag (1969) calls 'the love of the unnatural: of artifice and exaggeration', long before white pop stars began to exploit its 'shock-value'. Indeed, 'Thriller' is reminiscent of the 'camp' excesses of the originator of the combination of music and horror in pop culture, Screamin' Jay Hawkins. Horror imagery has fascinated the distinctly white male genre of 'heavy metal' in which acts like Alice Cooper and Ozzy Osbourne consume themselves in self-parody. But like Hawkins, whose 'I put a spell on you' (1956) borrowed from images of horror to articulate a scream 'that found its way out of my big mouth *directly* through my heart and guts' (quoted, Hirshey 1984: 3–22), Jackson expresses another sort of 'screaming', one that articulates the erotic materiality of the human voice, its 'grain'. Writing about a musical tradition radically different from soul, Barthes (1977) coined this term to give 'the impossible account of an individual thrill that I constantly experience in listening to singing'. 'Thriller' celebrates the fact that this thrill is shared by millions.

NOTES

1 The *Sun* (London), 9 April 1984.
2 Quoted in Nelson George, *The Michael Jackson Story* (London: New English Library, 1984) p. 106.
3 Quoted in Andy Warhol and Bob Colacello, 'Michael Jackson', *Interview* magazine, October 1982.
4 The 'Thriller' video is generally available as part of *The Making of Michael Jackson's Thriller*, Warner Home Video, 1984.
5 On personal modes of enunciation in pop discourse, see Alan Durant, *Conditions of Music* (London: Macmillan, 1984) esp. pp. 201–6. The 'fantasy of being a pop star's girlfriend' is examined in Dave Rimmer, *Like Punk Never Happened: Culture Club and the New Pop* (London: Faber, 1985) p. 112.
6 One of Freud's most famous patients, The Wolf Man, makes connections between animals and sexuality clear. The Wolf Man's dream also reads like a horror film: 'I dreamt that it was night and that I was lying on my bed. Suddenly the window opened of its own accord, and I was terrified to see some white wolves were sitting on the big walnut tree in front of the window.' Cf. Muriel Gardiner, *The Wolf Man and Sigmund Freud* (London: Hogarth Press and Institute of Psychoanalysis, 1973) p. 173. Freud's reading suggests that the terror in the dream manifests a fear of castration for a repressed homosexual desire.
7 The notion of 'cryptonymy' as a name for unconscious meanings emerges in Nicholas Abraham and Maria Torok's re-reading of Freud's Wolf Man. See Peggy Kamuf, 'Abraham's wake', *Diacritics*, Spring 1979, vol. 9, no. 1, pp. 32–43.

REFERENCES

Barthes, Roland (1973) *Mythologies*, London: Paladin.
—— (1977) 'The grain of the voice', in Stephen Heath (ed.), *Image–Music–Text*, London: Fontana.
Brophy, Philip (1988) 'Horrality', *Screen*, vol. 27, no. 1.
Brown, Geoff (1984) *Michael Jackson: Body and Soul*, London: Virgin Books.
Chambers, Iain (1985) *Urban Rhythms: Pop Music and Popular Culture*, London: Macmillan.
George, Nelson (1984) *The Michael Jackson Story*, London: New English Library.
Hirshey, Gerri (1984) *Nowhere to Run: the Story of Soul*, London: Pan Books.
Johnson, Robert (1984) 'The Michael Jackson nobody knows', *Ebony*, December.
Laing, Dave (1985) 'Music video: industrial product, cultural form', *Screen*, vol. 26, no. 2.

Neale, Stephen (1980) *Genre*, London: British Film Institute.

Prawer, S. S. (1980) *Caligari's Children: the Film as Tale of Terror*, Oxford: Oxford University Press.

Sontag, Susan (1969) 'Notes on Camp', in *Against Interpretation*, London: Eyre & Spottiswoode.

7

GENRE AND FORM: THE DEVELOPMENT OF THE COUNTRY MUSIC VIDEO

Mark Fenster

Given country music's ability to tell a story – simple and straightforward lyrics are still considered more important in a country song than complex or new rhythms, tempos and melodies – one would think that its adaptation to a short-form narrative music video would have been natural and easy. Country music also had the advantage of having appeared on screen since the time moves could first talk, from Jimmie Rodgers' 1929 movie-short *The Singing Brakeman* through thousands of singing-cowboy movies, the national television exposure that culminated in *Hee Haw* and recent films like *Honeysuckle Rose* (1980) and *Tender Mercies* (1983) that attempt to embody and represent the ethos of country music. With a visual history and a classical narrative style, country music would have seemed better able than rock music to take advantage of the promotional opportunities that music videos represented in the early part of the 1980s.

The development of country music videos, however, was not quite so simple, at least partially due to the fact that popular music videos were produced first and the form was quickly associated with the production values, aesthetic conventions and media outlets of rock videos. In a sense, the early history of country videos must be seen as a *response*: a response to the mainsteam music industry's success with rock videos as a source of promotion, and a response to the excitement and new possibilities that the form helped to raise for newer artists and kinds of music. Throughout its history, the country music industry, since the mid- to late-1950s based in Nashville, has had a tenuous relationship with the popular-music industry of Los Angeles and New York. While for the most part it has wanted to remain distinct and loyal to its stable audience base, Nashville has looked longingly and jealously at the larger, younger audiences that make pop music so much more lucrative.[1] Both the aesthetic and industrial development of country music videos, then, must be seen within this reactive relationship. As I will describe below, country videos simultaneously define themselves as distinct from those of popular music (*country* music videos) while at the same time both taking advantage of the new technological and promotional possibilities developed by pop music videos and leaving open the possibility of crossing over to a non-country audience (country *music videos*).

My concern will be with the ways in which the country video has evolved, and the ways that the industrial response to the perceived success of the rock and pop video, along with the conventions created through the history of the country music genre, have contributed to the current form. My analysis will begin with a history of the way the issue of the country video was presented in trade magazines, from the early days of suspicion towards the new form to the current situation, in which videos are perceived as another, established way of promoting an artists's newest release. I will then give an aesthetic analysis of country videos from the early experiments to the most recent, more 'mature' videos, in which the classical story-telling style of country lyrics has been adapted to a short narrative film format. In the concluding section I will use the development of the country music video to inform a theoretical model of the sets of relations – including those between music and technological, economic and ideological change; industry and audience; and different music genres – that determine the adoption and adaptation of a new form by an established genre.

THE INDUSTRIAL RESPONSE

The industrial response to the country music video was a three-step process: the identification of a successful medium of promotion in another genre; the development of both financial standards in the form of budget levels and industrial institutions such as cable television channels to present the videos to their intended audience; and finally the establishment of the music video as a promotional tool available for all artists, though not for all releases. Throughout each of these stages, there was a constant questioning of the developing medium, particularly in terms of its cost-effectiveness and the ability of the makers to translate a perceived pop music form to the country music genre. Even now, seven years since the first country music videos and five years since *Billboard* declared a 'video boom' in Nashville, the country music video is used far more sparingly and with greater industrial apprehension than in the pop/rock field.[2]

In October 1982, more than a year after the start of MTV (the most successful and most important pop/rock video outlet), a *Billboard* article asked, 'Will the success story for 1983 be country videos? No one is predicting, although MTV's runaway AOR [album-oriented rock] success has Nashville acts and executives casting a longing eye at the possibility' (Clayton 1982). But along with a 'longing eye', there was also apprehension based on cost: in the same edition of *Billboard*, an article on the country music industry's movement towards cutting costs stated,

> Video crept into many label marketing plans this year, but [a high-level label executive] sums up the general industry feeling on that point, at

least until a country MTV arrives: 'It isn't economical at $30,000 a clip but it is at $5,000 a clip because there are enough sources in terms of software users to cover that cost'.

(Millard 1982)

Five thousand dollars was an astonishingly low budget, even at that time, and it was only a fraction of what was being spent on the average pop video in 1982. The next year's *Billboard* annual country music yearbook dubbed the music video problem the 'Video Clip Game', and claimed that this 'game' was still being considered a 'gamble' (Simmons 1983).

While doubts lingered, the growth of suitable outlets, particularly the then new Nashville Network (TNN) and the Country Music Television Network (CMT), a 24-hour video channel that began in March 1983, was seen as an important new factor. One executive stated that 'the next six to twelve months is [*sic*] crucial because the new outlets are coming on and we'll be able to see the sales figures in a market after a clip has aired' (Simmons 1983). While the country music industry was moving forward in its use of the form, worries remained because the country genre was continually perceived as having a different set of needs and limitations when compared to mainstream pop/rock music.

For country music videos 1984 proved a pivotal year, as the two central elements that concerned executives – media outlets and budget levels – finally reached a level of stability. A *Billboard* article on the subject declared that a 'Video Boom' had come to Nashville, and stated that 'labels have stepped up production of country music videos in response to the spread of cable, syndicated and local television outlets programming the clips' (Roblin 1984a). Another important step was the levelling-off of budgets at the $35,000–50,000 range, which was expected to happen in the coming months (Roblin 1984b). A *Billboard* article later that year claimed that because 'change comes more slowly in Nashville', the video explosion which 'changed the face of rock' when MTV arrived was finally occurring in country music (Roblin 1984b). But despite this optimism, industry executives continued to question cost-effectiveness ('Record sales are the bottom line, and we can't say quantitatively that [videos] help with that') and the form's suitability for the genre ('We know what video has done for rock, but country may be the last market to come through').

As country music videos became institutionalized, the growth of suitable outlets and budget levels helped to dictate the aesthetic conventions of the form. In the early stages of development, when budgets were small and outlets were few, production quality was low, particularly in comparison with those being produced for rock and pop songs. But as outlets emerged and the need for higher production values became greater due to wider dissemination and higher expectations, budgets rose to the point at which Willie Nelson's and Merle Haggard's 'Pancho and Lefty' (1983) looked, and was budgeted and exhibited like a movie-short.

111

When the only available outlets for country music videos were small country music cable stations and local television shows, the videos were less able to pay for themselves as promotion and there was less need to produce a high-budget video. If television outlets and other users complained that the quantity and quality of country music videos were not adequate, the record labels claimed there was not enough exposure to warrant videos' production (Millard 1984). But as country outlets eventually grew in size and number, and national, non-country outlets (like VH-1, MTV and the USA Network's *Nightflight* programme) began to open their playlists to country music, the industry had to produce videos with higher production values for a wider audience. This was particularly important in cases where a label hoped for a crossover to larger, non-country outlets, as these videos competed with and played next to pop and rock videos.

As country videos began to crossover in outlets and in audiences, the form began to be perceived as a way in which country music could reach more lucrative markets. By 1985, an article claimed, 'country videos are finally reaching the wide – and young – audience labels hope will return sales to the high-water levels of the early eighties', with the key being 'programming that appeals to younger, active record buyers' (Roblin 1985). One record executive, commenting on the growth of the cable county music stations, said, 'I'm very encouraged as I see these outlets looking for younger and broader demographics' (Wood 1987). In this way, videos became a way in which country music could reach audiences that were more familiar with pop and rock music videos and that would not be exposed to country music except through that medium.

The mid-1980s' crossover success of Alabama, Kenny Rogers and Anne Murray on VH-1, and Hank Williams Jr's more limited success on MTV and rock outlets, enabled these artists to gain exposure to a wider and more demographically attractive audience than would normally be the case. A delegation sent from VH-1 to the 1985 Country Music Association awards seemed to indicate that the crossover of country videos to non-country outlets would grow; as the CMA's Judi Turner announced, networks like VH-1 promised 'the greatest hope for exposure to country videos' (Bessman 1985). At that time, according to a VH-1 executive, the cable channel's commitment to country was 'equal to [its commitment to] other genres', and its playlist was approximately 25 per cent country. Jim Fogelsong, president of the Nashville division of Capitol/EMI America, called VH-1's programming 'the most dramatic thing to happen in video as far as country music is concerned' (Bessman 1985). But the promise of video crossover was never fully realized; currently, even a country-rocker like Steve Earle can only get very limited play on MTV, and VH-1, which has adapted its format to a more up-scale, urban, *thirtysomething* market, no longer adds videos from Kenny Rogers, Anne Murray and Willie Nelson to its rotation.

112

Indeed, the current situation in the country music industry, in terms of who is popular and what new artists are getting the largest promotion budget, has had a great effect on the kinds of songs being made into videos and the kinds of videos presently being produced. As the recording careers of crossover artists like Rogers, Murray and Nelson have declined since the mid-1980s and the industry has experienced a 'whiplash against crossover' (Holley 1988), country music has achieved a new sense of stability and success through its commercially successful return to a more traditional sound. In addition, the large numbers of new, younger artists being signed by labels and finding success on the charts – thirty-eight new performers reached the charts for the first time over the period from January 1986 to August 1988, compared to an average of six to seven prior to that (Goldsmith 1988) – have helped to signify the re-affirmation of country music as a separate genre of popular music with a distinct sound and a loyal, identifiable market. If anything, recent years in country music have seen younger, more up-scale audiences seek out country music rather than vice versa: a writer in the *Village Voice* pronounced that 'country music is more exciting than rock, than rap, than jazz, than any popular, semi-popular or anti-popular music' (Tucker 1987), while *Time* pronounced that 'There is a bumper crop of new talent around, making personal, adventurous, uncompromised music' (Cocks 1988). This has led the industry to more actively seek out younger audiences; for example, CBS-Nashville has designed a promotional and 'alternative marketing' campaign in order to obtain college and 'youth' radio airplay for their younger artists (Holley 1989). As I will argue below, recent country videos have worked within this trend towards younger stars singing more traditional songs in recognizably country narratives and iconographic backgrounds.

The effects of these videos on sales remain unquantifiable, and instead of perceiving videos as directly causing sales, Nashville currently sees them as one among a variety of avenues of exposure for new artists and new releases. The president of a Nashville company that distributes and tracks video airplay claimed that the form can 'help break new acts, establish visual identity, give exposure, . . . and offer tremendous promotion and publicity' (Holley 1987), and thus, presumably, increase sales. In February 1987, a *Billboard* article stated that, 'One by one, most well-known country singers have come to terms with music video', and country singer John Anderson said, 'I want to get my name and sound out where all the other country artists have been going. [I want] all that exposure they've been getting on VH-1 and TNN and all the other good country outlets' (Roblin 1987).

The recent success of such new artists as K. T. Oslin, Kathy Mattea and Clint Black has been directly associated with their videos. Oslin's '80's ladies' (1987), her first single and video, was placed in heavy rotation by CMT and TNN and enabled her to construct a popular and widely acknowledged image of herself that would never have otherwise been possible. As she said in accepting an award for '80's ladies', 'I felt I could have been made into a tacky piece of junk with the wrong video' ('Hank Williams, Jr . . .' 1987). In a similar way, the success of Clint Black's debut album has been tied to his videos. CMT's airing of 'A better man' (1989) helped to create awareness and interest in him before his album was released, and the 'fan mail' that the cable channel received in support of him increased the frequency with which it played his videos. In some cases, then, even what *Billboard* terms a 'modestly budgeted, run-of-the-mill production' like 'A better man' can help to make an artist successful more quickly than had the previously exclusive sources of exposure for country artists, radio and personal appearances (Morris 1989; Lambert 1989).

Although doubts remained, particularly in 1986, when even the pop music industry began to question the video's impact on record sales (Roblin 1986), country video has continued to grow. With the establishment and success of The Nashville Network and Country Music Television – as of 1987, TNN was in 35 million, or 81 per cent of homes with cable and was the fastest growing cable network, while CMT was in 9.4 million homes through cable, satellite dishes and broadcast services (Holley 1987) – country music videos have attained a stable position on cable television nationally. Between the CMT's 24-hour rotation of videos and TNN's shows *Country Clips* and *Videocountry* (recently expanded to an hour), there are a number of effective outlets for country videos. Because there are far fewer reasonably professional-looking county videos available for television than there are country singles available for radio, most new videos are virtually assured national exposure – something that radio cannot promise. Although there is no longer much possibility for the crossover of country videos to non-country outlets, country outlets are perceived as important enough to warrant the continued production of well-produced videos. In response to the success of this new form of promotion, then, the country music industry moved from identification through development into the establishment of a relatively distinctive music video. The following section will sketch how this form developed aesthetically.

AESTHETIC DEVELOPMENT

The development of the way country music videos look and the kind of narrative, concept of performance that frames their content has, for the most part, been determined by the industry's response to the form. As labels have become more accustomed to authorizing the production of one (or in some cases two) videos for many albums, budgets have risen and video production companies have grown in Nashville. Part of what I will trace in this section, then, will be the changes over time in the production quality of country videos: a change from the use of video stock to the more professional look of film stock, from the use of stock footage and still photography to elaborately photographed and dressed sets, and a movement towards the warm, orange

114

tones that have become the dominant 'look' of many contemporary country videos.

In addition to visual quality, the development of a country video aesthetic includes the successful establishment of a classical narrative style that suits the genre's lyrical content. Unlike the more disjointed, fragmented narratives of pop/rock videos, which owe more to experimental films and advertising, most country video narratives are more directly descended from the classical Hollywood style. In fact, the tendency of country lyrics towards a character-centred, personal/psychological narrative can be traced back further than cinema, to their folk and blues roots, but country videos have rather neatly taken up many of the visual conventions that were initiated in silent film and that continue to predominate in commercial cinema and television.[3] My description and analysis, then, will follow the establishment and refinement of a narrative style in country video.

Finally, the most important role of the country video is neither to look professional nor tell a story, but to promote records and present and circulate a performer's image. The refinement of the aesthetics must be seen as the refinement of the visual representation of a series of commodities: the particular single, the album, the star and country music in general. What has ultimately been developed, then, has been the ability to present the performer in a series of roles – actor, performer, 'real human being' – that defines him or her attractively in the country music marketplace.

Early videos

Early country videos reflected the industry's hestitancy towards the form. They were generally shot on video, which was less expensive than, and, particularly during the early 1980s, visually inferior to, the 16mm and 35mm film stock used by most pop videos of the time. And their stylistic qualities seemed to reflect these shortcomings in their production values: 'conceptual' and narrative storylines seemed bound by both budgetary limitations and the inability to successfully translate the country music 'drama' to this 'foreign' form. These early videos immediately employed the visual iconography of country lyrics like bars, small towns, traditional values, rodeo cowboys and the like, but seemed uncomfortable in creating a suitable and plausible frame for these icons.

An early narrative video encapsulates many of the problems of the first attempts at the new form. In George Strait's 'You look so good in love' (1983), the singer plays a cuckolded lover following his former girl and her new boyfriend while commenting upon them in song. The video is striking in its ordinariness and simplicity, particularly in terms of its exposition, characters and locations. It begins and ends in a bar, the location of an infinite number of country songs, yet the bar scenes appear in full daylight, diminishing the romantic drama that the bar in a country song represents. Strait himself is shot in such a way that he does not seem to transcend the seeming banality of the situation; he is continually found in strange positions in the bar and in a park as he watches the couple. He seems the common cuckold, devoid of star persona. The simplicity of the country music milieu and lyric translates directly here into mundane visuals, indistinct locations and the exposition of a complex concept in a simple, almost banal way. Whether due to budgetary contraints or aesthetic choice, this video cannot survive in competition with either pop videos (current and of its own time) or country videos that have been produced since. The simple production values are also 'poor' production values that are disconcerting for a sophisticated viewer.

One of the most successful frames developed in early country videos was the performance/concept combination, in which the central part of the video is a filmed or taped performance, and intercut within the performance are various segments that somehow illustrate the message or the plot of the lyrics. This structure is particularly suited for country videos in their performance aspect: a performance video satisfies industrial budgetary constraints in its simplicity of shooting, and it also gives the sense of immediacy inherent in country music's direct emotional appeal.[4] In the performance format, the performer seems to be singing 'to' the viewer, as opposed to merely being an actor in a skit that illustrates the narrative, as in the Strait video above.

Both Merle Haggard's 'Are the good times really over?', which won the 1982 Academy of Country Music Award for Best Video, and Strait's 'Amarillo by morning' (1982) employ this structure, using identifiable imagery associated with country music that either comments upon or visually translates part of the lyrical content. The Haggard video intercuts Norman Rockwell illustrations and stock television news footage to illustrate its 'message'. But these images do more than simply illustrate: because of the enormous cultural significance Rockwell carries and the careful pairing of image to lyrics (an illustration of a little girl bending in front of a stove accompanies the lines, 'Before microwave ovens/When a girl could still cook and still would'), as well as footage of Richard Nixon and Vietnam that reflect lyrical content, the images strengthen the sense that this song is *intended as a message*. This message is inherently a country music message in its traditional values (particularly in its views towards sexuality, drugs and labour) and its small-town iconography, making this a *country* music video through the use of images that are *not* those of a popular music video, and that *are* firmly within the realm of country music.

In 'Amarillo by morning', as opposed to the later 'You look so good in love', Strait's performance is 'real'. Instead of the conventional lip-syncing technique, Strait and his band are recorded live, and the sound is rougher than on the actual recording, with a bluesier and louder guitar solo and a more traditional honky-tonk fiddle solo. In addition, Strait seems far more at ease than when he was an 'actor' in the previous video. He seems more like a country singer with his unshaven, smiling face singing live with his band behind him. The intercutting of rodeo footage illustrates the song's story-line of the life of a rodeo cowboy, yet does so only conceptually in that we never follow any one particular cowboy or develop any sense of a narrative within these images. Instead we see 'slices' of the rodeo life: the parades, clowns, falls from a bull's back, etc. The effect is not as strong as the Haggard video, yet it works by stringing together two important aspects of both the song and the genre, the heartfelt honky-tonk performance and the mythological rodeo figure. This structure of combining live performance and conceptual icono-graphic elements was an important step in the development of a country music video aesthetic. The visual representation complements and enhances the music; it works within established country music iconography to define itself as a country music video and its performer as a particular kind of country star.

A transition to a more exalted position for the country music video was begun by Haggard's and Willie Nelson's 'Pancho and Lefty' (1983). Shot on location in Texas, its narrative followed the lyrics' story-line in a somewhat undefined yet still obviously historical setting in the old West. In addition, the video was exhibited in ninety-six movie theatres across six states (Millard 1984). 'Pancho and Lefty' proved that there was a market for high-budget, high-quality country music videos, and that to continue to make the kinds of low production value videos described above would merely keep the country video ghettoized in the smaller outlets that catered directly to it. Whether or not 'Pancho and Lefty' directly affected record sales (the single and album were two of the top sellers of that year) is debatable; what is certain is that the video changed the stature of the recording into an event with its professional, film-quality look, and it changed the perspective of the industry to the form by revealing the additional audiences a music video could reach.

By 1986, the country music video had reached a kind of industrial and aesthetic maturity. With video production houses in Nashville and elsewhere that could make satisfactory country videos within prescribed budgetary allowances, cable television outlets with large subscription bases, and a set of established aesthetic conventions, the form was becoming as much a part of the genre as it was for rock and pop. Thus maturity, in the context of the country music video, can be defined as the acceptance of the new form by the industry and the marketplace as an effective form of promotion. Though not itself a 'commodity', the mature country video is an accepted extension of the genre into a visual form that helps to define and sell the industry's products. What follows is an attempt to categorize some of the types of country videos, and to analyse them with respect to their production values, narrative and presentation of the performer. I will end this section by giving a close reading of two videos which illustrate the form's attempts at defining the star and employing a classical narrative frame.

Iconography of traditional values/small towns

With the rise of the new, 'neo-traditional' country stars and the 'return' to country music's roots in lyrical content, 'traditional' values and small towns have been a major set of themes and locations for recent country videos. Ricky Skaggs' 'Country boy' (1984), though filmed in New York City, celebrates the 'country' by making fun of the 'city'. Skaggs plays a character who is uncomfortable in his urban surroundings, and who tries to prove to his Uncle Pen (played by bluegrass pioneer Bill Monroe) that despite his formal attire he is, as the refrain repeats, 'a country boy at heart'. Although both Skaggs and Monroe look ill-at-ease among the tall buildings and in the subway, they are able to prove that the 'country' can survive even within the city as Monroe shows some young black breakdancers some country dance steps. John Anderson's 'Countrified' (1987), which takes place mostly in the small town through which Anderson escorts the camera and the viewer, also satirizes big-city conventions in short sequences shot in New York. We watch as Anderson, the bemused and slightly bewildered country boy, is refused admission to a chic downtown club and then inadvertently interrupts a high-fashion modelling session taking place by an abandoned building. But the focus of the video is on Anderson's small town, its farms, its old folk sitting around talking, and its restaurant/dance hall that Anderson leads us through. In these videos, the conventional country lyric story-line that extols the virtues of the small town over the dangers of the big city is both translated and examined through the use of visual imagery associated with country music. Simplicity and ordinariness become iconographic and almost mythological elements through this visual representation and are associated with the performers' celebrations of their country 'roots'.

Traditional values and romantic emotions in the country music lyric are visually translated in videos that focus on the family and rituals associated with it. Randy Travis sings 'Forever and ever, amen' (1987) at his sister's wedding, and the familial traditions and rituals are displayed in the warm orange glow of the video's colours. Children, grandparents and young couples dance about and pose for the photographer in a kind of small-town community ritual, all participating except the singer himself. The Forester Sisters' 'I fell in love again last night' (1985) also takes place at a family/community gathering, with the group singing while different generations interact. Two of Patty Loveless's videos, 'If my heart had windows' (1988) and 'Don't throw us away' (1989), deal explicitly with marriage. The former focuses on a newlywed couple moving into their new house, while in the latter, Loveless 'experiences' the pain of an estranged marriage while she watches a friend's wedding. All of these videos visualize scenes as traditional as Rockwell illustrations and translate important aspects of the country music mythology: the home, the family and the 'older' ways of life they seem to represent.

118

The country music tradition

The current presence of the 'Neo-traditionalists', whose music hearkens back to the country singers of the past, makes clear country music's tradition of tradition, its continually evolving remembrance of its own past. Throughout the genre's existence, performers have canonized their historical influences in song: in the 1950s, Lefty Frizzell paid tribute to Jimmie Rodgers' songs of the 1920s, while Merle Haggard similarly treated both Frizzell's and Rodgers' songs in the 1970s. This awareness of and emphasis on tradition has appeared in many videos, perhaps most notably George Jones' 'Who's gonna fill their shoes?' (1985), in which the venerable singer visits the home of a gas station owner whose room is decorated with the memorabilia of country stars of the past. Inspired, Jones sings a song which recalls these stars' careers and asks the title question while the video shows television clips of the old stars. Asleep at the Wheel's 'Way down Texas way' (1987) uses clips of Texas performers like Bob Wills, George Strait, Ernest Tubb and even the rock group The Fabulous Thunderbirds to illustrate the song's thesis that there's always music playing in Texas. Several Hank Williams Jr videos use photos and footage of his legendary father to evoke both the singer's and country music's traditions, culminating in 'There's a tear in my beer' (1989), in which Hank Jr is seen 'accompanying' his father through special visual and musical effects.

In fact, the preservation of the country tradition is so strong that it serves as a cause or crusade in some videos. 'Will the circle be unbroken?' (1989), from a double-album project led by the Nitty Gritty Dirt Band to celebrate country roots (a similar triple album had been recorded in 1972), features older country stars like Roy Acuff and Johnny Cash accompanied by younger stars such as Ricky Skaggs and Rosanne Cash. Like the 'We are the world' video's format of isolating star performances, 'Will the circle' 'captures' the studio recording and focuses on various performers, including more pop-oriented performers like Bruce Hornsby, John Hiatt and Roger McGuinn, singing a verse or chorus of the old Carter Family song. But rather than serving as a charity project for famine relief – or, as Greil Marcus (1985) has characterized 'We are the world', working to celebrate the rock stars who are singing – 'Will the circle' takes as its object the country tradition and *its* 'survival'. The 'circle' – within the context of the song the family that must endure the death of one of its members – becomes in this case country music's past, and the video dramatizes its importance and visually captures, through the committed faces of star performers, country music's tradition of tradition.

Performance videos

As in the pop music video field, performance videos have remained a part of country music videos from their inception because of their simplicity and generally low cost. Country performance videos tend to differentiate

119

themselves from those of pop or rock not only through the song, but also through set design, costume and the singer's style or performance. The videos of Holly Dunn, a relatively new female singer, are examples of performance videos that lie within the country genre both musically and visually without as 'strong' a thematic or narrative statement as Skaggs' 'Country boy' or even Travis's 'Forever and ever, amen'. Dunn's 'Two too many' and 'Daddy's hands' (both 1986) feature high-production values and filmed 'performances', as Dunn sings with only part of the band that can be heard on the recording. 'Two too many' shows Dunn performing in a barn filled with hay, a conventional country setting, while the visual elements of 'Daddy's hands', a song that evokes memories of Dunn's hard-working father, focus so strongly on Dunn's face and her emotional performance that the visuals are de-emphasized in favour of the traditional familial values expressed in the lyrics. Dunn is thus portrayed as a 'sincere' young female singer who expresses 'traditional' sentiments in an 'authentic' manner.

Clint Black's 'Killing time' (1989) uses the singer's performance to construct an image of Black as an authentic honky-tonk singer. The video takes place in a 'genuine' Texas honky-tonk where old men play dominos during the day and couples dance to live country bands at night. Black, dressed in a T-shirt and jeans, pulls into the parking lot in his pick-up truck, greets and jokes with the bartender, then joins his band onstage to rehearse 'Killing time' for the night's performance. A brief focus on one of the bar's customers, who drinks alone at a table with a series of photographs of his estranged family spread out before him, briefly dramatizes the song's theme of broken love. The video then dissolves to later that night as Black, dressed in more formal stage attire, and his band play the same song. Many of the dancers know the lyrics and sing along, and Black seems at home in the honky-tonk milieu. In a very simple and direct way, the video has presented an image of Black that positions him as a recognizable figure – the Texas dance hall singer – within the country music marketplace.

Rosanne Cash's 'I don't know why you don't want me' (1985), though, expands the horizons of a country performance and a country video. Cash has, throughout her career, attracted young audiences through a mix of rock and country musical elements, and this song is an even greater departure from the genre than Cash's previous releases. This 'performance' video, in which she lip-syncs for the camera without a band behind her, can be seen as Cash's attempt to translate that rock sound into the visual form. This is apparent mainly in dress (her attire is more contemporary than that of most female country singers), her almost 'new wave' hairstyle, and the video's urban locations. Both the video and the song were more successful in the country market, but this video was an obvious attempt to place Cash in a position to crossover to pop/rock markets. The more recent 'Tennessee flat top box' (1987), however, shows her performing the more traditional country song (actually, a cover of a song originally recorded by her father, Johnny) in a more conventional country setting, an old-time music festival. Country performance videos, then, are not in themselves definable within the genre; their visual content proves to be the central signifying factor in terms of the positioning of the performer as 'traditional', 'contemporary', 'crossover' or some combination thereof.

Crossing over to the suburban audience

Some country music videos attempt to represent performers in situations that are less associated with the conventions of country music in order to open up for them the possibility of gaining a wider audience. One demographic group in particular that has become an important part of the country music market and represents part of the genre's potential for growth in market share is the suburban middle class. Rather than celebrating a rural past, many of the recordings and videos that are aimed at this audience represent and celebrate a suburban lifestyle, white-collar occupations rather than blue-collar or farm labour, and relative economic security.

In the video for her song 'Whoever's in New England' (1986), Reba McEntire plays a housewife whose husband is having an affair with a business associate in New England. Reba plays a 'typical' suburban housewife, pictured alone in a brand-new house with an ultra-modern kitchen and a comfortable living room while her husband frolics in the Boston snow with his lover. Because of the conventional country narrative (the trials of the wounded lover, like George Strait in 'You look so good in love'), her position as a 'new traditionalist' country star, and the traces of country instruments in the arrangement, McEntire's video is obviously a *country* video. Yet what this video represents is not the mythical 'country' roots of the genre, but the suburban middle-class lifestyle of many of McEntire's listeners.

Two videos that are equally suburban though less explicitly tied to country are Anne Murray's 'Are you still in love with me?' (1986) and K. T. Oslin's '80's ladies' (1987). Like 'Whoever's in New England', the narrative in Murray's video concerns the wife/mother (Murray) questioning the husband/father's love for her, but in this case, the setting is a family holiday at a picturesque, remote beach house. The family seems quite prosperous and wears nice, somewhat cosmopolitan clothes, and the video as a whole looks like a Ralph Lauren commercial. The song itself has few ties to country conventions, and neither does the video; it seems to be 'country' only because that is how Murray is being marketed currently. In '80's ladies', the character played by Oslin (despite the narrative's 'realism', the story is fictional) is returning home for a high-school reunion, where she stays overnight with one of her best friends. After the reunion, the two stay up through the night and reminisce about a third friend, whose grave they visit in the morning. As Oslin sings 'We were the girls of the fifties/Stone rock'n'rollers of the sixties', the video's use of home movies recalls a 'baby boom' childhood and adolescence.

The video's characters are in their thirties or forties and live a 'typically' middle- or upper-middle-class existence in comfortable surroundings and drive foreign cars. The success of the video, album and performer are testament to this kind of evocation of a suburban upbringing and lifestyle which, although not traditionally 'country', is more typical of an important part of the contemporary country music audience.

'New' traditions and young audiences: 'Honky-tonk man'

Dwight Yoakum's 'Honky-tonk man' (1986) brings together a number of the different currents and categories described above, particularly in the way that it is able to both seem in some way untraditional and yet remain defiantly 'hard' country. In his cowboy hat and boots, his tight jeans, his vocal stylings and overall sound, Yoakum is a symbolic leader of the 'new traditionalists', rebelling against the Nashville gloss by strongly evoking the honky-tonk rebels of the past. The 'Honky-tonk man' video intercuts between a romantic vision of a country dance hall and the Las Vegas strip. It is, in structure, not far removed from the intercut performance of 'Amarillo by morning' and 'Are the good times really over?' However, the production quality is comparable to rock videos, particularly in its use of editing and special visual effects.

'Honky-tonk man' is, in one sense, directed towards a young audience that might not necessarily follow country music and does not fall within its assumed share of the popular music market. The video attempts to connect with the rock audience in a number of ways. Most obviously, the 'audience' for the 'performance' at the dance hall is young and identifiable, in its 'punkish' clothing and dance styles, as a rock audience. Dwight Yoakum is in this sense playing for the same crossover audience in his 'live' performance as he is in the video as a whole. His physical presence evokes, particularly in his hip movement, the sensuality of a young Elvis Presley and similar male rock singers. And the attributes of the honky-tonk-man myth, as constructed in this video, are not foreign to current rock mythology (are in fact among its antecedents), so that the bright lights and gambling scenes in Las Vegas lie comfortably within the iconography of rock music and rock video.

In another sense, however, the use of country motifs in 'Honky-tonk man' makes it acceptable as a country video as well. Its most important element in this context is the song itself, which instrumentally, vocally and culturally (it is an old Johnny Horton tune) *is* a country song. Yoakum is being marketed as a 'hard country' neo-traditionalist, one who hearkens back 'directly' to such honky-tonk singers of the pre-pop crossover/Nashville sound era as Hank Williams. As such, he is a kind of 'rebel', one who is fighting to maintain a 'pure country' sound. Thus, the imagery that might enable the video to be attractive for a young rock audience also works to support the image of Dwight Yoakum as an old-style honky-tonk singer. His physical presence can be decoded differently – the swivel-hips look like the old kinescopes of Hank

Williams' television appearances – as can the nightclub and Las Vegas – the country-boy's sinful paradise. 'Honky-tonk man' is an example of a mature country music video not merely because of its production values but also because of the accessibility of its imagery and its ability to be decoded in ways that broaden its audience while remaining true to country music convention.

The classical narrative: 'Cathy's clown'

I will return to my beginning focus on narrative to discuss a recent video which, like 'Honky-tonk man', epitomizes the emergence of the country music video. Reba McEntire's 'Cathy's clown' (1989) is a relatively elaborate and expensive production which draws heavily from the imagery and narratives of the western film genre, and uses these conventions to evoke a formal tradition in a similar way to much of contemporary country music. It thus not merely employs the classical narrative frame that the country video adapted from Hollywood films, but celebrates this heritage by honouring the conventions of the western, arguably the most classical and 'American' of cinematic genres.

The visual imagery of 'Cathy's clown', and particularly its very filmic sets of a western frontier town and its saloon, refer less to some real American past than to the sets of western films and television shows with which much of McEntire's audience grew up. Indeed, the extended use of the long establishing shots in both locations evoke similar locations in previous westerns. Similarly, McEntire's very vibrant full-length dress, as well as her hairstyle and lace choker, do not evoke memories of pioneer clothing but of the apparel of the heroine of the fictional western. This imagery thus refers back to a stable set of generic conventions from the past – the western remains a relatively 'dead' genre – and suggests the traditions of a mythic, represented past, not of a 'real' one. In a sense, this resonates with country music's relationship to its own past, which it evokes as much to maintain the tradition of musical forms and mythical representations as to recall the 'real' past.

The video is framed by a psychological narrative explicitly told in the song's lyrics and implicitly followed in the video. McEntire's rendition of the Everly Brothers' song retains the storyline of a girl (Cathy, who never appears in the video) who plays with the affections of a boy (her 'clown'). But the McEntire's cover version shifts the perspective from that of the boy to that of a third woman who is in love with the boy. In the video, McEntire assumes the character of the third woman and watches the man as he rides into town, enters the saloon and is laughed at by many of the other patrons because, presumably, of his inability to stand up to his girl. McEntire's character trades a meaningful glance with the man as he finishes his drink, and then she is left alone again as he leaves. The narrative frame is thus classical in its centring of character, psychological motivation and the heterosexual relationship, as well as in its use of the glance and the shot–reverse shot sequence to establish physical space and character relations.

The very generic traditions that 'Cathy's clown' evoke establish the video's connection to the signifying practices of Hollywood's past and older, more classical ways of telling a story. This contrasts sharply with a pop video like Madonna's 'Express yourself' (1989), which evokes a different cinematic past (the German Expressionism of Fritz Lang's *Metropolis*) in order to play with images of transgression and violence and create associations with a tradition of formalistic experimentation.[5] 'Cathy's clown', on the other hand, celebrates both the formalistic and moral traditions of the classical western, and thus is emblematic of the successful adaptation of the new form of music video to the established conventions of country music. By effectively matching the visual and story-telling conventions of the classical Hollywood cinema with the narrative and lyrical style of country music, many country videos resolve the 'problem' of constructing a successful visual form for the musical genre.

CONCLUSIONS

Thus far, I have based my essay on the following premises: first, that the country music industry began the production of music videos as a response to the format's success as a promotional tool for rock and pop records; and second, that the aesthetics of country music videos are an attempt to adapt conventions established by and associated with rock and pop videos to the established conventions of country music. In terms of the latter, the iconography and narrative form associated with that genre's lyrical content were particularly important. In this final section, I will use this aesthetic and industrial development of a new form in order to inform a theory of genre (the *country* music video) and music video (the country *music video*).

My analysis thus far has focused explicitly on three different sets of determinate relations: the relations between music and extra-musical determinants, in this case the recent shifts in country music in response to economic, technological and ideological change; relations between musical producers – in this case, the country music industry – and consumers; and relations among different musical genres, in this case country music and mainstream rock and pop. Although I will separate these levels for the purpose of analysis, the development of the country music video has shown that these relations exist simultaneously and are inextricably bound in history.

First, the development of country music videos clearly displays the ways in which genres work as constructed systems or orders of meanings and signifying practices that must continually be restructured, redefined and adapted in order to remain culturally and economically viable. Country music has a received, widely circulated history, but like any history it is continually struggled over and reformulated in the face of economic, technological and ideological change. The text of country music – that is, the boundaries of difference that help to constitute that which is and is not within the genre – is constantly articulated in different directions: now 'modern', now 'traditional'; in this song rural, in that song suburban; first defiant, then repentant.

Country music is thus built on a series of contraditions and conflicts that are elided in each song and video. These contradictions include (from the categories of country videos described above): the possibility of traditional values and the small town in the midst of late capitalism; the maintenance of a musical tradition in the face of the multi-national leisure corporations that control the major record companies and publishing houses; the potential for the 'personal' performance in mechanically reproduced forms; the opportunity of an 'authentic' life in the reified existence of suburban consumerism; and, ultimately, the possible construction of an autonomous individual subject, the 'star', within all of these constraints. The successful resolution of these conflicts ties country music to greater structures of ideology. But as in any hegemonic system, country music's resolution is not guaranteed; it has gaps and points at which the contradictions raised cannot be resolved within the form.

Country music is thus not a given, coherent whole in itself, but must be continually refigured and reconstructed in order to make sense and remain meaningful to its audience. In Rick Altman's words, 'Genres are not neutral categories, . . . rather they *are ideological constructs masquerading as neutral categories*' (1987: 5). In this sense the necessary work involved in adapting music video to country music was bound to the ideological constraints of the genre as a cultural construct – that is, resolving the ideology of the content of country music with the ideology of the form of music video. The successful development of industrial structures and aesthetic conventions for country music videos was a struggle to construct a coherent form within the cultural constraints of the genre and its audience and the economic constraints of industrial capitalism. The genre is thus rearticulated in the face of economic, technological and/or cultural change in order to continue to cohere and remain culturally viable.

Second, the development of the country music video provides insight into the ways in which the genre's meanings are circulated between producers and consumers. The industry's apprehension towards the new form was partially but not wholly due to economic reasons; had the video been perceived or immediately proven itself as a new and drastic way of building the country music market, the entire history of country videos would have been drastically different. Instead, the industry's invocation of the marketplace as determinant – if they help in sales, we'll make more of them – is indicative neither of the democracy nor the fascism of the 'free market'; instead, the cultural viability of a form produced by the culture industries is dependent upon the form's acceptance within its culture. Thus Stephen Neale defines genre in two ways, working simultaneously in two directions: on one hand, genres are 'systems of orientations, expectations and conventions that circulate between industry, text *and* subject' (Neale 1980: 19; emphasis added), while on the other hand the industry uses genres to 'institutionalize a set of expectations which it will be able, within the limits of its economic and ideological practices, to fulfil' (1980: 54). The country audience's 'expectations' in this sense are not simply created full-blown by the industry, but are instead circulated, institutionalized and directed towards the replication of the experience of pleasure through the further purchase of country records and other commodities. But again, such institutionalization is neither given nor guaranteed but must continually be won. The country video cannot merely 'appear' but must be developed in such a way that the cultural and aesthetic forms that it articulates make sense and prove attractive.

Finally, the development of country music videos displays how musical genres interact. Rather than suggesting a free 'inter-textuality' within this form – as though the country video was the result of a combination of neutral forms and texts colliding in an essentially meaningless pastiche – this development was a very specific historical conjuncture in which country music's relation to mainstream popular music provided a set of both aesthetic and industrial determinations. Specific genres like country and heavy metal define themselves by such relations, most specifically by their differences from other forms of popular music. A genre, as an ordered system, only has meaning in opposition to that which is outside it. In this way, the existence of a genre presupposes other genres against which it can react and define itself. A genre without differences, one that merely repeats other forms, would be inconceivable. A genre's texts, then, work through the repetition of such differences or, as Neale puts it, through 'repetition *in* difference' (1980: 48). Thus, as I've argued above, the interaction between country and pop music in the development of the country music video reveals the ways in which a particular genre attempts to articulate a form associated with another genre in order to create a new form that works within a system of repetition in difference.

Genres thus interact in their circulation among audiences and the culture industries and through their continual reformulation in relation to each other as ordered systems of meaning. It might seem 'natural' that country music would refine a classical visual story-telling style to match its lyrical content, but the actual historical progression through which these videos developed proves how the end result is anything but 'natural'. The specific histories and qualities of genres like country music and cultural forms like music videos provide insight into the continuing development of popular music as an industrial and aesthetic phenomenon.[6]

NOTES

1   For more extensive accounts of this history, see Malone (1985) and Hemphill (1970).
2   On the week ending 17 June 1989, the *Billboard* charts showed that 19 of the top 50

country singles were accompanied by a video. Although this shows an increase from two years earlier, when the proportion was 9 of 40, the corresponding proportion on the pop charts was 45 of 50, while on the black music charts, the percentage was also much higher, 36 of 50.

3 For more on the development of the 'classical Hollywood style' in American cinema, see Bordwell, Staiger and Thompson (1985).

4 The performance/concept combination seems particularly well suited for specific genres like country music and heavy metal, which also employs it regularly. In both genres, live performance is seen as a crucial aspect of the music's communicative and emotional powers.

5 As Thomas Elsaesser has argued, the very distinctive visual quality of *Metropolis* and other German silent films associated with the Expressionist movement was an attempt to differentiate German film from the large influx of foreign films (particularly American) that flooded Germany after the First World War. In addition, the movement was consciously marketed by German film studios to attract bourgeois audiences with the promise of distinctive 'works of art' made by 'authentically creative' *auteurs* like Lang (1984: 70–2).

6 And the history of country music video has, of course, continued since this paper was written in 1989.

REFERENCES

Altman, Rick (1987) *The American Film Musical*, Bloomington: University of Indiana Press.
Bessman, Jim (1985) 'VH-1 turnout sparks CMA awards', *Billboard*, 2 November, pp. 43, 46.
Bordwell, David, Janet Staiger and Kristin Thompson (1985) *The Classical Hollywood Cinema: Film Style and Mode of Production to 1960*, New York: Columbia University.
Clayton, Rose (1982) 'Country sheds cowboy image for multi-media sophistication', *Billboard*, World of Country Music (WOCM), 18 October, p. 28.
Cocks, Jay (1988) 'Trippin' through the crossroads', *Time*, 25 July, pp. 68–71.
Elsaesser, Thomas (1984) 'Film history and visual pleasure: Weimar cinema', in *Cinema Histories, Cinema Practices*, Patricia Mellencamp and Philip Rosen (eds), University Publications of America and the American Film Institute, pp. 47–84.
Goldsmith, Thomas (1988) 'New-artist goldmine: will record number of break-throughs make it tough for next wave?', *Billboard*, WOCM, 15 October, pp. 4, 12.
'Hank Williams, Jr keeps entertainer title', *Austin American-Statesman*, 22 March, 1988, p. B6.
Hemphill, Paul (1970) *The Nashville Sound: Bright Lights and Country Music*, New York: Simon & Schuster.
Holley, Debbie (1987) 'Country video: 'tis better to be seen and heard', *Billboard*, WOCM, 7 October, pp. 6, 14.
—— (1988) 'Beyond labels: marketers search for fresh ways to promote new, improved country', *Billboard*, WOCM, 15 October, pp. 6, 14.
—— (1989) 'CBS promo hinges on "Hitchhiker". Nashville division woos youth market', *Billboard*, 27 May, p. 36.
Lambert, Pam (1989) 'Clint Black: country music's "Better Man" ', *Wall Street Journal*, 1 June, p. A28.
Malone, Bill C. (1985) *Country Music USA*, Austin: University of Texas.
Marcus, Greil (1985) 'Number one with a bullet', *Artforum*, November, p. 99.
Millard, Bob (1982) 'Labels fight costs of consolidating gains of recent boom years', *Billboard*, WOCM, 15 October, p. 5.

—— (1984) 'Country music video budgets rise as more outlets open', *Variety*, 14 March, p. 74.

Morris, Edward (1989) 'Clint Black succeeds via singles scene', *Billboard*, 13 May, p. 37.

Neale, Stephen (1980) *Genre*, London: British Film Institute.

Roblin, Andrew (1984a) 'Video boom comes to Nashville', *Billboard*, 26 May, p. 4.

—— (1984b) 'Video set for wider exposure', *Billboard*, WOCM, 12 October, p. 4.

—— (1985) 'Videos roll on more outlets', *Billboard*, WOCM, 13 October, p. 4.

—— (1986) 'Video verdict: doubts linger, but labels continue to vote with their pocketbooks', *Billboard*, WOCM, 18 October, p. 4.

—— (1987) 'John Anderson gets "clipped": makes video for "Countrified"', *Billboard*, 7 February, p. 34.

Simmons, Jan (1983) 'Country gambles on video clip game', *Billboard*, WOCM, 15 October, p. 5.

Tucker, Ken (1987) 'Country music's sophomore class: flex them neck muscles, boys', *Village Voice*, 7 July, p. 71.

Wood, Gerry (1987) 'Country music networks flourish', *Billboard*, 20 June, p. 76.

8

BEING DISCOVERED: THE EMERGENCE OF FEMALE ADDRESS ON MTV

Lisa A. Lewis

Since MTV's inception in 1981, the issue of sexism has been a recurring and insistent theme in both popular and academic criticism.[1] But the charge of sexism, while it importantly foregrounds issues of textual politics, too frequently treats MTV as a monolithic textual system, and sexism as a static and ahistorical mode of representation written into media textuality. Music video does bring together two cultural forms that have notorious histories as promulgators of female objectification – rock music and televisual imagery. And specific textual examples of women in chains, in caged boxes and strewn across sets in skimpy leather outfits can certainly be called upon to justify such claims. But focusing exclusively on the sexist representations present in many male-addressed videos overshadows the emergence on MTV of an aggregate of videos produced to songs sung by female musicians, and their enormous popularity among female fans.

MTV'S ROLE IN THE RISE OF FEMALE MUSICIANSHIP

In the years leading up to the start of music video promotion, female rock musicians were struggling for recognition both as vocalists (the traditional female niche) and as instrumentalists and composers.[2] The contemporary women's movement in the late 1960s and early 1970s provided momentum for change, as did the early punk movement in Britain at the end of the 1970s. Although punk emerged essentially as a working-class male subculture, Hebdige (1983) makes the point that punk included a minority of female participants who aggressively tried to carve out a specifically female form of expression, a sharp contrast to the usual subsuming of women by subcultural phallocentricism:

> Punk propelled girls onto the stage and once there, as musicians and singers, they systematically transgressed the codes governing female performance. . . . These performers have opened up a new space for women as active participators in the production of popular music.
>
> (Hebdige 1983: 83–5)

Punk's advocacy of 'defiant amateurism' (Swartley 1982: 28) undermined the devalued status of the amateur musician, in the process granting women unprecedented access to musical information and audiences. The start of MTV represents another conjunctural moment in female pop and rock musicianship. The channel's origination of a music video format and distribution mechanism played an important role in providing female musicians with the opportunity to gain industry backing, assert a subjective textual vision and build audience recognition.

Under the capitalist economic system that operates rock'n'roll as an entrepreneurial enterprise, professional musicianship is defined largely in terms of a record company contract. The largest audiences and the financial backing to produce and promote one's music, and thus the aspirations of most rock musicians, women included, lie with commercial distribution. But in 1979, just when new female musicians were preparing to break into the music scene, the US recording industry went into a tailspin as the combined effects of a sluggish economy, home-taping and the diversification of the home entertainment market began to be felt. The years 1976 to 1978 had been boom years for record companies, but 1979 became known as 'the year of the Platinum Goose's downfall' (Sutherland 1980: 96). Any individual or group without a proven track record, and this especially applied to women musicians, was hard pressed to win a record company contract, an essential step in the quest for a large audience. That began to change, however, in the summer of 1981 with the introduction of music video programming.[3]

Six weeks after MTV went on the air in selected test markets like Tulsa, Witchita, Peoria, Syracuse, Grand Rapids and Houston, there was an increase in record sales of certain musical artists getting heavy play on the channel. Retailers in these areas received requests for music that was not getting radio airplay in their communities. By 1983, a Neilson survey commissioned by MTV owner, Warner-Amex, showed MTV to be influencing 63 per cent of its viewers to buy certain albums. For every nine albums bought by MTV viewers, four purchases could be directly attributed to the viewing of the record company-produced music videos (Levy 1983: 34). Lee Epand, vice-president of Polygram Records, one of the companies originally reticent about turning over free copies of music videotapes to MTV, admitted that the cable channel had proved to be 'the most powerful selling tool we've ever had' (Levy 1983: 78). Album and singles sales rose to all-time highs, in some cases surpassing industry sales records, and record companies renewed financing for new and unknown bands and vocalists, women musicians included.

In 1982, the Go-Gos became the only all-female vocal and instrumental group ever to make the Top 10. Their first album, *Beauty and the Beat*, was also the first album by an all-women rock band to hit number one on the charts. Cyndi Lauper's debut album *She's So Unusual* remained in the Top 30 for more then sixty weeks, having sold close to 4 million copies in the US alone. The album produced four Top 5 hit singles, a new record for a female singer. Madonna sold 3.5 million copies of her album, *Like a Virgin* in just 14 weeks. The album was 'triple platinum' before its artist had even set foot on a touring stage. By 1985, the album became the first by a female artist to be certified by the Recording Industry Association of America (RIAA) for sales of 5 million units. The 1985 winner of the top grammy award, Tina Turner, was a woman without a record deal one year, and with a hit single the next. Her album *Private Dancer* sold 10 million copies around the world. Pat Benatar, Chaka Khan and the Pointer Sisters all reached a million in sales with albums promoted by music video.[4]

Entering the world of professional musicianship is not necessarily an invitation to create the music of one's choice. Musicians who work within the record industry must constantly negotiate contradictory roles as self-expressing artists and paid workers in an industrial mode of production. Female rock musicians additionally contend with their subordinate position as female social subjects whose mode of promotion is highly tied to sexist standards of representation and musical niches. The ascendancy of music video as a promotion vehicle, and final stage in the song production process, however, suggested certain strategies whereby female musicians could expand their struggle for authorship over both their image and their music.

Formally, music video, as presented by MTV, is characterized by two broad devices − by the use of a pre-recorded popular music song and by the appearance of musicians in on-screen roles. Vocalists are called on, most conventionally, to lip-sync the song's lyrics while being visually featured as the musical performer, and sometimes additionally, as actor in the video's narrative scenarios. Female musicians' traditional musical role as vocalists is thus turned into an asset in music video promotion. In narrative videos, the soundtrack provided by the female vocalist can operate like a narrator's omnipotent voice-over to guide the visual action. Sometimes, she manages to literally put words in the mouths of other characters (sometimes male) through the use of a common music video device whereby a selected lyrical phrase is lip-synced as if it were dialogue. In Cyndi Lauper's first MTV video, 'Girls just want to have fun', the burly ex-wrestler Lou Albano, as Lauper's father, lip-syncs Cyndi's lyric, 'What you gonna do with your life?' as she is shown pinning his arm behind his back in a wrestling manoeuvre. The replacement of the father's scolding voice with the daughter's parodies and undermines the authority of the father, and by symbolic extension, patriarchy[5] itself. Although feminist critics, in their desire to broaden the spectrum of female musicianship, have sometimes criticized the vocalist niche, in music video the prerogative rests most squarely on the vocalist's shoulders.

The visual appearance of the musician in music videos affords a greater range of performance than that offered on the concert stage. Eye-contact and facial gestures available to only the few concert-goers at the front are equally accessible to video viewers. Role-playing, limited to costuming changes and the use of props on the stage, can be intricately elaborated in music video through location shooting, the use of sets, and interactions with actors. In other words, the gamut of devices available to television productions is opened up to musicians in music video. Many female musicians have proven to be quite adept at manipulating elements of visual performance, utilizing music video's formal characteristics as authorship tools.

Cyndi Lauper was one of the first female musicians to achieve mass popularity as a direct result of her exposure on MTV. 'Girls just want to have fun', released on MTV in 1983, was the culmination of an intricate set of initiatives designed to create a woman-identified image for herself and her music. When Lauper's producer, Rick Chertoff, first suggested Robert Hazard's 'Girls just want to have fun' for Lauper to sing, she thought it was sexist and refused to consider it:

> he played me 'Girls ...' and I said, well I ain't doing *that* song ... because it wasn't what it ended up to be – which is something that I'll never forget that Rick did for me. I was so headstrong and so set. It was basically a very chauvinistic song. He said, 'but wait, think about what it *could* mean, just think about it for a minute, forget all this other stuff, and think about what it could mean.' I said, 'Well how could I do that? Look at this and look at that.' He said, 'so change it.'
>
> (The Meldrum Tapes 1986)

Hazard's original version had been fashioned as an inflated male fantasy of female desire with lyrics that read:

> My father says, 'My son, what do they want from your life?'
> I say, 'Father, dear, we are the fortunate ones.
> Girls just want to have fun.'

But Lauper's alteration of the song's lyric text resulted in a custom-made vehicle for the expression of her views on female inequality:

> My mother says, 'When you gonna live your life right?'
> 'Oh, Mother, dear, we're not the fortunate ones.
> And girls just want to have fun.'

The change was subsequently used as a cornerstone for the song's video interpretation with Lauper's own mother in a leading role. The video's design was an affirmation of Lauper's appropriation of Hazard's song, a means of extending her authorship. The appearance of Lauper's mother also encouraged an autobiographical interpretation of the song's text.

On Lauper's album, Hazard receives songwriting credit, an indication that he was duly compensated. In the informal notes Lauper includes in the album's jacket, she thanks Hazard 'for letting me change your song'. Essentially, Lauper traded in 'ownership' of the song for the right to be its author, and as it turns out, initiated a commercial success which translated into dollars down the line. Hazard was put in the somewhat embarrassing, although financially rewarding, position of accumulating royalties from the sale of a song which no longer speaks his creative vision. He maintains ownership, but is robbed of authorship. While it is not uncommon for song-writers to remain all but invisible in the wake of a vocalist's rendition, the case of 'Girls' represents an extraordinary political intervention by Lauper, one which clearly worked to her benefit.

Lauper's participation in the production of the video was also substantial, although she was not the director of the clip. In Shore's (1984) day-by-day account of the making of the video, Lauper's name appears over and over as a contributor at virtually every stage of production. It is 'Cyndi' who picks the video's producer Ken Walz, and director Ed Griles, based on her prior experience of working with them on videos for her first (commercially unsuccessful) band, Blue Angel. 'Cyndi' suggests the video's concept, picks location sites in New York City, brings in choreographer Mary Ellen Strom and finds extras to appear in the video. The construction workers, who serve as pivotal symbols in the video's snake-dance sequence, were actual workers who Lauper coaxed into the on-camera action. Shore (1984) describes her coaching of the other passers-by she drew into the scene:

> Cyndi, who appears to be doing as much directing as Griles or anyone else, runs them through their paces several times while waiting for the new chorus-line members to return to the location.
>
> (Shore 1984: 171)

As the account eloquently demonstrates, the division of labour suggested by the official title of 'director' did not preclude Lauper's collaborative accomplishments.

Shore's story of Lauper's involvement in the shoot continues. 'Cyndi' suggests the antique boutiques where campy items used in the creation of interior sets were purchased. She spends hours splatter-painting furniture for the bedroom scene. Her input even extends to post-production work, as she screens rushes, approves the rough cut, and checks in on the progress of the time-consuming special effect that appears mid-way through the video. In his diary-like chronicle, Shore is attentive to Lauper's many initiatives and interventions, and even includes snatches of interviews that allow her to voice her intentions:

> Finally, there is the artist herself: Cyndi is not just a pretty face onstage, a pretty voice on record. She's an experienced actress as well. ... Cyndi plays an unusually large creative role in the conceptualizing and staging of the video itself, from start to finish ... says Cyndi ... 'I know what I want and don't want – I don't want to be portrayed as just another sex symbol.'
>
> (Shore 1984: 167)

Lauper's self-consciousness about representation, her ability to use visual language to overturn staid images, create song authorship and build a musical career is indicative of new directions in female musicianship and the important role played by music video.

MTV has also facilitated new and different relationships between female musicians and female audiences. The distribution of music video into cable-wired homes created a domestic outlet for musician promotion. Prior to the advent of MTV, the concert tour had been a primary means for promoting rock musicians, an event overwhelmingly identified as a male adolescent cultural activity. MTV's promotion of musicians on its home-based distribution channel (television) included a larger female audience and helped sponsor a female entry into concert arenas. According to Pat Benatar, who performed on concert stages both before and after the start of MTV, a clear shift in female concert attendance occurred once MTV began distribution of her image into the home:

> When we first began, most of our concerts were probably 80/20 male-oriented. There were very few women. Very few women used to go to concerts no matter who was playing, male or female. I saw that really change about 1982. It became like 60/40, and the next thing I knew, it was 50/50, then 60/40 the other way. Now there are more women in the audience than men.
>
> (Benatar 1987)

The opportunity to build a female audience through music video promotion was seized by female musicians as an occasion to develop an address to girls and women.

CULTURAL CONTRADICTIONS IN MTV'S TEXTUAL ADDRESS

Although the formal characteristics of music video and its distribution on MTV served as enabling devices for female musician authorship, it is to the credit of female musicians such as Lauper and Benatar that MTV became a touchstone for female address. Overall, the textual system of address developed by MTV did not accommodate the need of the rising number of female musicians for a vehicle of self-representation, nor was it geared to female audiences. By the time 'Girls just want to have fun' was aired on MTV in 1983, the channel's system of discourse had largely solidified around the representation of male adolescent experiences and desires.

MTV was a product of demographic thinking (Marc 1984). It was conceived with a specific target audience in mind, the broadly stated age group of 12–34-year-olds (Wolfe 1983). In translating its perception of youth into a textual address, MTV chose the path, not surprisingly, of reproducing the culturally-salient and ideological category of adolescence. Hudson (1984) describes adolescence as a system of discourse which fundamentally incorporates assumptions and definitions of *male* experience, activity and desire. The attitudes and practices typically associated with adolescence – socially-sanctioned retreats from parental surveillance and the constrictions of domestic life, aggressive attention to leisure practices and associated peer activities, pursuit of sexual experiences and experimentation with social roles and norms – serve boys in the assumption of their position in patriarchy. Adolescence and masculinity are ideologically united to support a social system of male privilege. The social authorization of adolescent licence is specific to one's gender and does not fully extend to girls.

Textually, MTV enacts male adolescence discourse through a broad system of images that evokes boys' privileged position with respect to both their female adolescent peers and the adult male role. Symbolic representations of adolescent boy culture, its distinct peer relationships, leisure activities, sexual fantasies and, on occasion, contradictory experiences, celebrate the distinctiveness of male adolescence. Towards this end, the image of the street is developed as an overarching sign system. Male musicians are shown loitering on sidewalks, strolling along avenues and travelling in cars, in keeping with the male youth attachment to the street. The representation of street-corner activities valorizes leisure, the arena in which adolescent boys carve out their own domain in the world (McRobbie 1980). It facilitates the textual presentation of the expansive parameters of rebellious play, of male adolescent licence, which only in the extreme becomes socially-classified as deviant. Even when the image of the street is physically absent from an individual video, it is an implied presence, for, as a sign system, it perfectly summarizes male adolescent quests for adventure, rebellion, sexual encounter, peer relationships and male privilege. Male adolescent viewers who formulate a symbolic equation between the representation of the street and their own privileged access to public space and patriarchal prerogatives are empowered by the address.

Male address videos draw fundamentally on the connection between male adolescent licence and adult male rule by activating textual signs of patriarchal discourse. Reproducing coded images of the female body, conventionally positioning girls and women as objects of male voyeurism, are effective strategies for associating male adolescent desire and male dominance. Representations of females are inflected in ways that facilitate their integration into the specific vision of male adolescent discourse. Girls, when they appear, are not represented as equal participants in the symbolic system of the street, but function instead to delineate male adolescent discourse.

This textual enactment of gender ideology and social discourse is what feminist and moralist critics are observing when they raise objections to sexual stereotyping and misogynous imagery on MTV. The charges of sexism, however, are never directly related by opponents of MTV to the channel's reliance on the notion of target audience, or to the ideological privileging of

135

male adolescence which pervades MTV's interpretation of its target audience. This is alarming given the defence offered by MTV spokespersons that its policies result from its need to cater to a youth audience. Bob Pittman, MTV's concept originator, consistently responded to allegations of sexism by naturalizing the highly ideological category of adolescence that MTV's format attempted to reproduce:

> It's not the Barry Manilow channel. . . . Some songs are unhappy. Some have a dark message. It's the essence of rock. It mirrors the issues of people moving from adolescence.
>
> (Levy 1983: 76)

His response illustrates the disparity between MTV's rhetoric (that it was enacting an address to a broad demographic category of youth of both genders), and its textual practice (the representation of male adolescence). It also reveals how problematic the social complexities underlying certain demographic categories can become for producers of televisual content.

By identifying a 'preferred' textual system of male address on MTV, I, too, raise the issue of 'sexism in the text', but in the broader terms of hegemonic preference discussed by Hall (1980, 1982). Applying Gramsci's (1971) theory of hegemony to signification practices, Hall (1982: 70) argues that the power to signify, to control 'the means by which collective social understandings are created' is fundamental to the ability of the ruling power to maintain consent from subordinates. In the case of male address on MTV, the hegemony of gender inequality and male adolescence is manifested in the exclusion of girls from male discourse, and in their coded and semiotically-improverished textual representation. In Hall's (1982: 81) terms, MTV's male adolescence discourse became 'the primary framework or terms of an argument', requiring parties interested in creating a female voice (select female musicians and audiences) 'to perform with the established terms of the problematic in play'. A number of female musicians took up the challenge of re-articulating the text, appropriating MTV's male youth address to produce a new address to female adolescents. Their videos engage in 'struggle over meaning' by offering representations that resonate with female cultural experiences of adolescence and gender in the United States.

Female address began to coalesce on MTV, in my estimation, around the year 1983, with the release of Lauper's video, 'Girls just want to have fun'. The music videos of a number of female musicians cohered in this and following years to form a distinct textual practice predicated on the representation of female adolescence within the social condition of gender inequality. Female address videos use two interrelated textual sign systems, which I call respectively: (1) Access signs, and (2) Discovery signs.[6] Access signs are those in which the privileged experience of boys and men is visually appropriated. The female video musicians textually enact an entrance into a male domain of activity and signification. Symbolically they execute take-overs of male space, the erasure of sex-roles, and demand parity with male privilege. In this way, the video texts challenge assumptions about the boundaries which gender, as a social construct, draws around men and women.

Discovery signs coexist and interact with access signs. They reference and celebrate distinctly female modes of cultural expression and experience. Discovery signs attempt to compensate in mediated form for female cultural marginalization by drawing pictures of activities in which females tend to engage apart from males. In female address videos, access signs open out into discovery signs that rejoice in female forms of leisure and cultural expression, and female sources of social bonding, to which adolescent boys have little access. By representing girl practices, the videos set a tone that celebrates female resourcefulness and cultural distinctiveness.

Music videos from four female musicians, appearing in 1983 and 1984,[7] will serve as examples of the textual strategies of female address. The videos of Cyndi Lauper, Madonna, Pat Benatar and Tina Turner unite behind a similar visual treatment of gender experience, and a nuanced, yet consistent, use of both access and discovery signs.

ACCESS SIGNS: APPROPRIATING THE MEANING OF THE STREET

The image of the street, exploited as a textual strategy in MTV's male adolescent discourse, summons up different and distinct connotations for female adolescents. Females are socialized to avoid streets for fear of harassment and rape, to expect to become objects of the male gaze if they make themselves too visible by loitering or even walking slowly. Girls are discouraged from participation in much of the leisure activity, social bonding practices and subcultural formations associated with male street culture. McRobbie (1980) describes gendered standards of leisure within youth culture as a consequence of a broader social system of gender inequality. Female address videos rework the ideological stance of male privilege by appropriating the image of the street for the production of access signs.

In 'Girls just want to have fun', the bouncing Lauper leads her band of girlfriends through New York City streets in a frenzied snake-dance that turns women's experience of foreboding streets upside-down in a carnivalesque display. Their arms reaching out for more and more space, the women push through a group of male construction workers who function as symbols of female harassment on the street. The lyrical refrain, 'Girls just want to have fun', enacts a powerful cry for access to the privileged realm of male adolescent leisure and fun.

Madonna's 'Borderline' immerses the star and female extras in male street-corner culture. Madonna is shown street dancing, spraying graffiti on urban walls and loitering on a street corner with female peers. She blows kisses and initiates flirtation with street boys, and leads her girlfriends into the male turf of the pool hall. In short, she appropriates activities and spaces typically associated with male adolescence.

Pat Benatar's video 'Love is a battlefield', presents a more militant version of the street take-over. The video begins by referring to women's usual experience on the street. Benatar, playing a homeless teenager, is shown being bumped and harassed by male passers-by, a scenario extended to the male space of the bar. A turning point in the video is marked by the scream of a woman who is being physically reprimanded by her pimp. Her voice, laid unconventionally over the musical soundtrack, shrieks out, 'Leave me alone!' Thus, the call to access begins. As lyrics sung by Benatar are heard: 'we are strong, no one can tell us we're wrong', Benatar and the other women in the bar burst forth with aggressive chest thrusts and kicks, forcing the pimp back against the bar. Benatar violently splashes a drink in his face, a moment that is formally prioritized by the addition of a sound effect. Retreating to the street, Benatar and her female companions demonstrate their solidarity and celebrate their defeat of the male ego. Benatar turns and saunters down the street, at last its rightful owner.

Tina Turner enacts signs of access in the video, 'What's love got to do with it?' by taking a long, slow walk down a New York City street. Unlike the other videos, Turner's does not amass a group of females for a final scene of appropriation of male space. It is as if this has already happened. Rather, the video picks up where the Benatar video ends; Turner is from the beginning alone on the street, already at one with it. Proceeding down the avenue, she encounters the gaze of a male onlooker. Far from averting her eyes, Turner matches his gaze with one of her own, and they circle momentarily in an equal exchange of looking. She comes across a group of men shooting craps on the sidewalk, a representation of male street-corner culture. Pushing them aside, she recalls a similar action by Lauper in 'Girls just want to have fun'. Magically, Turner has acquired the status and power to transcend the female experience of streets.

Female address videos take advantage of another code of male adolescence that the image of the street allows to surface – that of delinquency. Brake (1985: 23) has testified to discrepancies in the ways male and female youth are articulated as social problems. 'Males have usually been involved with illegal activities such as theft or violence or vandalism, and females with sexual misbehaviour'. The perception that girls are somehow 'less delinquent' than boys has generally resulted in the greater provision of social programmes to male youth (Nava 1984). Prostitution is considered to be the predominant mode of female delinquency, a form of behaviour that is less visible than many male delinquent activities and easily misidentified. Girls who engage in street loitering or walking, so-called 'normal' behaviour for boys, can become associated with delinquency, even find themselves institutionalized. Female address videos focus on the attention and resources that male youth, who are perceived as social problems, have historically received. They challenge the double standard that regards female adolescent delinquency primarily in terms of sexual transgression and appropriate the richness of signification that the image of the street holds out to boys and men.

In 'Girls just want to have fun', social responses to the 'problem girl' are explored. Lauper's character bounds home one morning after apparently staying out all night. Upon entering the home, she finds her mother (played by Lauper's own mother), hard at work preparing food in the kitchen. The lyric 'when you gonna live your life right?' speaks for the mother. Her distress over the daughter's flagrant disregard for appropriate feminine behaviour is expressed as she breaks an egg over her heart.

'Borderline' places Madonna squarely in the role of male adolescent delinquency by showing her defacing property, loitering in 'bad neighbourhoods', and entering the pool hall. The combined images of street-corner loitering and flirtation confuse the iconography of the prostitute. Building a tension between the two representations implicitly raises questions about how the code of prostitution is elaborated and about how representations of females on the street might be revisioned.

'Love is a battlefield' investigates the code of the prostitute by placing Benatar's character in the situation of a teenager, cast out onto the street by an angry father. Unlike Madonna, she remains unassociated with the activities of male youth street culture, and as merely a young woman walking the street, she is consequently represented as even closer to the coded prostitute image. But the reappearance of the street as a site for female camaraderie and displays of female style redirects expectations. The access sign seems to say, 'if women could share equally in the male adolescence discourse, then the code could be rewritten'.

In 'What's love got to do with it?' Tina Turner challenges the prostitute code head on. Strutting down the street, her mini-skirt, show of leg and spiked-heeled shoes could operate to code her as a spectacle of male desire. Instead, the image she projects struggles for a different signification. It's easier to imagine the spikes as an offensive weapon than as a sexual lure or allusion to her vulnerability. Turner's control over her own body and interactions with others in the video, particularly with men, encourages a revaluation of her revealing clothes and high heels from indices of her objectification to signs of her own pleasure in herself.[8]

Overall, the system of representation that constitutes access signs – female take-overs of streets, men pushed aside and out of the way, equal exchanges of looks and co-participation in leisure practices among boys and girls – references the differences girls experience as a result of gendered social inequalities and textually proposes solutions. In isolation, access signs argue in the language of role-reversal and utopianism for equal rights and recognition. In combination with discovery signs, however, the politics of female address are made more complex, pushing beyond the mere

139

transposition of sex roles and practices to accommodate and lend value to the specific culturalism of female adolescence.

DISCOVERY SIGNS: CREATING MEANING FROM GIRL CULTURE

Girl culture is often described in terms of a negative relation to male street culture and a functional relation to female gender oppression, rather than as a distinct cultural form in its own right. Frith (1981), for example, in the following passage, acknowledges girl culture modes of dance and dressing up, but only as a manifestation of a socially objectified position:

> all this female activity, whatever its fun and style and art as a collective occupation, is done, in the end, individually, for the boy's sake. It is the male gaze that gives girls' beauty work its meaning.
>
> (Frith 1981: 229)

But it is precisely the 'fun and style and art as collective occupation' which speaks to the expressiveness of girl culture, the complementary world of leisure and social bonding it creates for girls. To reduce these activities to an overdetermined desire to please boys is to reproduce male bias in cultural criticism.

McRobbie (1984: 145) describes dance as an activity of control, pleasure and sensuality for girls. Dance, she suggests, offers girls 'a positive and vibrant sexual expressiveness and a point of connection with other pleasures of femininity such as dressing up or putting on make-up'. The girl practice of learning and teaching specific dance steps is part of a wider participation by girls in the orchestration of body movement. Girls often spend hours with girlfriends practising cheerleading routines, synchronized swimming moves, jump-rope patterns. Choreographed movement provides a critical bond between girls and a means for negotiating social restriction on the presentation and signification of their female bodies. Discovery signs contribute to female address by referencing and revaluing such female modes of cultural expression.

In 'Girls just want to have fun', Lauper and her girlfriends are shown chatting on the phone in shots of luxuriously long duration. The video summons up the pleasure that many girls find in choreographed movement with a shot of Lauper and friends swaying rhythmically to the music, wrapped in intimate arm embraces. Dance is the mode through which Lauper and her female followers accomplish their symbolic take-back of the street. And, at the video's end, the men encountered on the street, their threatening status alleviated, are brought back to the Lauper character's home to experience female fun: dancing with wild abandon to records in one's bedroom. In 'Love is a battlefield', dance is the vehicle for the women's militancy. Their choreographed chest thrusts and kicks combine a wild sexual energy with self-

140

defence moves to mock and threaten the pimp figure. And in 'What's love got to do with it?' Tina Turner adds to the sense of control over her body through distinctive steps and a calculated mix of gestures. The video also includes a shot of girls doing the 'double dutch', a jump-rope pattern, to textually complement the shot of men shooting craps.

McRobbie (1984) has also commented on the irony in subculture critics' preoccupation with style as male expression given girls' historical investment in style and fashion. In female address videos, style is reclaimed for girls and richly articulated as a symbolic vehicle of female expression. Madonna's video, 'Borderline' moves into discovery signs in its presentation of the female fantasy of becoming a fashion model. In the video, a fashion photographer 'discovers' the character played by Madonna during the first street-dance scene. She participates in the excitement and pleasure of wearing glamorous clothes and make-up, until the male photographer begins to assert his authority over her 'look'. Desiring to manage her own image, she returns to participate with boys in street culture. Later Madonna videos rely on discovery signs to a greater extent, dwelling on the recognition that fashion and made-up faces achieve for women. In 'Material girl', Madonna, draped in jewels and male attendants, rewrites the tragic Marilyn Monroe image she references into a decidedly female image of recognition and power.[9]

Appearance, style and fashion have long been arenas of female cultural production and knowledge in the United States. From birth, the imposing of a gendered appearance by parents, largely in the form of clothes, constructs and enforces gender identities. Purchasing and dressing up in feminine clothes accompanies every major event in a girl's life from confirmation to prom night, until the arrival of the most fussed-over ritual, the wedding with its expensive and rigidly-defined attire. It is the regiment of dress codes and restrictions on hairstyle and application of make-up that often first expose girls to gender contradictions. They learn that wearing particular clothes is a highly charged activity which situates one's own desires against a host of social approval ideologies. The desire to dress like a boy is an early form of resistance to the physical and mental restraints that gender definitions seek to impose on girls. As girls age and their physical body changes, they discover additional relationships between modes of displaying the body and social response. They learn not only to please and to placate by manipulating their appearance, but also to shock and to subvert.

In *Interview* magazine (Stanton 1985), Madonna reveals that as a young girl, she adopted strategies of subversive self-presentation. She describes how she and a best girlfriend developed a sexual persona in order to subvert their parents' authority, an image which interestingly enough was inspired by their identification with a female musician:

M: . . . it was a private joke between my girlfriend and me, that we were floozies, because she used to get it from her mother all the time, too . . .
[Interviewer]: So somewhere you did like the floozy look.

141

M: Only because we knew that our parents didn't like it. We thought it was fun. We got dressed to the nines. We got bras and stuffed them so our breasts were over-large and wore really tight sweaters – we were sweater-girl floozies. We wore tons of lipstick and really badly applied makeup and huge beauty marks and did our hair up like Tammy Wynette.

(Stanton 1985: 60)

Madonna's distinctive star style is an allusion to the resistive stance she practised as a girl. Her visual image engages with and hyperbolizes the discourse of femininity, enacting what Barbara Hudson (1984) asserts is a familiar tactic devised by girls to undermine the discourse of femininity – a set of expectations that attempts to restrict girls' behaviour and choices at the time of adolescence. Madonna combines contradictory accoutrements of a feminine presentation with the affected attitude of a cinematic vamp. Bleached blonde hair proudly displays its dark roots. Glamour eye make-up and lipstick create a look that is compared to Marilyn Monroe's, but a cocky demeanour exudes a self-assuredness and independence to counter the outdated, naïve image. Skin-tight, lacy undergarments and crucifixes add up to a blasphemous, 'bad girl' affectation, particularly in a woman who, we are told in the promotional press, hated the uniforms at her own Catholic school.

Lauper's image is more an ode to the adolescence discourse, enacting an alignment girls make in yet another attempt to counter the restrictive femininity discourse. She presents a rebellious, anti-feminine, 'she's so unusual' image. Lauper's display of odd colour combinations in dress and hair, her wearing of gaudy fake-jewellery, application of striped and sequined eye make-up, mock socially appropriate modes of female attire and behaviour. It is this sense of bucking the norm that *Ms.* magazine applauded by awarding Lauper a 'Woman of the Year' citation in 1985, in explanatory notes, characterizing her rebellious style as a feminist stance.

Girls' stake in their appearance involves them intensely in shopping and consumer culture. Critics have been reluctant to consider consumption practice as a site of cultural production. Culture critics, in fact, have been typically averse to forms of commercial culture, coding the marketplace as the antithesis of authentic cultural expression, as essentially a mechanism of capitalist economic reproduction. Such assumptions have proved to be obstacles to the analytical treatment of girl cultural forms, operating to reduce girl participation in consumption to a kind of false consciousness, useful only in preparing girls for reproductive social roles. Carter (1984) develops McRobbie's (1976, 1980) critique of male bias in the theoretical work on youth subculture,[10] citing the way culture critics have aligned commercialism and female gender with the effect of depreciating both simultaneously:

Like the phenomena which they examine, the analyses themselves are founded on a number of unspoken oppositions: conformity and

142

resistance, harmony and rupture, passivity and activity, consumption and appropriation, femininity and masculinity.

(Carter 1984: 186)

Close analysis of the overlap between consumption practice and female gender reveals far more complicated patterns of use and considerable activity between the opposed characteristics that Carter identifies in the assumptions of critics.

In the United States, consumer culture helps define and support female adolescent leisure practice, and forms a basis for common gender experience. The shopping mall is a popular female substitute for the streets of their male counterparts. Like the street, the mall offers an active, semi-anonymous site for adolescent loitering and gatherings of friends, but within a more restricted and supervised setting. Girls at the mall have the option to retreat into stores which offer the added attraction of shopping, an activity girls like to do together. For some girls, knowing what looks are in vogue, tracing cultural influences on designs and designers, participating in the popularity of certain fashions, becomes a form of private communication much like male sports talk. Fashion talk circulates as a kind of female knowledge at which boys and men are typically less competent.

Madonna and Cyndi Lauper have expertly created styles to address adolescent girls' involvement in fashion and consumer girl culture. Madonna manipulates the look of glamour and codes of high fashion into appropriations and recombinations that tap into viewer fascination with fashion models and the ability of celebrities to direct trends. Lauper wears thrift-store and boutique renditions that recirculate fashions from the past. They call attention to the circularity of consumption, point out ways to construct personal style on a budget, and suggest how to exercise control over the terms of prevailing fashion. The styles of the two stars articulate the tensions between conforming and resisting codes of gendered appearance, between following marketplace dictates and innovating fashion trends.

Discovery signs, then, address girls by referencing modes of female adolescent fun and leisure, the way girls engage in peer associations, and female methods for creatively negotiating the specific difficulties that result from being female at the time of adolescence. In this way, female address videos suggest to female spectators that access to the privileged realm of male cultural experience is partially a matter of discovering their own cultural agency.

FEMALE FAN RESPONSE: STYLE IMITATION

Discussion of female address in music video is incomplete without some attention to how the videos are acknowledged and made meaningful as female address by an actual social audience of girls.[11] I have already suggested ways in which the manipulation of appearance is fundamental to a host of cultural

143

exchanges and affective practices by girls, how it is that discovery signs incorporate style into the creation of female address. Style is also a mode through which girls formulate their response to the videos and the associated female stars.

Dressing alike is a familiar practice at the time in a woman's life before heterosexual desire is rigidly channelled, when girl friendships are most valued. Griffin (1985: 61) describes the expressing of female 'best friend' relationships as integrally bound up with the wearing of '*exactly* the same clothes, shoes, hairstyles, even jewellery'. Female fans of female address videos extend the status of 'best friend' to their favourite musician by displaying imitations of her dress and by mimicking her mannerisms.

Style imitation of stars also relates to the broader practice of fandom. Fans, characteristically, make themselves into authorities of texts, not by selecting them as subjects of research, but through their intense engagement with texts over time. The reiteration of a favoured star's style serves to demonstrate the fan's knowledge of the intricacies of textual references. Girls are particularly prone to using style imitation as a means of expressing textual competency, having learned some of their first lessons in producing and interpreting texts by studying fashion magazines. Style imitation as a female fan practice complexly intersects both the fan's characteristic display of textual knowledge and the female adolescent's involvement in style as a form of female knowledge.

The shopping mall is a site around which female fan participation in female address videos coalesces. 'Madonna is everywhere,' writes one biographer, 'there is even a mall in California that people have nicknamed "the Madonna mall" because so many girls who shop there try to look just like her' (Matthews 1985: 8). In response to the popularity of 'MadonnaStyle', Macy's Department Store created a department called 'Madonnaland' devoted to selling the cropped sweaters ($30), cropped pants ($21) and a variety of jewellery accessories such as crucifix earrings and outsize 'pearl' necklaces ($4–59) resembling those worn by Madonna.[12] The department became the location for the mobilization of Madonna fans in the summer of 1985 when Macy's sponsored a Madonna look-alike contest to coincide with the star's New York concert date.

To provoke attendance, Macy's ran a full-page advertisement in the *Village Voice* with text designed to capitalize on fan familiarity with Madonna's video, 'Material girl', and the movie, *Desperately Seeking Susan* in which she co-starred and performed the song, 'Into the groove':

JRS!
DESPERATELY SEEKING MADONNA LOOK-ALIKES
Join our Madonna Day contest, Thurs, June 6 in Madonnaland on 4,
Macy's Herald Square. If you're a brassy material girl, get into the
groove and prove it . . .

('JRS' 1985: 24)

The overwhelming response was featured on both MTV and the ABC Evening News where Madonna 'wanna-bes' revelled in their new-found fame. On camera, they gushed that they 'wanted to be famous' and 'to be looked at' like their idol, Madonna. For one magical moment, in front of Peter Jennings and ABC viewers, it came to pass.

The desire for fame and attention that girl fans express relates back to their experience of gender inequality, back to the fact of their exclusion from male forms of cultural expression and privilege. These are the conditions that access signs attempt to speak about and resolve symbolically in female address videos. Girls' desire for recognition as expressive cultural subjects in their own right is what discovery signs articulate and try to fulfil. Female fans of female address videos interact with the text in ways that are consistent with, and even celebrate, the system of address represented in the text. They demand access to male privileges of fun, money and authority, what they find embodied in celebrities, but refuse to dispose of the expressive forms that female culture has provided.

The popularity of female address video among girls helped define and create a distinctive, gendered textual practice on MTV. Female audiences participated in the struggles of female musicians for authorship in an industrial and textual system which prefers male musicians and male adolescent discourse, by providing audience consent, accepting the musicians as authors of a subjective textual voice. Fandom proved to be an effective vehicle for girl audiences to organize in support of female musician authors and female address textuality. The fans' intense displays of identification with the text created structures of popularity which extended the usual measure of textual success, ratings or, ultimately, product sales. Through their fan practices, girl fans produced a surplus of popularity, a kind of popularity excess, which functioned to win consent for female musician authorship and the alternative system of meaning represented in female address videos.

The audience's participation, then, involved more than an interpretation of meaning against a preferred address, the terms in which much cultural theory locates resistive textual practice. Rather, it was the result of a complex and dynamic interaction of decoding *and* encoding practices. Authors and audiences aligned at the site of the text and cooperated to make changes that were in their own respective social interests. The struggle over meaning took a material form as new texts were created with a revised address. Female address satisfied female musicians who were in search of a more complex and subjective mode of self-representation, female audiences who wanted a system of textual discourse comparable to the prominent male adolescent address, and it even served MTV whose primary prerequisite was the delivery of a youth audience to advertisers. As a result, the preferred encoding of male address was unable to fully sustain its ideological dominance. The creation of an alternative address strained the hegemony of male adolescent discourse inscribed in rock music and music video. The controlled entry of women to modes of cultural production, both as authors and as audiences, was undermined by their engagement in the struggle over authorship and meaning on MTV.

One of the driving forces behind this essay has been my desire to examine and refute the charge that MTV's visual discourse constitutes an overwhelmingly and uniformly sexist address, to suggest how such claims risk reducing complex textual and social processes to simplistic and one-dimensional characterizations of how meaning is generated and exchanged. When critics look only at textual examples of social reproduction, they fail to consider the conditional and historical character of textual meaning and the role of human agency in signification practices. In the case of MTV, they overlook how issues of sexism and gender inequality are contested within individual videos, across the channel's schedule of videos, and at the points where the videos converge with the social practices of producers and audiences.

NOTES

1   In the popular arena, the Parents' Music Resource Center, headed by wives of prominent government officials, organized to focus attention on so-called 'pornographic' rock music lyrics and album covers, persuading Congress to hold hearings on the enactment of a system for rating records similar to the one used for rating movies. Male musicians and bands came under the most fire, although Cyndi Lauper made the list for 'She bop', her song about female auto-eroticism (The Women Behind the Movement, 1985). The Parents' Choice Foundation distributed a review of sexism on MTV in their newsletter, lumping Benatar's video, 'Love is a battlefield', with its 'worst cases' videos, describing it in the following terms: 'one performer fights with her ornery parents then leaves home to become a hooker' (Wilson 1984: 3). Other examples of popular criticism that describe music video as sexist include Levy (1983) and Barol (1985).

In academic criticism, the arguments are more sophisticated, but frequently lead to the same charge. Brown and Campbell (1984) used content analysis to argue for a lack of positive female images on MTV, without ever addressing the issue of female musicianship. Kaplan (1985, 1986) has explored female representation in music video in several papers. Although she points out 'alternative' representations in some of the same videos I analyse, ultimately she argues for the overdetermination of male address. Holdstein (1985) provides a textual reading of Donna Summer's 'She works hard for the money', arguing against a feminist interpretation.

2   Rieger (1985) dates the institutional exclusion of women from musical composition and performance back to the beginning of institutions themselves. Churches in the Middle Ages made it an official practice to bar females from participation in liturgical rites, effectively creating a gender boundary to 'high music' culture. Early educational institutions reserved musical training and opportunities primarily for their male students. Women's music-making was forced into popular culture forms, and with respect to the formation of the bourgeoisie in the eighteenth century, into domestic space. Female piano-playing and singing were designed as appropriate forms of musical expression for women and incorporated into the bourgeois woman's role in the family. 'It was important to a man's prestige that his wife could entertain his guests with music, and of

course a musical education for his daughter served as a good investment for an advantageous marriage' (Reiger 1985: 141). Music by women was conceived as a service provided for fathers, husbands and children, not as a source of pleasure for themselves, or as a career direction, a means of making money. Prior to the influx of women, men were accustomed to performing music in the home. But as music in a domestic setting became associated with bourgeois female roles, men responded by establishing professional standards and devaluing the amateur status. The legacy of too little institutional support and the ideological attitudes pertaining to the suitability of musical expression for women is the basis of male-dominated musical forms today, including rock'n'roll.

3   The following sources enabled me to trace the decline of the record industry and to feel justified in crediting the start of music video cable distribution with its subsequent turnaround: Henke (1982), Hickling (1981), Kirkeby (1980), Loder and Pond (1982), Pond (1982), Sutherland (1980) and Wallace (1980).

4   Information about sales and rankings of female musicians were constructed from the following sources: Brandt (1982), Grein (1985), Loder (1984), Miller et al. (1985), Swartley (1982), Turner and Loder (1986).

5   I use the term 'patriarchy' loosely, as have many feminist critics, to describe an institutional system of male privilege and female subordination under capitalism, not as a strict anthropological description.

6   I am indebted to Nava's (1984) discussion of youth service provision to girls in Britain for providing the initial impetus behind my identification of these two categories of sign types.

7   A fuller discussion of the videos described below and other female address videos from 1985 and 1986 is included in Lewis (1990).

8   Kleinhans (1985: 30) adds to my analysis of 'What's love got to do with it?' the suggestion that the video continues a tradition of black woman's blues. 'As black feminist critics, Michelle Russell and Michele Wallace discuss, black women's blues insist on the woman's integrity – she won't love someone who doesn't love her'.

9   A recommended analysis of this video is Brown and Fiske (1987).

10   Carter (1984) cites the work of Hoggart (1957), Cohen (1972), Hall and Jefferson (1976), Hebdige (1979) and Willis (1977) as examples.

11   Kuhn (1984) suggests the use of the term 'social audience' to refer to the group of people (social subjects) who actually view the media texts under discussion. I adopt the term to make a distinction between actual viewership groups and target audience, the term used by media industries to signify a perceived or projected audience.

12   Pricing information for Madonna ready-to-wear clothing and accessories obtained from an article in Seventeen ('Funky frills': 1985).

REFERENCES

Ardener, S. (1975) 'Sexual insult and female militancy', in S. Ardener (ed.), Perceiving Women, New York: John Wiley, pp. 29–83.

Barol, B. (1985) 'Women in a video cage', Newsweek, 4 March, p. 54.

Benatar, P. (1987) Phone interview with author, 25 February.

Bessman, J. (1985) 'How clips helped break Cyndi', Billboard, 9 March, p. 38.

Brake, M. (1985) Comparative Youth Culture, London: Routledge & Kegan Paul.

Brandt, P. (1982) 'At last . . . enough women rockers to pick and choose', Ms., September, pp. 110–16.

Brown, J. D. and Campbell, K. C. (1984) 'The same beat but a different drummer: race and gender in music videos'. Paper presented at the University Film and Video Association Conference, Harrisonburg, VA, January.

Brown, M. E. and Fiske, J. (1987) 'Romancing the rock: romance and representation in popular music videos', *OneTwoThreeFour – A Rock'n'Roll Quarterly*, 5, 61–73.

Carter, E. (1984) 'Alice in the consumer wonderland', in A. McRobbie and M. Nava (eds), *Gender and Generation*, London: Macmillan, pp. 185–214.

Caughie, J. (1981) *Theories of Authorship*, London: Routledge & Kegan Paul.

Cohen, P. (1972) 'Subcultural conflict and working-class community', *Working Papers in Cultural Studies*, 2 (Spring).

Fiske, J. (1986) 'Television: polysemy and popularity', *Critical Studies in Mass Communication*, 3 (4), pp. 391–408.

Feuer, J., Kerr, P. and Vahimagi, T. (1984) *MTM: 'Quality TV'*, London: BFI.

Frith, S. (1981) *Sound Effects: Youth, Leisure, and the Politics of Rock'n'Roll*, New York: Pantheon Books.

—— and McRobbie, A. (1978/79) 'Rock and sexuality'. *Screen Education*, 29, 3–19.

'Funky frills: take center stage in Cyndi Lauper and Madonna-inspired extras' (1985) *Seventeen*, July, p. 34.

Gardiner, J. (1979) 'Women's domestic labor', in Z. Eisenstein (ed.), *Capitalist Patriarchy and the Case for Socialist Feminism*, New York: Monthly Review Press, pp. 173–89.

Gramsci, A. (1971) *Selections from the Prison Notebooks*, in Q. Hoare and G. Nowell-Smith (eds and trans), London: Lawrence & Wishart.

Grein, P. (1985) 'Hot Madonna', *Billboard*, 10 August, pp. 1, 71.

Griffin, C. (1985) 'Leisure: deffing out and having a laugh', in *Typical Girls? Young Women from School to the Job Market*, London: Routledge & Kegan Paul, pp. 58–71.

Grossberg, L. (1984) 'I'd rather feel bad than not feel anything at all: rock and roll, pleasure and power', *Enclitic*, 8 (1–2), 94–111.

Hall, S. (1980) 'Encoding/decoding', in S. Hall, D. Hobson, A. Lowe and P. Willis (eds), *Culture, Media, Language*, London: Hutchinson, pp. 128–38.

—— (1982) 'The rediscovery of "ideology": return of the repressed in media studies', in M. Gurevitch, T. Bennett, J. Curran and J. Woollacott (eds), *Culture, Society and the Media*, London: Methuen, pp. 56–90.

—— and Jefferson, T. (eds) (1976) *Resistance Through Rituals: Youth Subcultures in Post-war Britain*, London: Hutchinson.

Hebdige, D. (1979) *Subcultures: The Meaning of Style*, London/New York: Methuen.

—— (1983) 'Posing . . . threats, striking . . . poses: youth, surveillance, and display', *SubStance*, 37/38, 68–88.

Henke, J. (1982) '1981: another bad year for the record industry', *Rolling Stone*, 4 March, p. 51.

Henley, N. (1977) *Body Politics*, Englewood Cliffs, NJ: Prentice-Hall.

Hickling, M. (1981) 'Record sales hold steady with last year's', *Rolling Stone*, 15 October, p. 52.

Hoggart, R. (1957) *Uses of Literacy: Changing Patterns in English Mass Culture*, Fairlawn, NJ: Essential Books.

Holdstein, D. H. (1985) 'Music video messages and structures', *Jump Cut*, 29 (1), 13–14.

Hopkins, J. (1972) 'The fans', in H. R. Huebel (ed.), *Things in the Driver's Seat: Readings in Popular Culture*, Chicago: Rand McNally & Co., pp. 161–72.

Hornaday, A. (1985) 'Cyndi Lauper', *Ms.*, January, p. 47.

Hudson, B. (1984) 'Femininity and adolescence', in A. McRobbie and M. Nava (eds), *Gender and Generation*, London: Macmillan, pp. 31–53.

'JRS!' Macy's advertisement (1985) *Village Voice*, 11 June.

Kaplan, E. A. (1985) 'A post-modern play of the signifier? Advertising, pastiche and schizophrenia in music television', in P. Drummond and R. Paterson (eds), *Television in Transition*, London: British Film Institute, pp. 146–63.

—— (1986) 'History, the historical spectator and gender address in music television', *Journal of Communication Inquiry*, Winter, pp. 3–14.

Kirkeby, M. (1980) 'The pleasures of home taping', *Rolling Stone*, 2 October, pp. 62–4.

Kleinhans, C. (1985) 'Fashioning the fetish: the social semiotics of high heel shoe images', Unpublished lecture. Evanston, IL: Northwestern University.

Kuhn, A. (1982) *Women's Pictures*, London: Routledge & Kegan Paul.

—— (1984) 'Women's genres', *Screen*, 25 (1), 18–28.

Laing, D. (1985) *Power and Meaning in Punk Rock*, Milton Keynes, UK: Open University Press.

Leach, W. R. (1984) 'Transformations in a culture of consumption: women and department stores, 1890–1925', *Journal of American History*, 71 (2), 319–42.

Levy, S. (1983) 'Ad nauseam: how MTV sells out rock and roll', *Rolling Stone*, 8 December, pp. 30–7, 74–9.

Lewis, L. A. (1990) *Gender Politics and MTV: Voicing the Difference*, Philadelphia: Temple University Press.

Loder, K. and Pond, S. (1982) 'Record industry nervous as sales drop fifty percent', *Rolling Stone*, 30 September, pp. 69, 78–9.

McRobbie, A. (1980) 'Settling accounts with subcultures: a feminist critique', *Screen Education*, 34, 37–49.

—— (1983) 'Jackie: an ideology of adolescent femininity', in E. Wartella and D. C. Whitney (eds), *Mass Communication Review Yearbook*, Beverly Hills: Sage, vol. 4, pp. 273–83.

—— (1984) 'Dance and social fantasy', in A. McRobbie and M. Nava (eds), *Gender and Generation*, London: Macmillan, pp. 130–61.

—— and Garber, J. (1976) 'Girls and subcultures', in S. Hall and T. Jefferson (eds), *Resistance Through Rituals: Youth Subcultures in Post War Britain*, London: Hutchinson.

Marc, D. (1984) *Demographic Vistas*, Philadelphia: University of Pennsylvania Press.

Marchetti, G. (1982) 'Documenting punk: a subcultural investigation', *Film Reader*, 5, 269–84.

Matthews, G. (1985) *Madonna*, New York: Wanderer Books/Simon & Schuster.

Meehan, E. R. (1986) 'Conceptualizing culture as commodity: the problem of television', *Critical Studies in Mass Communication*, 3 (4), 448–57.

Miller, J., McGuigan, C., Uehling, M. D., Huck, J. and McAlevey, P. (1985) 'Rock's new women', *Newsweek*, 4 March, pp. 48–57.

Nava, M. (1984) 'Youth service provision, social order and the question of girls', in A. McRobbie and M. Nava (eds), *Gender and Generation*, London: Macmillan, pp. 1–30.

Newcomb, H. M. (1984) 'On the dialogic of mass communication', *Critical Studies in Mass Communication*, 1, pp. 34–50.

—— and Hirsch, P. M. (1983) 'Television as a cultural forum', *Quarterly Review of Film Studies*, 8 (2), pp. 45–55.

Pond, S. (1982) 'Record rental stores booming in US, *Rolling Stone*, 2 September, pp. 37, 42–3.

Reiter, R. R. (1975) 'Men and women in the South of France: public and private domains', in R. R. Reiter (ed.), *Toward an Anthropology of Women*, New York: Monthly Review Press, pp. 252–82.

Rich, A. (1983) 'Compulsory heterosexuality and lesbian existence', in A. Snitow, C. Stansell and S. Thompson (eds), *Powers of Desire*, New York: Monthly Review Press, pp. 177–205.

Rieger, E. (1985) ' "Dolce semplice"? On the changing role of women in music', in G. Ecker (ed.), *Feminist Aesthetics*, London: The Women's Press Ltd, pp. 135–49.

Ross, E. and Rapp, R. (1981) 'Sex and society: a research note from social history and anthropology', in A. Snitow, C. Stansell and S. Thompson (eds), *Powers of Desire*, New York: Monthly Review Press, pp. 51–72.

Rubin, G. (1975) 'The traffic in women: notes on the "political economy" of sex', in R. R. Reiter (ed.), *Toward an Anthropology of Women*, New York: Monthly Review Press, pp. 157–210.

Shore, M. (1984) *The Rolling Stone Book of Rock Video*, New York: Rolling Stone Press.

Stanton, H. D. (1985) 'Madonna', *Interview*, December, pp. 58–68.

'State of the industry: Part I: the cable numbers according to broadcasting' (1981), *Broadcasting*, 30 November, pp. 36–52.

Sutherland, S. (1980) 'Record business: the end of an era', *Hi Fidelity*, May, p. 96.

Swartley, A. (1982) 'Girls! Live! On stage!' *Mother Jones*, June, pp. 25–31.

The Meldrum Tapes (1986) Interview with Cyndi Lauper and David Wolff, MTV Cablecast.

'The Women Behind the Movement', (1985), *Broadcasting*, 15 July, p. 42.

Turner, T. and Loder, K. (1986) *I, Tina*, New York: William Morrow & Company, Inc.

Vener, A. M. and Hoffer, C. (1965) 'Adolescent orientations to clothing', in M. E. Roach and J. B. Eicher (eds), *Dress, Adornment & the Social Order*, New York: John Wiley & Sons, pp. 76–81.

Volosinov, V. N. (1973) *Marxism and the Philosophy of Language*, New York: Seminar Press.

Wallace, R. (1980) 'Crisis? What crisis?' *Rolling Stone*, 29 May, pp. 17, 28, 30–1.

Weinbaum, B. and Bridges, A. (1979) 'The other side of the paycheck: monopoly capital and the structure of consumption', in Z. R. Eisenstein (ed.), *Capitalist Patriarchy and the Case for Socialist Feminism*, New York: Monthly Review Press, pp. 190–205.

Williams, R. (1977) *Marxism and Literature*, Oxford: Oxford University Press.

—— (1981) 'Analysis of Culture', in T. Bennett, G. Martin, C. Mercer and J. Woollacott (eds), *Culture, Ideology and Social Process*, London: Open University Press, pp. 43–52.

Willis, P. (1977) *Learning to Labour: How Working Class Kids get Working Class Jobs*, London: Saxon House.

Wilson, S. (1984) 'So there it all is: rock TV 1984', *Parents' Choice*, pp. 3, 14.

Wolfe, A. (1983) 'Rock on cable: on MTV: Music Television, the first video music channel', *Popular Music and Society*, 9 (1), 41–60.

Wolmuth, R. (1983) 'Rock'n'Roll'n'Video: MTV's music revolution', *People Magazine*, 17 October, pp. 96, 99–104.

VIDEOGRAPHY

Cyndi Lauper, 'Girls just want to have fun', *She's So Unusual* (Epic records: Ken Walz, producer; Ed Griles, director; 1983).

Madonna, 'Borderline', *Madonna* (Warner Bros: Simon Fields for Limelight Productions, producer; Mary Lambert, director; 1984).

Pat Benatar, 'Love is a battlefield', *Live From Earth* (Chrysalis Records: Mary Ensign, producer; Bob Giraldi, director; 1983).

Tina Turner, 'What's love got to do with it?' *Private Dancer* (Capital Records: John Caldwell, producer; Mark Robinson, director; 1984).
Madonna, 'Material girl', *Like a Virgin* (Warner Bros: Mary Lambert, director; 1985).

9

FORGING MASCULINITY: HEAVY-METAL SOUNDS AND IMAGES OF GENDER

Robert Walser

The spectacle is not a collection of images, but a social relation among people, mediated by images.

Guy Debord[1]

Orpheus, the god-like musician of Greek mythology, was a natural figure for opera plots, which must reconcile heroics and song; his legendary rhetorical powers made him the most popular subject of early seventeenth-century dramatic music, with settings by Monteverdi, Peri, Caccini and many other composers. But his story contains a built-in contradiction: Orpheus must sing in such a way as to demonstrate his rhetorical mastery of the world, yet such elaborate vocal display threatens to undermine Orpheus' masculine self-control. Flamboyant display of his emotions is required as evidence of his manipulative powers, but such excess makes him into an object of display himself, and suggests a disturbing similarity to the disdained emotional outbursts of women. Western constructions of masculinity often include conflicting imperatives regarding assertive, spectacular display and rigid self-control. Spectacles are problematic in the context of a patriarchal order that is invested in the stability of signs and which seeks to maintain women in the position of object of the male gaze.[2]

Today's heavy-metal musicians must negotiate the same contradiction. Like the story of Orpheus, heavy metal often stages fantasies of masculine virtuosity and control. Musically, heavy metal often depends upon a dialectic of controlling power and transcendent freedom. Metal songs usually include impressive technical and rhetorical feats on the electric guitar, counterposed with an experience of power and control that is built up through vocal extremes, guitar power chords, distortion and sheer volume of bass and drums. Visually, metal musicians typically appear as swaggering males, leaping and strutting about the stage, clad in spandex, scarves, leather and other visually noisy clothing, punctuating their performances with phallic thrusts of guitars and microphone stands. The performers may use hyper-masculinity or androgyny as visual enactments of spectacular transgression. Like opera, heavy metal draws upon many sources of power: mythology,

153

violence, madness, the iconography of horror. But none of these surpasses gender in its potential to inspire anxiety and to ameliorate it.

Heavy metal is, inevitably, a discourse shaped by patriarchy. Circulating in the contexts of Western capitalist and patriarchal societies, for much of its history metal has been appreciated and supported primarily by a teenage, male audience. But it is crucial to specify not only age and gender, but the corresponding political position of this constituency: it is a group generally lacking in social, physical and economic power, but one besieged by cultural messages promoting such forms of power, insisting on them as the vital attributes of an obligatory masculinity. As John Fiske concluded from his study of 'masculine' TV shows such as *The A-Team*, 'our society denies most males adequate means of exercising the power upon which their masculinity apparently depends. Masculinity is thus socially and psychologically insecure; and its insecurity produces the need for its constant reachievement. . . .'[3] I would emphasize in Fiske's analysis the words 'apparently' and 'socially', for I see sex roles as contradictory, mutable social constructions, rather than as normative formations somehow grounded in biology or an ahistorical psychology. Moreover, it is not only masculinity that is insecure; none of the components of identity are stable or natural. Heavy metal, like all other culture, offers occasions for doing 'identity work': among other things, for 'accomplishing gender'.[4] That is, notions of gender circulate in the texts, sounds, images and practices of heavy metal; and fans experience confirmation and alteration of their gendered identities through their involvement with it.

For Fiske, the contradictions built into male sex roles and the insecurity that men feel as a result help explain the episodic and generic aspects of male culture. Television shows such as *The A-Team* are structured as repeated enactments of paradigmatic narratives and representations because their function is to address anxieties that can never be resolved. Fiske's ideas are easily transferable to music and music video, where repetition and genre are also crucial phenomena. The purpose of a genre is to organize the reproduction of a particular ideology, and the generic cohesion of heavy metal until the mid-1980s depended upon the desire of young white male performers and fans to hear and believe in certain stories about the nature of masculinity. But metal's negotiations of the anxieties of gender and power are never conclusive; that is why, as Fiske says, these imaginary resolutions of real anxieties must be re-enacted over and over again. That such representations can never be definitive or totally satisfying also means that they are always open to negotiation and transformation. But social circumstances may change such that particular forms of culture are no longer relevant: metal fans tend mostly to be young because much of metal deals with experiences of powerlessness that may be, to some extent, overcome. As they get older, fans may acquire some amount of economic power, or they may beget children who replace them at the bottom of the familial and social ladders, whose physical power and mobility is far less than theirs and who thus assuage some of their culturally-produced anxieties.[5]

Such a theoretical perspective cannot be a comprehensive one for the study of gender in heavy metal, though, for there are many female metal fans, for whom such explanations are inadequate. Indeed, since around 1987, concert audiences for metal shows have been roughly gender-balanced. But metal is overwhelmingly concerned with presenting images and confronting anxieties which have been traditionally understood as peculiar to men, through musical means which have been conventionally coded as masculine. Since the language and traditions of heavy metal have been developed by and are still dominated by men, my discussion of gender in metal will initially be an investigation of masculinity; I will return later to issues of the reception of these male spectacles by female fans.

Heavy metal, for two decades, has offered a variety of compensatory experiences and opportunities for bearing or resolving the contradictions of masculinity as they have been constructed by societies which are aligned by patriarchy, capitalism and mass-mediation. Thus one of the most important items on the heavy-metal agenda has long been to deal with what patriarchy perennially perceives as the 'threat' of women. I will be framing my discussion of heavy-metal songs and videos in terms of a loose list of strategies concerning gender and power: misogyny, exscription, androgyny and romance. Heavy-metal musicians and fans have developed tactics for modelling male power and control within the context of a patriarchal culture, and metal's enactions of masculinity include varieties of misogyny as well as 'exscription' of the feminine – that is, total denial of gender anxieties through the articulation of fantastic worlds without women – supported by male, sometimes homoerotic, bonding. But heavy metal also participates in rock's tradition of rebellion, and some metal achieves much of its transgressiveness through androgynous spectacle. Until recently, one of these three strategies – misogyny, exscription, androgyny – tended to dominate each heavy-metal band's 'aesthetic'. A fourth approach, increasingly important in recent years, 'softens' metal with songs about romance; this kind of music has drawn legions of female fans to metal since the mid-1980s.

In spite of the fact that this categorization of metal might look like a menu for sexual abuse, I intend neither to denounce utterly, nor to try to rescue wholesale, heavy metal's politics of gender. To do only the former would be to ignore the politics of critique, particularly the fact that criticism of popular culture never takes place apart from implicit comparisons with more prestigious culture. Like racism, sexism is sustained and naturalized across class lines. Writers who expose racism and sexism in popular culture must take care that their critique does not collude with those who want to identify such barbarisms with an economic and cultural underclass which can thus be more self-righteously condemned and oppressed. Critics of popular music must take care to acknowledge the politics of their work: while it is imperative to be critical, to avoid bland enthusiasm or dispassionate positivism, analyses of popular culture must also be empathetically drawn if they are to register accurately the contradictions and subtleties of popular practices. Otherwise they too easily serve as mandates for elitist condemnation and oppression. It is beyond dispute that some of the images and ideologies of heavy metal are violent and irresponsible. But of course the violence and irresponsibility of much so-called 'high' culture, and of the economic elite that underwrites its existence, is also demonstrable. The politics of prestige work to position 'high' culture beyond scrutiny, and 'low' culture beneath it. But in either case the effect is to forestall critique by mythologizing constructions that are in fact never natural, no matter how powerfully they work to constitute subjectivity. It is less important simply to denounce or defend cultural representations of gender than to critique them in the context of an explanation of how they work, what social tensions they address, where they come from, and why they are credible to particular audiences.

Gender constructions in heavy-metal music and videos are significant not only because they reproduce and inflect patriarchal assumptions and ideologies, but more importantly because popular music may teach us more than any other cultural form about the conflicts, conversations and bids for legitimacy and prestige that comprise cultural activity. Heavy metal is, as much as anything else, an arena of gender, where spectacular gladiators compete to register and affect ideas of masculinity, sexuality and gender relations. The stakes are as high in metal as anywhere, and they are more explicitly acknowledged there, both in visual and musical tropes and in the verbal and written debates of fans. By taking the trouble to distinguish carefully among the varieties of representation within heavy metal, we can gain a better understanding of larger interrelationships of gender and power.[6]

BEHIND THE SCREEN: LISTENING TO GENDER

In her pathbreaking study of music video, *Rocking Around the Clock*, E. Ann Kaplan makes two main points about metal videos: that their violence and rebelliousness place them in the 'nihilistic' category of her typology of videos, and that their reputation for blatant sexism is well deserved.[7] Neither of these might seem particularly bold assertions; but taken together, I think, they are contradictory. Sexism is in fact a major ideological constituent of much heavy metal, but sexism is never nihilistic: the intensity and variety of modes of sexist discourse must be understood as indices of the urgency and influence of patriarchal ideals. To call such discourse nihilist is to obscure its real ideological functions.

Kaplan's readings of videos as texts embedded in the contexts of MTV and consumer culture are sometimes acute and illuminating. But two serious methodological shortcomings flaw her comments on heavy metal. First, beyond her observation that metal audiences are made up of 'young males' (not entirely true even when her book was written, and certainly not now), Kaplan's comments appear to be uninformed by any ethnographic or personal contact with the heavy-metal musicians and fans whose texts and lives she presumes to explain. While Kaplan's conclusions are based on her analysis of MTV as a spectacular reinforcement of universal decentredness and passivity, the interviews and questionnaires I have received from heavy-metal fans point to a wide range of activities connected to their involvement with the music. *Headbangers' Ball*, the weekly three-hour MTV programme devoted to heavy metal, is quite popular with the fans I surveyed, but it is hardly the most important aspect of their involvement with metal. Concerts, records, radio, fan magazines and quite often playing an instrument figure as primary components of metal fans' lives. A significant number of fans (especially male) watch MTV seldom or never, and for many (especially female) the glossy photographs of rampant musicians to be found in the copious fan literature are more important sources of visual pleasure than videos. This is not to argue that metal videos are unimportant, but rather to say that they do not operate in a social vacuum: their analysis must be inflected by knowledge of the lives and cultural investments of the viewers.

Second, certainly the most serious shortcoming of Kaplan's book is the almost total absence of analysis pertaining to the *music* of music video. Kaplan's few comments addressing musical details of heavy-metal songs are hardly helpful: she characterizes heavy metal as 'loud and unmelodious', filled with 'relatively meaningless screaming sounds'.[8] Though musical discourses are invisible, they are nonetheless susceptible to analysis, and musical analysis is crucial for music video analysis because aural texts are indisputably primary: they exist prior to videos and independently of them, and fans' comments make it clear that it is the music of music video that carries the primary affective charge. That is, it is the music that is mostly responsible for invoking the libidinal and corporeal investment that intensify belief, action, commitment and experience. The challenge of analysing music videos is that of interpreting and accounting for *both* musical and visual discourses, simultaneous but differently articulated and assuming a variety of relations.

If the cinema, as Laura Mulvey asserts, 'has structures of fascination strong enough to allow temporary loss of ego while simultaneously reinforcing the ego', the same was surely true of music long before cinema was invented.[9] Musical constructions, in metal or elsewhere, are powerful in part because they are made to seem so natural and unconstructed. We experience music's rhetorical pull apart from language, seemingly apart from all social referents, in what is usually thought a pure, personal, subjective way. Yet that impression of naturalness depends on our responding unselfconsciously to complex discursive systems that have developed as historically and socially specific practices. It is not only lyrics or visual imagery, but the music itself that constructs gendered experiences.[10] The musicians I will discuss have used musical codes to articulate visions of the world that are filled with the pleasures of energy, freedom, power and a sense of community. Discursively, specific details of rhythm, pitch and timbre *signify* – some of them through the conventions of heavy metal proper, some as part of a complex, mutable tradition of musical semiotics that stretches back centuries. Such signification always occurs in social contexts structured through political categories such as gender, class and race; and musical meanings are thus inseparable from these fundamental constituents of social reality.

Only with its complex sonic texts and ethnographic contexts disregarded, as in analyses such as Kaplan's, can heavy metal be casually characterized as both sexist and nihilistic, or as a monolithic, adolescent deviance. For 'heavy metal' is a genre label which includes a substantial and growing female audience, a number of distinctive and sophisticated musical discourses, and many different 'solutions' to complex problems of gender relations. As I discuss several heavy-metal songs and their videos, I hope to delineate their musical and ideological strategies more precisely than is accomplished by such vague but pervasive terms of dismissal. As I work through the various gender strategies I have identified in heavy metal, I will be arguing on the one hand that music videos cannot reasonably be analysed without the musical component of such texts being examined; and on the other hand, that it is crucial for the cultural critic to develop an understanding of the interests and activities of the communities who find meaning in their encounters with these texts.

NO GIRLS ALLOWED: EXSCRIPTION IN HEAVY METAL

The most distinctive feature of heavy-metal videos is that they typically present the spectacle of live performance; bands are shown on stage, performing in sync with the song. Other kinds of pop music videos also frequently feature 'live' synced performances, but pop songs are less often 'performed' on a stage than mimed in front of fantastic or arty backgrounds, or in unlikely locations; often only vocals are synced, as only the singer is visible. In the typical metal video, however, actual concert footage is often used, and when it is not, sets, backdrops and musicians' posturings usually imitate the spectacle of an arena concert. Bands as different in their styles and constituencies as Guns N' Roses, Poison and Metallica all rely on scenes of 'live' performance for most of their videos. Heavy metal has long had the most loyal touring support of any popular musical genre, and the arena concert experience of collectivity and participation remain the ideal which many videos seek to evoke.

Besides the videos of metal singles to be seen on programmes like MTV's *Headbangers' Ball*, full-length heavy-metal concerts are popular rentals at video stores. Since a favourite performer might come through town once a year at best, and since many younger fans are not allowed by their parents to attend concerts, heavy-metal videos make more widely available the singular events which are most highly valued by fans. The video in a concert setting, with or without fans, presents the performers in all their glory, as larger-than-life figures whose presence is validated by feelings of community and power, and evoked by venue and music.

Many such performance videos offer for the pleasure of young males a fantasy not unlike that constructed by *The A-Team*, as John Fiske describes it: a world of action, excess, transgression, but little real violence; one in which men are the only actors, and in which male bonding among the members of a 'hero-team' is the only important social relationship. As Barbara Ehrenreich has pointed out, for young men maturing in a patriarchal world where men dominate the 'real' world while women raise kids, growing up means growing away from women.[11] Fiske's analysis of the television show stresses the value of male bonding for creating close social ties while excluding the threat of the feminine: 'Feminine intimacy centers on the relationship itself and produces a dependence on the other that threatens masculine independence. . . . Male bonding, on the other hand, allows an interpersonal dependency that is goal-centered, not relationship-centered, and thus serves masculine performance instead of threatening it.'[12] Even in many non-performance metal videos, where narratives and images are placed not on a stage but elsewhere, the point is the same: to represent and reproduce spectacles that depend for their appeal on the exscription of women.

Even exceptions to the metal concert video format emphasize the performative. In Judas Priest's 'Heading out to the highway', a song from 1981 that was still popular as a video in 1988 and 1989, performance is not literally represented. The band's two guitar players drag race on an empty highway in the middle of nowhere, flagged on by the singer, whose macho stances, gestures and singing are the only elements of the real performance retained in the fantastic setting. The song and the images are about freedom and adventure, and we don't even need the initial 'Hit 'em, boys' to know that we're talking about a specifically male kind of freedom. There are no women to be seen in this video, and what is there to be seen – the cars, the road, the leather, the poses – have long been coded as symbols of male freedom, linked as signs of aggressiveness and refusal to be bound by limits.

The performance enacts this in musical terms as well. The vocals and guitars constantly anticipate the downbeats, punching in ahead of the beat defined by the bass and drums throughout the song. Halford's rough, powerful voice finds support in harmony vocals that sound as menacing as a gang's chant. He sustains triumphant high notes at the end of each chorus, in a display of power that has counterparts in the guitar's solo section and the bass pedal under the verse. Not only his voice, but the singer's writhing and posing provide a spectacle of male potency for a male audience, including both the band on screen and the presumed male viewer of the video.[13]

But images of masculine display are available to be construed in a variety of ways. Gay heavy-metal fans sometimes celebrate forthrightly the homoeroticism that is latent in such displays of exclusive masculine bonding. This can be seen, for example, in the activities of the Gay Metal Society, a social club of over 100 members, based in Chicago. In addition to sponsoring and organizing parties and nights out on the town for its members, GMS publishes a monthly newsletter, which contains commentary on the history, criticism and discography of heavy metal. The GMS *Headbanger* also functions as a forum for debate of issues involving sexuality and music. Gay fans celebrate metal musicians whom they believe are gay, such as Judas Priest's Rob Halford, and confirm and contest each other's 'negotiated' readings of popular texts. They may see metal videos as erotic fantasies, while straight fans resist the homoerotic implications and insist on identification with the power and freedom depicted.[14] Of course, straight fans must negotiate their readings, too. Some of Accept's lyrics are explicitly homosexual if studied closely; despite this, the band is quite popular among heterosexual, often homophobic, men. As with classical music, heterosexual and even homophobic audiences can negotiate their reception and find the constructions of gay composers powerfully meaningful.

Male bonding itself becomes crucial to the reception of metal that depends on masculine display, for it helps produce and sustain consensus about meaning. Exscripting texts do occasionally refer to sexuality, but typically as just another arena for enactments of male power. Mutual erotic pleasure rarely appears in the lyrics of heavy metal, just as it is seldom discussed by men in any other context. Metal shields men from the danger of pleasure – loss of control – but also enables display, sometimes evoking images of armoured, metallized male bodies that resemble the Freikorps fantasies analysed by Klaus Theweleit.[15] The historical context and social location of these fantasies marks them as very different from heavy metal, but the writings and drawings of the German soldiers Theweleit studied evince a similar exscription of women, and a concomitant hardening and metallic sheathing of the male body as a defence against culturally-produced gender anxieties. Such images from heavy-metal lyrics and album cover art could be cited by the hundreds, in a tradition that goes back to one of the founding texts of heavy metal, Black Sabbath's *Paranoid* (1970), which included the song 'Iron man'.[16]

The seductive women who sometimes intrude into otherwise exscripting videos signify in several ways. First, these shots function just as they do in advertising: to trigger desire and credit it to the appeal of the main image. But the sexual excitement also serves as a reminder of why exscription is necessary: the greater the seductiveness of the female image, the greater its threat to masculine control. Moreover, the presence of women as sex objects stabilizes the potentially troubling homoeroticism suggested by the male display. I will have more to say about the anxieties produced by homoerotic display in my discussion of androgyny below. There are, however, many videos which attempt to manage gender anxieties more overtly, through direct repre- sentations of women.

THE KISS OF DEATH: MISOGYNY AND THE MALE VICTIM

Blatant abuse of women is uncommon in metal videos. There are unequivocal exceptions, such as the brutal stage shows of W.A.S.P., or the forthrightly misogynistic lyrics in some of the music of Guns N' Roses and Mötley Crüe. But despite heavy metal's notorious reputation among outsiders, few heavy-metal videos have ever approached the degree of narcissistic misogyny routinely displayed by, for example, pop star Michael Jackson (e.g., his videos for 'Dirty Diana', or 'The way you make me feel'). If the exscripting music of Judas Priest or AC/DC conflates power and eroticism, making pleasure contingent upon dominance, many of heavy metal's critics have similarly confused the issue. Tipper Gore, for example, makes it clear that she considers rape and masturbation equal threats to 'morality'. And William Graebner has offered an analysis of 'the erotic and destructive' in rock music that too often fails to distinguish between the two themes.[17] But articulations of gender relations in contemporary patriarchy are complex, and if constructions of sexuality in popular music are to be understood, their relationship to structures of power and dominance must be delineated, not crudely presumed.

Like heavy metal, sexually explicit films have an undeserved reputation for physical violence, according to a recent historical study of hard-core pornographic films. Building on the observation that sex is more shocking than violence in the United States, Joseph W. Slade explains the rampant violence in 'legit' films as a result of prohibitions of dealing with eroticism. Violence is often used as a metaphor for passion, Slade maintains, in discourses where explicit depiction of sexual activity is banned. In X-rated films, on the other hand, where representation of sex is not only permissible but primary, power relations are articulated through sexual relations rather than violence. The central purpose of pornography, Slade summarizes, has been 'to assuage male anxieties about the sexuality of females'.[18] Male authority is characteristically made secure through porn because that authority is represented as being founded in love: women are seen to submit themselves voluntarily and gladly, and force is unnecessary.

While non-violent fantasies of dominance might be, for some, no less repugnant than blatant misogyny, it is important to recognize that they are different. As is typical of hegemonic constructions, overt force is not only unnecessary in pornography, but it would be disruptive of a representation that depends on presenting itself as natural and uncoerced. Heavy metal too relies much less on physical violence against women than on a number of more hegemonic representations. Because metal has developed discourses of male victimization, exscription and androgyny, its power to reproduce or adapt patriarchy is often contingent on the absence of overt violence. Although some of these discourses embody challenges to or transformations of hegemonic ideology, some reproduce rather directly the hegemonic strategies of control and repression of women that pervade Western culture.

For example, there is the strategy of confronting the 'threat' head-on: one of the more successful representations of women in metal is the *femme fatale*. Such images are quite popular, from Mötley Crüe's 'Looks that kill' to Whitesnake's 'Still of the night', but the metal band Dokken could be said to have specialized in such constructions, embedded in narratives of male victimization. Many of their best-known songs enact the same basic story of the male entrapped, betrayed or destroyed by the female: 'Heaven sent', 'Prisoner (chained by love)', 'Just got lucky', 'Into the fire' and 'Kiss of death'.[19] Dokken's success with this formula was enabled by two of the band's particular assets: singer Don Dokken's voice and face are clean and soulful, the perfect complement to his tragic, self-pitying lyrics; and guitarist George Lynch is a powerful rhetorician whose solos and fills demonstrate a perhaps unmatched command of the semiotics of frantic but futile struggle.

Dokken's 'Heaven sent' (1987) is reminiscent of nineteenth-century operatic constructions such as Salome and Carmen in the way it locates women at a nexus of pleasure and dread.[20] Dokken sings of a woman who is simultaneously angel and witch, temptress and terror. A slim young woman in the video appears inexplicably, metamorphosed from a much heavier and older woman. She never speaks, but walks alone through the night, sometimes in black mini-skirt and leather, sometimes in a flowing white gown, holding a candelabra; she is followed by a rushing, tipping camera until she mysteriously dissolves. Jump-cuts and shifts in point of view fragment the video, but the decentring and transformations are precisely the point: the boys in the band, first seen playing chess in a bar (in an unlikely portrait of innocence), wind up doing their onstage posturing in a graveyard, to the tune of their own victimization. Of course, the woman in the video never actually does anything threatening; it is enough that she exists. Women are presented as essentially mysterious and dangerous; they harm simply by being, for their attractiveness threatens to disrupt both male self-control and the collective strength of male bonding.

Musically, 'Heaven sent' constructs this victimization through images of constraint and struggle. The song opens with the repetition of a pair of open fifths, a whole step apart. But the fifths are not the usual power chords – they lack sufficient sustain and distortion. Instead, they sound haunting and ominous, and their syncopation and sparseness give them an anticipatory air, in contrast to the rhythmic control and driving energy of the rest of the song (and of most other metal songs). Once the song gets under way, the rhythm is inexorable and precise, in that articulation of power and control that is one of the primary musical characteristics of heavy metal. In tension with the rhythmic stability, though, are the sudden and unexpected harmonic shifts that articulate 'Heaven sent' formally. Like the jump-cuts in the video, these key changes are initially disorienting; but since the song stays in its gloomy Aeolian/Dorian mode throughout, each new section is affectively felt as the same scene, however distant harmonically – just as the various manifestations of 'woman' in the video are linked by an aura of mystery and dread.

The guitar solo, often the site of a virtuosic transcendence of a metal song's constructions of power and control, is in 'Heaven sent' a veritable catalogue of the musical semiotics of doom. As with 'ground bass' patterns in seventeenth-century opera, the harmonic pattern uses cyclicism to suggest fatefulness; as in certain of Bach's keyboard pieces, the virtuoso responds to the threat of breakdown with irrational, frenzied chromatic patterns.[21] The guitar solo is an articulation of frantic terror, made all the more effective by its technical impressiveness and its imitations of vocal sounds such as screams and moans. After the solo, the song's chorus intensifies these images through ellision: seven measures long instead of the normal, balanced eight, the pattern cycles fatalistically, without rest or resolution.

Visual images, narrative and the music itself combine in this video to represent women as threats to male control and even male survival. The mysteriousness of women confirms them as a dangerous Other, and their allure is an index of the threat.[22] Female fans, who now make up half the audience of heavy metal (though only a very small fraction of metal musicians are women), are invited to identify with the powerful position that is thus constructed for them; it is a familiar one, since women are encouraged by a variety of cultural means to think of appearance as their natural route to empowerment. Men, on the other hand, are reassured by such representations that patriarchal control is justified and necessary. Such constructions are by no means to be found only in heavy metal, of course; not only do they belong to a long and esteemed tradition of Western cultural history, but their success in the 1980s has been widespread in a political context marked by reactionary governmental policies and a significant backlash against feminism. It is crucial to recognize that heavy metal itself, then, is not the aberrant 'Other' that many conservative critics would have it be. The sexual politics of heavy metal are a conflicted mixture of confirmation and, as we will see, contradiction of dominant myths about gender.

LIVING ON A PRAYER: ROMANCE

Heavy metal changed a great deal in the last half of the 1980s, and one particular album of 1986 is a good register of the shift, as well as a major factor in precipitating it. With *Slippery When Wet*, one of the biggest-selling hard-rock albums of all time (over 13 million copies), Bon Jovi managed to combine the power and freedom offered by metal with the constructed 'authenticity' of rock and, most important, the romantic sincerity of a long tradition of pop. Though Bon Jovi offered typical experiences of the heavy-metal dialectic of absolute control and transcendent freedom in a performative context of male bonding, lead singer Jon Bon Jovi also projected a kind of sincerity and romantic vulnerability that had enormous appeal for female fans. It is this discursive fusion that enabled the band's Top 40 success, and which helped spark the unprecedented entry of much heavy metal and metal-influenced music into the Top 40 of the late 1980s.

Bon Jovi was certainly not the first to achieve this fusion; bands like Van Halen, Boston, Journey, Foreigner, Loverboy and others were engaged in similar projects some time before. But Bon Jovi's music was a phenomenal success, and it helped transform what had long been a mostly male subcultural genre into a much more popular style with a gender-balanced audience. The fusion was developed and managed very deliberately: once a standard leather/chains/eye-liner heavy-metal band, with lots of tragic, macho songs about running, shooting and falling down, the band sought to capture a wider audience for *Slippery When Wet*. The most obvious change was in the lyrics: abandoning heavy-metal gloom, doom and creepy mysticism, they began cultivating a positive, upbeat outlook, where the only mystical element was bourgeois love. Writing songs about romantic love and personal relationships, they tempered their heavy-metal sound and image and pitched their product to appeal as well as to a new female market.

There is still a lot of metal in Bon Jovi's music, although the question of his inclusion in the genre is vigorously contested among various factions of metal fans. Features of heavy metal are evident in the timbres and phrasing of both instruments and vocals, the emphasis on sustain, intensity and power, the fascination with the dark side of the daylit respectable world. But by not wearing makeup anymore, and by wearing jeans, not leather or spandex, Bon Jovi abandoned much of heavy metal's fantastic dimension in favour of signs of rock 'authenticity'. Moreover, from pop music the band got its constructed sincerity, just the right degree of prettiness, and a conscious appeal to a female audience. The sustained and intense sounds of heavy metal are channelled behind the romantic sincerity of pop, while smooth, sometimes poignant synthesizer sounds mediate the raw crunch of distorted guitars.

The biggest hit song from *Slippery When Wet* was 'Livin' on a prayer', which invites us to sympathize and identify with Tommy and Gina, a young couple who are good-hearted but down on their luck. Tommy, now out of work, is a union man, working-class, tough – but also tender, caring and musical. He used to make music, that is, until he had to hock his guitar; Tommy's loss of his capacity to make music is a sign of the couple's desperate circumstances. The lyrics of the song fall into three groups, each with a different sort of text and musical affect: the verses of the song tell the story of Tommy and Gina's troubles; the pre-choruses are resolutions not to give up, the pair's exhortations to each other about the power of love; and the choruses are Tommy's affirmation that such hope and faith in love is justified, that love really can transcend material problems.[23]

The source of the song's main pleasures is its musical construction of romantic transcendence. As with most pop songs, the transcendent moment is the place in the chorus where the title hook is presented, where the affective charge is highest: it is there, if ever, that we are convinced that Tommy and Gina *will* make it, that love *must* triumph over adverse social conditions, that bourgeois myths *can* survive even the despair of joblessness. Such affirmative stories have led to critical dismissal of Bon Jovi as fatuous rock 'perfect for the Reagan era'.[24] But such disparagements typically ignore gender as a site of political formation, and critical sneering does little to help us understand the tensions that are mediated by such a vastly popular song.

There are at least three ways of understanding how this sense of transcendence is constructed musically. First, and simplest, it is at this moment that the piece moves out of its minor key and into its relative major. Such a key change accomplishes a tremendous affective change, moving from what is conventionally perceived as the negativity or oppression of the minor key to the release and affirmation of the major. Experientially, we escape the murk that has contained us since the beginning of the song. Second, this moment in the chorus offers an escape from the C–D–E pattern that has been the only chord progression the song has used until this point, and which thus has seemed natural and inevitable, however cheerless.[25] 'Livin' on a prayer' breaks out of its gloomy treadmill at this point of transcendence, moving from C to D to *G*, not E. By breaking free of its oppressive minor tonality, and by doing so through a brand-new progression, the song leaps into an exciting new tonal area and constructs a transcended context for Tommy and Gina, and for the song's audience. To clinch it, a background group of voices joins in here to support Tommy's tough solo voice; the rest of the social world seems to join in this affirmation.

Finally, this new progression C–D–G has discursive significance. This pattern has been one of the most important formulas for establishing resolution and closure in Western music from Monteverdi to the 'Monster mash'; it is not, however, a common progression in heavy metal. The C–D–E progression upon which most of 'Livin' on a prayer' is built, on the other hand, is strongly associated with metal. Thus when 'Livin' on a prayer' reaches its moment of transcendence, the shift in affect is marked by the use of a different harmonic discourse. The transcendence is in part an escape from heavy metal itself, with all its evocation of gloominess, paranoia and rebellion. 'Livin' on a prayer' breaks away from the musical discourse of heavy metal at the point where it offers its bottom line: transcendence through romantic love. To offer such a payoff, it *must* break away from metal.

The success of the song depends on the contrast of and tension between two affective states: the Aeolian grunge of the beginning, which sets up the story of Tommy and Gina's hardship; and the transcendent change to G major in the chorus, which symbolically and phenomenologically resolves it. For most of the song, the grunge frames and contains the chorus. It seems more realistic, since it returns as though inevitable whenever Bon Jovi's fervent vocalizing stops. The utopian promise is thus made contingent on the singer's efforts. Only at the end of the song, where the chorus endlessly repeats through the fade-out, does it seem that the transcendence might be maintained – and then only if the singer never ceases. At the same time that the magical power of romantic love, transcending material conditions, is being touted as the solution to what are in fact social problems, the Horatio Alger solution of hard individual work is also suggested. In the end the utopian moment wins out, keeping the realistic grunge at bay and even suggesting that the transcendent fantasy is more real. But all of this is possible only because Bon Jovi has created these realities: a bleak, resonant social landscape, the power of romantic love to offer transcendence, and a tough but sensitive male to make it work. The patriarchal premises of Bon Jovi's fusion are clear.

Towards the end of the song the transcendent moment is kept fresh through a key change, up a half step. Not only does the pitch rise, creating an overall affective elevation, but it also forces Bon Jovi's voice higher, charging it with even more effortful sincerity and, since he meets the challenge successfully, utopian promise. Moreover, the key change is made to coincide with a dropped beat, so the music jumps forward suddenly, unexpectedly, onto this new, higher harmonic plateau. In the concert footage used in the video of 'Livin' on a prayer', Jon Bon Jovi sails out over the audience on a wire at precisely this moment, tripling the transcendent effect.

The rest of the video seems to have little to do with the song as I have analysed it. It consists mostly of grainy black-and-white footage of Jon and the band backstage and in rehearsal, without any visual connection to the romantic narrative of the song. Neither is it a typical performance video like the ones I discussed above, since more camera time is devoted to backstage and rehearsal scenes than to actual or even faked (synced) performance. Yet the video is closely connected to the music; the biggest visual gesture is the sudden switch to colour film and a live concert audience, which occurs two-thirds of the way through the song, precisely at the climactic moment of transcendence indicated by the song's chorus. The video marginalizes the literal narrative of the lyrics, in accordance with the way that typical heavy-metal videos cater to fans' enjoyment of live concerts. The transcendence constructed by the music, originally mapped onto the story of Tommy and Gina, has now become the transcendence available through Bon Jovi: the music, the concert and even the grainy black-and-white footage that purports to let the fan in on the behind-the-scenes lives of the musicians. What was framed by the lyrics as a moment of transcendence for a romantic, heterosexual couple, made possible by the male narrator, is now a celebration of the band members as objects of desire, and of the concert as an experience of collective pleasure. The 'Livin' on a prayer' video is less a romantic story than a spectacle of masculine posturing, and the musically-constructed transcendence of the song is linked to patriarchy through both narrative and visual pleasure.

It has been argued that the cinema has only recently begun to present the masculine as spectacle, in something like the way that women have been so presented. This is in contrast to theorizations of earlier cinematographic practice, where women were typically presented as erotic objects of the male gaze, but representations of men functioned as embodiments of a powerful, ideal ego.[26] Such a development is of great interest, because the contradictions historically coded into representations of gender result in an almost androgynous glamour being attached to male objects of desire. Bon Jovi's image has been carefully managed so as to simultaneously maintain two different kinds of appeal to male and female fans. For example, the release order of singles from *Slippery When Wet* was carefully balanced between romantic and tougher songs, in order to sustain interest in the band from both genders.[27] But we will see more serious problems of managing desire in the face of gender blurring in a sub-genre of heavy metal distinguished by blatant visual androgyny.

NOTHING BUT A GOOD TIME? ANDROGYNY AS A POLITICAL PARTY

Androgyny in heavy metal is the adoption by male performers of the elements of appearance that have been associated with women's function as objects of the male gaze – the visual styles that connote, as Laura Mulvey put it, 'to-be-looked-at-ness'.[28] The members of bands like Poison or Mötley Crüe wear garish make-up, jewellery and stereotypically sexy clothes including fishnet stockings and scarves, and sport long, elaborate, 'feminine' hairstyles. Though they are normally included within the genre of heavy metal, such 'glam' bands are considered by most fans to be less 'heavy' than the mainstream. This is due less to musical differences than to their visual style, which is more flamboyant and androgynous than heavier metal.[29]

Androgyny has a long history in music; I have already mentioned problems of gender and representation in Baroque opera. (And one could also mention the seventeenth-century castrati – perhaps the most dedicated androgynes in history.) Recent examples of male androgyny outside of heavy metal range from Liberace to Little Richard to Lou Reed, not to mention the androgynous glamour of many country-and-western stars.[30] Some of this history has faded through supercession: some thought the Beatles' hair, for example, threateningly androgynous in 1964. But in glam metal, androgyny has found popular success to a degree unique in the rock era. And it's a particular sort of androgyny; unlike the 1970s' great androgyne, David Bowie, heavy metal lacks ironic distance. It is this absence of irony more than anything else that leads rock critics to scorn glam metal, for the ridiculous seriousness of metal's gender constructions is at odds with the patriarchal premises undergirding the ideologies and institutions of rock.

Poison is a good example of a successful glam-metal band: one that boasts millions of fans and no critical approval. 'Nothin' but a good time', from

Poison's multi-platinum album *Open Up and Say . . . Ahh!* (1988), is shot almost entirely as a performance video, one that presents the band as though actually performing the song we hear. It includes, however, two framing scenes, which I will describe and discuss briefly before focusing on Poison's androgyny. The opening scene shows us a young man, with a metal fan's long hair, washing dishes in the back of a restaurant. He is swamped with work, surrounded by dirty plates and hot steam, and he is alone except for a small radio, which is playing a song by Kiss, the founders of spectacular metal. Next we meet his boss, loud and rude, who has stomped back to apply a verbal whip; he threatens and insults the dishwasher, flipping off the radio as he leaves. Disgusted and exhausted, the kid sullenly turns the radio back on as soon as the boss leaves. Then he kicks open a nearby door, as though to grab a bit of air before returning to the grind. When the door opens, we are instantly plunged into a Poison performance, taking place just outside. 'Nothin' but a good time' begins with that door-opening kick, and while it lasts, the framing narrative is suspended; we don't see the dishes, the washer or the boss until the song is over. Afterwards, we are returned to the same scene as at the beginning. Having heard the music, the boss storms back into the frame to lash again at the kid; he suddenly notices, however (at the same time that we notice it), that all the dishes, miraculously, are clean. Confounded, he sputters and withdraws, as the dishwasher relaxes and smiles.

The framing scenes of this video call to mind cultural critics' debates about class and resistance in popular culture. The issue is whether or not popular narratives such as that presented by this song and video contain any oppositional potential or critical perspective, whether they offer viewers anything more than an experience of rebellion that is ultimately illusory and inconsequential. We must be wary of simply dismissing such 'unreal' resolutions of real social antagonisms; as Fredric Jameson has argued, although mass culture has conservative functions, though it commonly arouses utopian hopes but perpetuates their containment within hegemonic social forms, the very representation of social fantasies is risky, and maintenance of dominant ideologies is never complete.[31] However, the overt political lesson of the video's framing narrative may be far less important than the implications of the band's visual and musical styles for notions of authenticity and gender. 'Nothin' but a good time' can serve as an example of those subcultural challenges to hegemony which, as Dick Hebdige has argued, are not issued directly, but rather are 'expressed obliquely, in style'.[32]

In the 'Nothin' but a good time' video, the song itself is framed as a fantastic experience. Reality is the world of the frame, the world of work, steam, sweat and abuse; as in *The Wizard of Oz*, the real world is shot in muted colour so as to enable the fantasy to seem more real. When the dishwasher kicks open the door, Poison explodes in colour and musical sound, and the real world, the one which supposedly includes the fantasy, vanishes; the fantasy takes over as a more real reality. Even the dishwasher himself disappears for the duration of the song, in a kind of dissolution of the ego in the flux of musical pleasure. This fantasy is credited with magical agency as well: at the end of the song, we are returned to grey reality to find the dishes done, the impossible task fulfilled. The boss's torrent of abuse is plugged; something has been put over on him, though he can't say what or how.

When combined with the song's lyrics, the video's message seems fairly simple self-promotion: the good time being sung about is something that can be accessed through Poison's music, no matter what the 'real' conditions. As with many TV advertisements, Poison's fantasy is represented as more real than mundane reality, and the fantasy is to be enjoyed through involvement with a commercial product. Such an appeal, though, must evoke our desires for community and for greater freedom and intensity of experience than are commonly available in the real world. Poison, like Pepsi, uses narrative and image to arouse these longings and then present us with a particular kind of consumption as the means of satisfying them.

But it would be a mistake to exaggerate the importance of the narrative framing of the song; however obvious the 'political' message of the framing narrative may seem, it may be far less important than the gender politics of the song and its performance. Debates over the liberatory possibilities of mass culture all too often proceed in terms that neglect the gendered character of all social experience. Yet popular music's politics are most effective in the realm of gender and sexuality, where pleasure, dance, the body, romance, power and subjectivity all meet with an affective charge. The significance of the musical section of the video may be overlooked because it seems to be simply a representation of a live performance, whereas the frame is more arbitrary, and thus presumably more meaningful. But it is the band's performance that is privileged visually, through colour, free movement and spectacle – and through the transgressive energies of male display and flamboyance. Most tellingly, it is the performance rather than the framing narrative that benefits from the affective invigoration of the music. If the framing scenes address labour relations, they do so in a rather flat, pedantic way. It is the video of the song itself that deals with the issues of greatest importance to metal fans: the power, freedom, transcendence and transgression that are articulated through fantastic, androgynous display. The young man we meet in the frame finds his release from drudgery in Poison's spectacular androgyny.

Significantly, the video's 'live' performance of 'Nothin' but a good time' is neither live nor a real performance, but a constructed fantasy itself. The musicians undergo impossibly frequent and sudden changes of costume, without narrative explanation, through the invisible, extra-diegetic powers of editing. Along with similar metamorphoses of the guitar player's instrument, which is a different model and colour each time we see it, these unreal transformations contribute to the fantastic aura of the performance by offering an experience of freedom and plenitude. Moreover, there is no audience; the band 'performs' in an abstract space, a contextless setting for

169

pure spectacle. Such a location can serve as a 'free space' for Poison's play of real and unreal, authenticity and desire, and the ambiguous subversiveness of androgyny, supported by the energy of the music.

The lyrics of the song are fairly simple: they combine a lament about overwork with a celebration of partying. The music is similarly straightforward, built around a vigorous rock beat and standard power chords on the scale degrees I, ♭VII and IV. The musical mode is mixolydian, quite commonly used in pop-oriented hard rock or metal, as it combines the positive effect of the major third with the 'hard' semiotic value of the minor seventh.[33] 'Nothin' but a good time' derives much of its celebratory energy from the repeated suspension of the fourth-scale degree over this major third, and the conventional move to ♭VII adds to the song's rebellious or aggressive tone. The visual narrative and the musically-coded meanings are roughly parallel; the lyrics are supported by music that is energetic, rebellious and flamboyant.

But in 'Nothin' but a good time' we can also detect the association of androgynous visual styles with a particular set of musical characteristics. The song features compelling rhythmic patterns, it contains the requisite guitar solo, it utilizes the distorted timbres one would expect in the electric guitar and vocals of a metal song; in short, the song meets generic criteria in every way. It is, of course, successful music, deploying discursive potentials with skill and effectiveness. However, one would be hard pressed to find it very distinctive in any way; this is not especially innovative or imaginative music. Androgynous metal usually includes less emphasis on complexity and virtuosity than other styles of metal, and many arguments among fans are provoked by the collision of visual spectacle and transgression with metal's dominant aesthetic (masculine) valorization of sonic power, freedom and originality.

This alignment of androgynous spectacle with a musical discourse relatively lacking in sonic figurations of masculinity is crucial, for it signals the extent to which a linkage of 'feminine' semiotic instability with monolithic, phallic power is deemed impossible. To be sure, if the music of glam metal were separated from its visual context, it would still sound like hard rock. Compared to other kinds of popular music, glam rock is replete with constructions of masculine power. But within the context of heavy metal, glam metal's relative lack of virtuosity, complexity and originality are aural contributors to androgyny. Fans link visual signs of androgyny with an abdication of metal's usual virtuosic prowess. 'It seems like if you have the makeup you're thought of as less than a musician', complains Poison's guitarist C. C. Deville. 'It seems because of the image we can't get past that hurdle. Now we try to stay away from the glam thing. When we first came out we were a little extreme.'[34]

Indeed, I was quite surprised when I attended a Poison concert and discovered that their drummer, Rikki Rockett, was actually an excellent musician whose featured solo was marked by sophisticated polyrhythms and rhetorical intelligence. I was surprised by this because his playing on Poison's recordings had always been extremely simple, however accurate and appropriate. But Poison's simplicity is constructed, like that of much American popular music throughout its history. From Stephen Foster to Madonna (not to mention Aaron Copland), many musicians have used great skill to craft musical texts that communicate great simplicity. The musical construction of simplicity plays an important part in many kinds of ideological representations, from the depiction of pastoral refuges from modernity to constructions of race and gender. Poison succeeded in a genre dominated by virtuosity because their musical simplicity complemented their androgynous visual style and helped them forge a constituency. As Deville's comment indicates, the band now yearns to be respected musically as well, and though they have yet to make much progress towards this goal, they have drastically reduced the amount of make-up they wear, in pursuit of it.

'REAL MEN DON'T WEAR MAKE-UP'

In the case of bands such as Poison, we might understand androgyny as yet another tactic for dealing with the anxieties of masculinity. Androgynous musicians and fans appropriate the visual signs of feminine identity in order to claim the powers of spectacularity for themselves. But while it is certainly important to understand heavy metal androgyny as patriarchal, metal takes part in a rock'n'roll tradition of Oedipal rebellion as well: the musical and visual codes of heavy metal may function to relieve anxieties about male power, but they are incompatible with the styles previous generations of men developed for doing the same thing. Teenage boys and young men chafe under patriarchal control even as women do, and boys often develop innovative ways of expressing control over women as simultaneous proof of their achievement of manhood and their rebellion against dominant men. This internal tension is never entirely manageable or predictable, and heavy metal transgresses against patriarchal control in ways that sometimes undermine, sometimes affirm, its tenets.

Musicians themselves may notice how the ambiguities of androgyny provoke compensatory strategies. Aerosmith's hit song and video 'Dude looks like a lady' (1987) confronts the gender anxieties aroused by androgyny, airing the problem with a tone of mock hysteria. And singer David Lee Roth self-reflexively connects his enthusiasm for bodybuilding and martial arts training to his 'feminized' image on stage: 'A lot of what I do can be construed as feminine. My face, or the way I dance, or the way I dress myself for stage. . . . But to prove it to myself, to establish this [his masculinity], I had to build myself physically. I had to learn to fight'.[35]

Roth's private regimen allows him to go on being androgynous in public. His personal anxieties about masculinity are shaped by conventional patriarchy, yet the attraction of androgynous transgression is also strong.

Among the most leering of rock's lyricists, Roth seems neither personally nor artistically to have resisted sexist objectification of women, as is attested by his notorious paternity insurance policy, or the video for his swaggering remake of the Beach Boys' 'California girls'. Yet Roth has also publicly criticized the sexism of a society that discourages women from becoming professional musicians:

> What if a little girl picked up a guitar and said 'I wanna be a rock star'. Nine times out of ten her parents would never allow her to do it. We don't have so many lead guitar women, not because women don't have the ability to play the instrument, but because they're kept locked up, taught to be something else. I don't appreciate that.[36]

Roth's ideal of personal freedom is in conflict with the limitations of conventional gender definitions, though he doesn't grapple with the problem of how patriarchal power relations might be further strengthened by transgressions that rely on objectified representations of women.

In the journalism of heavy metal, the most heated debates are over 'authenticity', which often implicitly revolves around issues of gender and sexuality. Fans frequently write to the letters columns of metal magazines to denounce or defend glam-metal bands. Attackers label such musicians 'poseurs', implying either that the band is all image with no musical substance, or that they find androgyny fundamentally offensive, a perversion. As one female fan complained in a letter to a fan magazine, 'real men don't wear makeup'.[37] On the other side, defenders of glam metal are quick to respond, though they rarely defend androgyny *per se*:

> This is to Kim of Cathedral City . . . who said that real men don't wear makeup. I have just one question: Do you actually listen to the music, or just spend hours staring at album covers? True, Metallica and Slayer kick f?!kin' ass and Megadeth rules – but Poison, Mötley Crüe and Hanoi Rocks f?!kin' jam too.[38]

Unwilling to discuss gender constructions directly, or lacking cultural precedents for doing so, fans usually defend the musical abilities of the band's members or argue for the intensity of experience provided by the group. But they may also respect the courage that is required of those who disrupt the symbolic order through androgyny, those who claim social space by having 'the guts to be glam'.[39]

Male fans of 'harder' styles of heavy metal are often frantic in their denunciations of androgyny, seeing in it a subversion of male heterosexual privilege and linking it to the threat of homosexuality. On the cover of an album by MX Machine (*Manic Panic*, 1988), a picture of a grimacing boy with his fist in the air is accompanied by a sticker proclaiming 'No Glam Fags! All Metal! No Makeup!' Both homosexuality and symbolic crossing of gender boundaries threaten patriarchal control, and they are thus conflated in the service of a rhetoric which strives to maintain difference and power. Musicians who wear make-up often compensate in private for their transgressions with homophobic banter, insulting each other in order to call masculinity into question and provide an opportunity for collective affirmation of heterosexuality.[40] An interview with Charlie Benante, drummer in the thrash-metal band Anthrax, confirms that even instruments themselves are conventionally gender-coded, and that the use of a feminine-coded instrument in the context of heavy metal evokes the spectre of homosexuality. When an interviewer asked, 'Would you ever consider using keyboards as a major part of the song?' Benante replied, 'That is gay. The only band that ever used keyboards that was good was UFO. This is a guitar band. . . .'[41]

However, since many glam-metal performers appeal in particular to young women, an analysis of heavy metal that understands it only as a reproduction of male hegemony runs the risk of duplicating the exscription it describes. Heavy-metal androgyny presents, from the point of view of women, a fusion of the signs specific to current notions of femininity with musically- and theatrically-produced power and freedom that are conventionally male. Colourful make-up; elaborate, ostentatious clothes; hair that is unhandily long and laboriously styled – these are the excessive signs of one gender's role as spectacle. But on stage in a metal show, these signs are invested with the power and glory normally reserved to patriarchy. As usual, women are offered male subject positions as a condition of their participation in empowerment; but the men with which they are to identify have been transformed by their appropriations of women's signs. In their bid for greater transgression and spectacularity, the men on stage elevate important components of many women's sense of gendered identity, fusing cultural representations of male power and female erotic surface. At the symbolic level, prestige – male presence, gesture, musical power – is conferred upon 'female' signs which, because they mark gender difference and are used to attract and manipulate, adolescent men pretend are trivial but take very seriously.

Feminist scholars have long been concerned with investigating the gendered aspects of the relationship of symbolic and political orders, and the long-standing linkage of women with ephemeral spectacle is highly relevant to metal videos. Kaja Silverman has pointed out that the instability of female fashion has historically marked women as unstable, while male sartorial conservatism represents the stable and timeless alignment of men with the symbolic and social orders.[42] Heavy-metal androgyny challenges this 'natural' alignment, drawing on the power of musical and visual pleasures. It is true that there is no inherent link between subversive textual practices and subversive politics, but the relationships I have delineated among the lyrics, music, images, fans, musicians and ideologies of heavy metal, particularly with respect to gender, are intended to make the case for a conventional link.[43] Glam metal has prompted a great deal of thought and discussion about gender by demonstrating, even celebrating, the mutability of gender, by revealing the

173

potential instability of the semiotic or symbolic realms that support current gender configurations. In some ways, heavy metal reflects the impact of what Jane Flax has called the greatest achievement of feminist theory, the problematization of gender.[44]

Metal replicates the dominant sexism of contemporary society, but it also allows a kind of free space to be opened up by and for certain women, performers and fans alike. Female fans identify with a kind of power that is usually understood in our culture as male – because physical power, dominance, rebellion and flirting with the dark side of life are all culturally designated as male prerogatives. Yet women are able to access this power because it is channelled through a medium – music – that is intangible and difficult to police. Female performers of heavy metal can become enabled to produce and control very powerful sounds, if they meet other genre requirements and acquiesce in the physical display that is so sexist and widespread in society generally, but which may in fact seem less so in metal, where men similarly display themselves.[45] Thus when metal guitarist and singer Lita Ford brags 'I wear my balls on my chest', she combines her seemingly inevitable status as an object of sexual spectacle with her metallic stature as an object embodying the spectacle of power.[46]

Women's reception of these spectacles is complex, and female performers of heavy metal may be advancing provocative arguments about the nature and limits of female claims to power. I have observed and interviewed female fans who dress, act and interpret just like male fans, for example, particularly at concerts of bands like Metallica – bands which avoid references to gender in their lyrics, dealing instead with experiences of alienation, fear and empowerment that may cut across gender lines. Elements of rock music that had been coded as masculine, such as heavy beats, are negotiable, in so far as female fans are willing to step outside of traditional constrictions of gender identity.[47] It may well be, then, that the participation of female metal fans reflects the influence that feminism has had in naturalizing, to a great extent, the empowerment of women. Even in the 1970s, fewer women would have been comfortable identifying with power, when power was more rigidly coded as male. The choice was between being powerful and being a woman, a dichotomy which has since eroded somewhat.

But female fans also maintain their own distinctive modes of engagement with heavy metal, including practices which are often too quickly dismissed as degrading adoration. Sue Wise has argued that the young women who screamed and swooned over Elvis were not so much worshipping him, as so many male rock critics have assumed, as *using* him. Instead of a subject who caused his helpless fans to go into frenzies, Elvis was for many women an object, by means of which they explored their own desires and formed friendships.[48] Similarly, many female heavy-metal fans take great pleasure in collecting, owning and looking at pictures of male heavy-metal musicians. Predictably, male fans tend to be scornful of the pin-up magazines and their devotees.[49] But the enthusiasm of young women for glam styles of heavy metal is not simply an example of masochistic submission to male idols. Such spectacle also infuses with power the signs of women's hegemonically constructed gender identity, offers visual pleasures seldom available to women, and provides them with opportunities to form their own subsets of the fan community.

The channelling of so much masculine prestige through feminine forms thus represents a risky sexual politics, one that is open to several interpretations. Heavy metal's androgyny can be very disturbing, not only because the conventional signs of female passivity and objectification are made dynamic, assertive, transgressive, but also because hegemonic gender boundaries are blurred and the 'natural' exclusiveness of heterosexual male power comes into question.[50] For all its rhetoric of male supremacy – phallic imagery, macho posturing, the musical semiotics of male power – metal's rebellion and fantastic play offer its fans, both male and female, opportunities to make common cause against certain kinds of oppression, even as the same texts may enable each gender to resolve particular anxieties in very different ways. The level of discussion of gender among heavy-metal fans is impressive, in statements that reflect their awareness of the mutability of gender roles and other cultural constructions. Practically every issue of the fan magazine *RIP* in 1989 contained letters from fans protesting sexism, racism and even homophobia.[51] Glam metal fostered greater perception of the conventionality of gender roles, and thus helped lead to greater participation in metal by women, and to debates over gender stereotypes, masculinity, behaviour and access to power.

Androgyny offers male performers (and vicariously, male fans) the chance to play with colour, movement, flamboyance and artifice, which can be a tremendous relief from the rigidity expected of them as men. Philip Gordon argues that singer Dee Snider 'grew his hair and wore women's clothes and make-up, not merely to assert a difference between himself and his parents (as if any sign of difference would be equally effective), but as a carefully constructed style signifying attractiveness, energy and opposition to authoritative restrictions on particular pleasures.'[52]

Critics have not generally understood glam metal in this way. E. Ann Kaplan denies any significance to heavy metal's gender politics: 'Unlike the genuine Bakhtinian carnival, the protest remains superficial: mere play with oppositional signifiers rather than a protest that emerges from a powerful class and community base.'[53] But Kaplan can make such a statement only because she made no efforts to discover anything about the 'class and community base' of heavy metal. There is nothing superficial about such play; fans and musicians do their most important 'identity work' when they participate in the formations of gender and power that constitute heavy metal. Metal is a fantastic genre, but it is one in which real social needs and desires are addressed and temporarily resolved in unreal ways. These unreal solutions are attractive and effective precisely because they seem to step outside the normal social categories that construct the conflicts in the first place.

Like many other social groups, metal musicians and fans play off different possibilities available to them from mainstream culture, at the same time that they draw upon the facts of a social situation that is not mainstream. Androgynous metal's bricolage of male power and female spectacle, and its play of real and unreal, are complex responses to crucial social contradictions which its fans have inherited. Heavy metal's fantastic representations clash with the visions of many other social groups in the cultural competition to define social reality, and like the tensions to which they are a response, metal's fantasies are themselves richly conflicted. If male heavy-metal fans and musicians sometimes assert masculinity by co-opting femininity, what they achieve is not necessarily the same kind of masculinity that they sought, as the conflicting demands of masculinity and rebellion are mediated through new models, and the free play of androgynous fantasy shakes up the underlying categories that structure social experience.

However, androgyny is by no means a purely utopian sign. Capitalism, after all, feeds on novelty as a spur to consumption, and mass culture may colonize existing tensions and ambiguities for consumer purposes rather than to prefigure new realities. As Fred Pfeil points out, mass audiences are increasingly offered 'scandalously ambivalent pleasure', and the same 'de-Oedipalization' of American middle-class life that makes androgyny possible, attractive and thrilling can also block further development towards new collective social forms, beyond fragmentation.[54] Moreover, postmodern cultural 'decentring' can serve capitalism by playing to sensual gratification in ways that deflect people from making the connections that might enable critique.

But postmodern disruptions also open up new possibilities and enable new connections and formulations to be made by delegitimating conceptual obstacles; androgynous metal's defamiliarization of social categories that are still thought normative by many must be given its due. Poison's music and images reflect a concern with shifting boundaries of gender and reality that cannot simply be disregarded as nothing but inauthentic or commodified fantasies. For such fantasies are exercises in semiotic power, offering challenges at both the level of what representations are made and who gets to make them. Dismissing fantasy and escapism 'avoids the vital questions of *what* is escaped from, *why* escape is necessary, and *what* is escaped to.'[55]

Simon Frith and Angela McRobbie ended their early theorization of rock and sexuality with what they saw as a 'nagging' question: 'Can rock be nonsexist?'[56] The obvious answer would seem to be 'no', for there is no way to step outside the history of a discourse, and Frith and McRobbie's question begs for a kind of music that is recognizably – that is, discursively – rock, but which does not participate in the sexism that rock has articulated. Rock can never be gender-neutral, because rock music is only intelligible in its historical and discursive contexts. Rock can, however, be anti-sexist; instead of dreaming of a kind of music that might be both 'rock' and 'nonsexist', we can spot many extant examples of rock music that use the powerful codings of gender available in order to engage with, challenge, disrupt or transform not only rock's representations of gender, but also the beliefs and material practices with which those representations engage. The point of criticism should not be to decide whether rock music is oppositional or co-optive, with respect to gender, class or any other social category, but rather to analyse how it arbitrates tensions between opposition and co-optation at particular historical moments.[57]

I have ranged widely within heavy metal in this paper, turning to a number of very different bands, and to various visual and musical strategies for dealing with the contradictions inherent in the gender roles in the 1980s. The range of examples is necessary, I think, in order to demonstrate that heavy metal as a genre includes a great variety of gender constructions, contradictory negotiations with dominant ideologies of gender that are invisible if one is persuaded by metal's critics that the whole enterprise is a monolithic symptom of adolescent maladjustment. In fact, it is those most responsible for the very conditions with which metal musicians and fans struggle – the contradictory demands of subordination and socialization, of 'masculine' aggressiveness and communal harmony, the possibilities of transcendent pleasure and street pain – who insist on reading this music as impoverished and debased 'entertainment'.

Heavy metal, like virtually all cultural practices, is continually in a flux, driven by its own constitutive contradictions. Patriarchy and capitalism form the crucible, but human experience can never be wholly contained within such a vessel: there are aspects of social life that escape the organization of one or the other; there are also aspects organized in contradictory ways by the pair. Culture cannot transcend its material context, but culture very often transcends hegemonic definitions of its context: heavy metal perpetuates some of the worst images and ideals of patriarchy at the same time that it stands as an example of the kinds of imaginative transformations and rebuttals people produce from within such oppressive systems. Masculinity is forged whenever it is hammered out anew through the negotiations of men and women with the contradictory positions available to them in such contexts. It is also forged because masculinity is passed like a bad cheque, as a promise that is never kept. Masculinity will always be forged because it is a social construction, not a set of abstract qualities but something defined through the actions and power relations of men and women – because, with or without make-up, there are no 'real men'.[58]

NOTES

1   Guy Debord (1983) *Society of the Spectacle*, Detroit: Black & Red, §4.

2   See Susan McClary (1991) 'Constructions of gender in Monteverdi's dramatic music', in *Feminine Endings: Music, Gender, Sexuality*, Minneapolis: University of Minnesota Press, pp. 35–52.

3   John Fiske (1987) *Television Culture*, New York: Methuen, p. 202. See also Fiske (1987) 'British cultural studies and television', in *Channels of Discourse*, Robert C. Allen, (ed.) Chapel Hill: University of North Carolina Press, pp. 254–89.

4   See Arthur Brittan (1989) *Masculinity and Power*, New York: Basil Blackwell, especially pp. 36–41.

5   Deena Weinstein (1991) believes that heavy metal 'celebrates the very qualities that boys must sacrifice in order to become adult members of society'; see her *Heavy Metal: A Cultural Sociology*, New York: Lexington Books, p. 105. I argue the opposite of this: that the same patriarchal ideals are largely held in common by 'boys' and 'adult members of society'.

6   Heavy metal engages with many other social formations and historical tensions than those subsumable under 'gender'. For more comprehensive musical and social analysis of heavy metal, see my forthcoming book, *Running with the Devil: Power, Gender, and Madness in Heavy Metal Music*, Hanover, New England: Wesleyan University Press, 1993.

7   E. Ann Kaplan (1987) *Rocking Around the Clock: Music Television, Postmodernism, and Consumer Culture*, New York: Methuen.

8   Kaplan, *Rocking Around the Clock*, p. 107.

9   Laura Mulvey (1985) 'Visual pleasure and narrative cinema', in *Movies and Methods*, vol. 2, Bill Nichols (ed.), Berkeley: University of California Press, p. 308.

10 For a full discussion of this point, see Susan McClary, 'Introduction: a material girl in Bluebeard's castle', in *Feminine Endings*, pp. 3–34.

11 See Barbara Ehrenreich (1990) *The Worst Years of Our Lives*, New York: Pantheon, pp. 251–7. It is crucial to recognize that exscription is not subcultural deviance but a mainstream ideological convention. Daniel Patrick Moynihan once proposed that the 'character defects' of young black men be solved by removing them to a 'world without women' in the military. Adolph Reed Jr and Julian Bond (1991) 'Equality: why we can't wait', *The Nation*, 9 December, p. 733.

12 Fiske, 'British cultural studies', p. 263. Fiske properly discusses the links between such a concept of masculinity and its context of patriarchal capitalism.

13 Of course, some women also find such images attractive, as I will discuss below. But the point is that 'the social definition of men as holders of power is translated not only into mental body images and fantasies, but into muscle tensions, posture, the feel and texture of the body' (not to mention the music). R. W. Connell (1987) *Gender and Power: Society, the Person, and Sexual Politics*, Cambridge, MA: Polity Press, p. 85.

14 When I first started studying metal, a friend and I discovered we were reading a Judas Priest concert film in these two very different ways. Occasionally, the 'threat' (for straight men) of homoeroticism is addressed directly, as by metal star Ted Nugent, who remarking during a concert, 'I like my boys in the band, as long as they don't fucking touch me.' On the theory of 'negotiated' readings of popular texts, see Horace M. Newcomb (1984) 'On the dialogic aspects of mass communication', *Critical Studies in Mass Communication*, 1, pp. 34–50.

15 Klaus Theweleit (1989) *Male Fantasies*, vol. 2, Minneapolis: University of Minnesota Press.

16 For example, many Judas Priest songs, such as 'Hard as iron' and 'Heavy metal', from *Ram It Down*, and the album cover art from *Ram It Down*, *Screaming For Vengeance* and *Defenders of the Faith*.

17 Tipper Gore (1987) *Raising PG Kids in an X-rated Society*, Nashville: Abingdon

Press, pp. 17–18. William Graebner (1988) 'The erotic and destructive in 1980s rock music: a theoretical and historical analysis', *Tracking: Popular Music Studies*, 1 (2), 8–20.

18   Joseph W. Slade (1984) 'Violence in the pornographic film: a historical survey', *Journal of Communication*, 34 (3), 153. See also Linda Williams (1989) *Hard Core: Power, Pleasure, and the 'Frenzy of the Visible'*, Berkeley: University of California Press.

19   All from the album *Back for the Attack* (1987); further examples of this type of song can also be found on earlier Dokken albums, such as *Tooth and Nail* (1984). 'Looks that kill' is from Mötley Crüe's *Shout at the Devil* (1983); 'Still of the night' is on Whitesnake's *Whitesnake* (1987).

20   On this reading of the presentation of women in nineteenth-century opera, see Catherine Clément (1988) *Opera, or the Undoing of Women*, Minneapolis: University of Minnesota Press.

21   See, for example, the E Minor Partita; or see Susan McClary's (1987) analysis of the Brandenburg Concerto No. 5: 'The blasphemy of talking politics during Bach year', in *Music and Society: The Politics of Composition, Performance, and Reception*, Richard Leppert and Susan McClary (eds), Cambridge: Cambridge University Press, pp. 13–62. As I have argued elsewhere, such comparisons are neither arbitrary nor coincidental: album liner credits, published interviews with musicians and the musical analyses in guitarists' trade journals all make explicit the relation of Baroque musical discourse to that of heavy metal, a relationship resulting from the continuing circulation of classical music in contemporary culture, and metal guitarists' conscious and meticulous study. See Robert Walser (1992) 'Eruptions: heavy metal appropriations of classical virtuosity', *Popular Music* 11 (3), 263–308.

22   In a stunning projection of violence onto the victim, the lyrics of 'Midnight maniac', by Krokus (*The Blitz*, 1984), warn of a female sex maniac creeping about at night, breaking in and killing; the singer evokes the terror of the presumably male victim.

23   I have written elsewhere about the musical organization of this song; see Robert Walser (1989) 'Bon Jovi's alloy: discursive fusion in Top 40 pop music', *OneTwoThreeFour*, 7, 7–19.

24   Rob Tannenbaum (1989) 'Bon voyage', *Rolling Stone*, 9 February, pp. 52–8, 132–3.

25   This distinctive harmonic progression is more fully discussed in Chapters Two and Three of *Running with the Devil*.

26   See Steven Neale (1983) 'Masculinity as spectacle: reflections on men and mainstream cinema', *Screen*, November–December, 24 (6), 2–16; and Laura Mulvey, 'Visual pleasure and narrative cinema'.

27   Susan Orleans (1987) 'The kids are all right', *Rolling Stone*, 21 May, pp. 34–8, 108–11.

28   Mulvey, 'Visual pleasure and narrative cinema', p. 309.

29   See the album cover photos in Poison's *Open Up and Say . . . Ahh!* and the even more androgynous look on their first album, *Look What the Cat Dragged In*. See Mötley Crüe's photos on the albums *Shout at the Devil, Theatre of Pain* and *Girls, Girls, Girls*. Such images fill the pages of metal fan magazines like *Hit Parader, Metal Mania, Faces, Metal Edge* and *RIP*.

30   See Steven Simels (1985) *Gender Chameleons: Androgyny in Rock'n'Roll*, New York: Timbre Books. In 1987 the same costume designer was employed by both Liberace and the metal band W.A.S.P.; see Anne M. Raso (1987) 'Video: behind the reel', *Rock Scene*, July, p. 68.

31 Fredric Jameson (1979) 'Reification and utopia in mass culture', *Social Text*, 1 (1), 130–48.

32 Dick Hebdige (1979) *Subcultures: The Meaning of Style*, New York: Methuen, p. 17.

33 For explanations of the affective character of the various musical modes and their self-conscious deployment by heavy-metal musicians, see *Running with the Devil*, especially Chapters Two and Three.

34 John Stix (1989) 'Ready or not', *Guitar for the Practicing Musician*, March, p. 56.

35 Roberta Smoodin (1986) 'Crazy like David Lee Roth', *Playgirl*, August, p. 43.

36 Dave Marsh (ed.) (1985) *The First Rock & Roll Confidential Report*, New York: Pantheon, p. 165.

37 Kim of Cathedral City (1989) *RIP*, February, p. 6.

38 Ray R., Winter Springs, Florida (1989) *RIP*, May, p. 6.

39 Interview with Scott, 30 June 1989, St Paul, Minnesota.

40 Besides observing this behaviour among members of various bands, I discussed it openly with musicians during two interviews. Such behaviour is equally widespread among orchestral musicians; indeed, it occurs whenever men transgress against hegemonic norms of masculinity by acting expressive, sensitive or spectacular.

41 George Sulmers (1987) 'Anthrax: metal's most diseased band', *The Best of Metal Mania #2*, p. 24.

42 Kaja Silverman (1986) 'Fragments of a fashionable discourse', in *Studies in Entertainment*, Tania Modleski (ed.), Bloomington: Indiana University Press, pp. 139–52.

43 For a critical view of this position, see Rita Felski (1989) *Beyond Feminist Aesthetics: Feminist Literature and Social Change*, Cambridge, MA: Harvard University Press. Felski's criticism of avant-garde strategies of textual disruption as political action rests on her perception of a conflation of gender and class: avant-garde art is as elitist as anything it might challenge. It is worth noting that the same problem hardly exists with heavy metal.

44 See Jane Flax (1990) 'Postmodernism and gender relations in feminist theory', in Linda J. Nicholson (ed.), *Feminism/Postmodernism*, New York: Routledge, Chapman & Hall, pp. 39–62.

45 Pat Benatar discusses the difficulty of creating her own hard-rock image: 'I never considered the character [I play] to be a sex symbol. I just was looking for extreme strength and self-assuredness. . . . I listened to a lot of male-dominated groups like the Stones and Led Zeppelin. There weren't a lot of women around to emulate, no one female figure, so I took a shot in the dark and tried to figure out a way to do this without looking stupid and victimized.' Joe Smith (1988) *Off the Record*, New York: Warner Books, pp. 406–7.

46 Laurel Fishman (1988) 'Lita Ford', *Metal*, May, pp. 36–8. One fan told me that she was contemptuous of Ford and other female metal musicians because they are 'stupid sex objects', but also that she saw some of the male musicians the same way. Interview with Rita, 30 June 1989.

47 For writings which focus on female reception of heavy metal and hard rock, see Daniel J. Hadley, (1991) ' "Girls on Top": women and heavy metal', unpublished paper, Department of Communications, Concordia University, Montreal; and Lisa A. Lewis (1990) *Gender Politics and MTV: Voicing the Difference*, Philadelphia: Temple University Press, especially pp. 149–71. Both Hadley and Lewis discuss the fanzine *Bitch*, wherein female heavy-metal fans debated the meanings of their own involvement with metal.

48 Sue Wise (1990) 'Sexing Elvis', in Simon Frith and Andrew Goodwin (eds), *On Record: Rock, Pop, and the Written Word*, New York: Pantheon, pp. 390–8.

49　This was debated at length during an interview with Lisa, Tammy and Larry, 30 June 1989.

50　From her cross-cultural study of androgyny, Wendy Doniger O'Flaherty asserts that the androgyne expresses 'conflict between one sex's need for and fear of the other, . . . primarily the male's need for and fear of the female'. She concludes: 'Dangling before us the sweet promise of equality and balance, symbiosis and mutuality, the androgyne, under closer analysis, often furnishes bitter testimony to conflict and aggression, tension and disequilibrium. . . .' Wendy Doniger O'Flaherty (1980) *Women, Androgynes, and other Mythical Beasts*, Chicago: University of Chicago Press, pp. 331, 334.

51　See, for example, the letter from 'Hard rockin' and homosexual, Boston, Massachusetts', (1989) *RIP*, August, p. 5; and a letter decrying sexism in metal by a female musician in *RIP*, May, 1989, p. 5.

52　Philip Gordon (1989) 'Review of Tipper Gore's *Raising PG Kids in an X-rated Society* and Dee Snider's *Teenage Survival Guide*', *Popular Music*, 8 (1), January, p. 122.

53　Kaplan, *Rocking Around the Clock*, p. 72.

54　Fred Pfeil (1988) 'Postmodernism as a "structure of feeling" ', in *Marxism and the Interpretation of Culture*, Cary Nelson and Lawrence Grossberg (eds), Urbana: University of Illinois Press, pp. 381–403.

55　Fiske, *Television Culture*, p. 317. Moreover, such explorations are not unique to capitalist societies, nor are they reducible to epiphenomena of commerciality. From his study of the music of the Venda people of South Africa, ethno-musicologist John Blacking learned that fantastic music is not an escape from reality; it is a creative exploration of reality, and of other possibilities. John Blacking (1973) *How Musical is Man?*, Seattle: University of Washington Press, p. 28.

56　Simon Frith and Angela McRobbie (1978/9) 'Rock and sexuality', *Screen Education*, 29.

57　See George Lipsitz (1990) *Time Passages: Collective Memory and American Popular Culture*, Minneapolis: University of Minnesota Press, p. 102.

58　I would like to thank Susan McClary, George Lipsitz, Wendy Kozol, Carolyn Krasnow, Andrew Goodwin and Diane Shoos for their helpful comments on earlier drafts of this paper, and Metal Mark, Gary Thomas, Nancy Armstrong and many heavy-metal fans for illuminating conversations. For a fuller discussion of heavy-metal music and politics, see *Running with the Devil*.

Part IV
CONCLUSION

10

THE MEDIA ECONOMY OF ROCK CULTURE: CINEMA, POST-MODERNITY AND AUTHENTICITY

Lawrence Grossberg[1]

Two of the most obvious cultural developments in postwar Western societies are the emergence of televison and of rock culture. Because of their increasing domination of leisure time and popular taste, some people, myself included, have argued that the interactions and contradictions between these two cultural vectors offer a powerful map of the contemporary cultural situation. It is easy to understand, then, why some critics have privileged music video as not merely another example of various trends in contemporary society, but as the *ultimate* example: of commodification, of the incorporation of authenticity and resistance, of textual and psychological schizophrenia, of the 'postmodern' disappearance of reality, and of new forms of resistance.

Such apocalyptic interpretations of music video often avoid the real work necessary to understand the historical effects of music video: its relations to reality, experience and subjectivity (ideology), its place in everyday life, the ways it is 'plugged into' the material, social and cultural world. Music video exists in a complex set of relationship, even within any single domain of social life. Economically, it exists within an industrial–corporate structure as a particular sort of commodity implicated in the production of surplus value (profit). It has its own modes of production and distribution, and its own relationship to specific capitalist ideologies (corporatism, consumerism, etc.). Aesthetically, its texts construct meanings through specific practices, languages, syntaxes, iconographies and rhetorics. Music video, as a set of cultural practices, has historical, intertextual and intermedial ties with other cultural forms. And music video exists within a range of social relationships: it is consumed, by different social groups, for specific reasons and in specific ways.

Although music video is not limited to any single form of popular music, its impact and notoriety in contemporary society depend largely on its relationship to rock culture. I propose to look at some of the ways music video has intervened in, or more accurately, been caught up in, the changing relations and forms of rock culture (e.g., the changing relations between stars, music and fans). I have argued elsewhere (Grossberg 1988) that music television involves, in part, the reconciliation of the contradictions between the two dominant media of postwar popular culture: rock and television. In this essay, I want to extend that argument to suggest that music video is also about the changing ratio, in rock and youth cultures, between sound and vision. Music video is a billboard announcing a new media economy. The claim that the ratio between sound and vision, as sensorial relations to culture, is changing, is not the same as the common complaint that music video limits the imaginative freedom of its fans. Rather, I want to suggest that the popularity of music video has to be located in a larger context in which visual media and images are competing with, if not displacing, music and aural images as the site of salvation and transcendence in rock culture. Further, this changing topography of the media in people's lives points to an even more significant possibility: the increasing erosion of the form of the relationship between fan and music which has characterized rock culture, what I will call the ideology of authenticity. If the way in which fans are able to invest in their music tastes is significantly being altered, then understanding music video may lead us to at least speculate on whether we are witnessing the beginning of the 'death' of rock culture as it has existed for thirty-five years. I am not claiming that rock music (even great rock music) has ceased to exist, or that the music of the past was better. I am talking about how fans relate to the music, and how that relationship functions in the larger historical context. I am not claiming that we can conclude from contemporary tastes that the music does not matter (because, as has often been argued, the quality of the music cannot sustain the commitment). I am not even claiming that the music does not matter; rather, I am trying to describe the possibility that the ways in which the music matters are changing, and that these changes can be understood in part by examining the changing media economy of rock culture. I do not mean to suggest that music video has killed it. Rather, I am interested in how music video fits into the changing shape and power of rock culture in the contemporary world. Consequently, I will approach the question indirectly, using the history of rock cinema rather than music video to point to a part of the larger context within which music video has to be understood.

Discussions of music video are often plagued by the uncertainty of their object: what constitutes music video as a new cultural form? While the answer may seem intuitively obvious, there are good reasons for posing the question. For example, in a 1986 contract dispute between the Screen Actors' Guild and the major Hollywood production studies, the arbitrator ruled that music videos did not necessarily constitute a new form of entertainment; if they did, actors would have to be paid additional royalties. Instead the arbitrator argued that music videos produced in conjunction with films were just another form of exploitation or promotion (Gaines, 1991). This functional definition of music videos is in fact rather common: music videos are often assumed to be merely promotional clips – new forms of advertising – for songs, albums, films or products. Such a definition ignores everything but the economic relations organized around and by music video.

186

Alternatively, some critics start with the structural uniqueness of music video. But if we try to identify the text of music video, the 'unit of critical analysis', we seem to always fall back upon the measures of popular music and/or televisual texts. Whether it is the single isolated video clip (the 'fragment'), or the megatext formed by the conjunction of clips (the flow of programming which is never as fragmented as critics assume), such definitions tell us nothing about the specificity of music video. In fact, many commentators on music video are actually talking about specific television formations, and ignore the significant differences between different television formats (e.g., in the US, between MTV, VH-1, BET, Nashville, Nightflight, Night Tracks, etc.). They also ignore the other ways in which music videos are placed into television (on programmes like *Miami Vice*, on the Disney Channel, in cartoons, as advertisements, as fillers on movie channels, in televised films, etc.). Nor can they explain the attempts to package music video (as video albums, concerts, or CD-Vs), or the relative failure of these efforts. Having failed to find a structural definition, we might ask if there are any formal characteristics which enable us to identify music video as a cultural form. Is there any clear single aesthetic which dominates the internal dynamic of music videos? The answer is clearly no; for every video that exhibits a 'postmodern' aesthetic, there is another video built upon more classical narrative or romantic aesthetics.

But maybe we should not begin by seeking to define music video. After all, music video, however it is understood, is constantly and rapidly changing, for, like any commercial enterprise, it responds to changes in popular taste even as it helps to shape those tastes. Moreover, popular music has been available on television for a long time. So perhaps the real question is why it has recently been singled out as a crucial site of cultural activity. That is, rather than starting with music video as a specific body of texts, I want to explore the context within which it has appeared as a singular site of cultural production and consumption, an important site of cultural and historical effects. And, as I have said, I will approach this context through a consideration of the cinema's changing place in rock culture.

THE MEDIA ECONOMY OF ROCK CULTURE

It has often been repeated that rock is the soundtrack of the lives of postwar youth. As charming as this description may be, it is inaccurate for at least two reasons. First, the soundtrack of the postwar years is also replete with bits and pieces of the history of television, not merely from theme songs but also from the narratives and dialogues that have entered into popular memory and conversation: from *Father Knows Best* to *Peter Gunn*, from *The Twilight Zone* to *Candid Camera* (to take only one moment of television's history, and one generation of the rock audience). Similarly, the cinema has contributed its own musical and rhetorical 'riffs' to the soundscape of our collective memory:

from *The Sound of Music* to *The Graduate*, from *Space Odyssey* to *Jaws*. The fact that rock has a special place in that memory says something about the relations between different media, the ratio between different senses, within rock culture (a point to which I will return later).

Second, rock has always been more than just a soundtrack, more than just 'the noise'. It has involved images, and the memory of a song is always partly visual as well. For rock has – at least until the 1980s – always carried a great deal of shared visual baggage, which was linked, not only to particular songs, but to the contours of one's taste as well. When you heard rock, you saw it as well, whether live, or in films, or on television, or on record sleeves. And when you listened, you were also seeing the performers and other fans. You were seeing styles of clothing, make-up and hairstyles, images of the sexual body and the body dancing. You were seeing, as well as hearing, fantasies and social experiences, attitudes and emotions. It is precisely because of the complex entanglements surrounding rock music that it has played such a powerful role in the lives of its fans (or perhaps it is the other way round).

The image of the soundtrack fails just because it carries the suggestion of independence; it assumes that the music can be separated from its anchor in other media and forms, that it stands as a commodity in its own right, capable of being isolated, identified and bounded. Rock has always had its own relations to the larger visual media economy, but the way in which it has been inserted into this economy is different for different rock cultures across time and taste. At different moments, for different audiences, the importance of images, the particular forms they take, and the ways they are related to the music, have varied, not only across genres and generations, but also across structures of historical and social difference.

My argument depends upon the assumption that music video is implicated in part in the changing possibilities for connecting rock with images. Here we can see the contradiction of trying to talk about rock music: for it is, at one and the same time, a powerful agent in our lives and constantly receding into the background in favour of all the activities and images that it brings with it. This is not to say that we don't, on some occasions, intently listen to the music. But I think it is true that this is only one of the ways in which we relate to the music, and not necessarily the dominant one. Here we can begin to see the difference between acoustic and visual stimuli: the latter demand a sort of attention that we can grant to, or withhold from, the former. But curiously this differential investment does not necessarily diminish music's ability to have a significant impact on our lives. In fact, it seems somehow to have enabled the music to become a crucial place at which fans invest their energy, their commitment and themselves.

Rock culture has always been intimately connected with images – of styles, stars and attitudes. Rock is often precisely about such images, which exceed the sonorial performance itself. It is rather surprising that so little has been written on the relations between rock and film, and almost nothing on rock and television.[2] Considering the latter first, television has always been centrally implicated in the history of rock music and culture. In almost every period of rock, it has been on TV, albeit in different ways and forms, for different audiences. The relationship is made even more complex by the fact that different audiences may watch the same programme differently, not only because of their own history and relations to rock music, but also because of the uses to which they put particular media and images in the context of their everyday lives and rock fandom. Fans have learned to dance from television; they have learned how to dress and act; they have learned new organizations of desire and emotion, and sometimes they have found new objects and narratives for those desires and emotions. In fact, the generations of rock fans have always been doubly coded: they are also the television generations. And if, at different times, different audiences have had different relations to rock, the same is true, although not in necessarily corresponding ways, about their relations to television.

Sometimes, television has been, for some fans, their only access to 'live' performance: as occasional acts on variety shows (e.g., The Beatles on the *Ed Sullivan Show*), as regular activities of the characters (e.g., *The Monkees, The Partridge Family*), as programmes devoted to performance (e.g., *Midnight Special*) or to the rock audience (e.g., *American Bandstand*). Television has at times provided the stage on which rock stars are born (e.g., Shelly Fabares, Rick Springfield and even the Sex Pistols). And it has occasionally offered models of the relationship to rock music (e.g., *Happy Days, Square Pegs, Best of Times*) as well as interpretations of the dominant culture's relation to the music (e.g., the infamous episode of *Quincy* on punk, the music episodes of *Wiseguy*). Television has helped us to make sense of the attitudes (e.g., *Laugh-In, David Letterman*) and images (e.g., Kookie on *77 Sunset Strip, Miami Vice*) of the rock culture. Television has always helped to make sense of the experiences of youth, and of growing up in America (e.g., from the Nelsons to the Cosbys, from *Welcome Back Kotter* to *A Different World*). Finally, every generation, and every fraction within the generation, has had its own programmes which have become part of their own cultural identity (e.g., *Dragnet*, or *The A-Team*).

While television and rock were never simply or totally opposed, the relations between them have traditionally been rather cool. While they cooperated over time in shaping their audiences and the cultural practices they appropriated, their audiences did not precisely overlap; television traditionally attracted those at either chronological end of the continuum of rock fans. For most, it served as a secondary, albeit perhaps necessary, source of material. For many fans, television has often been seen as part of the dominant culture against which the rock culture is defined. This ambiguous relationship between rock and television was due in part to the low technological quality of the visual and aural imaging of the television apparatus. But even more importantly, it was determined by the domestic context of viewing which controlled, until recently, the social situatedness of television.

Television has rarely – until the 1980s – provided original definitions of rock and style. The medium has been unable to take up a place in the ideological construction of rock and youth culture. That is, it has failed to find narrative forms which address the experiences at the centre of contemporary rock. Television has always been most successful at representing youth within the domestic context. There have been very few successful programmes, until recently that is, which have focused on youth as a peer culture; and when there were such programmes, they were (and to some extent still are) inevitably located within schools and built around the figure of the teacher. Recently, a new mode of representing youth has become very popular on television: youth via flashback. Here youth is often given its own social and cultural space, but only by virtue of having already disappeared (e.g. *thirtysomething*, *The Wonder Years*, *Almost Grown*).

The recent changes in the relations between rock and television are not solely dependent on these new narrative representations, nor on music video programming, although these are both crucial. But the relationship is deeper and more pervasive than these forms may suggest. The proliferation of advertisements and promotions using rock music as background seems to successfully speak to the diverse generations and fractions of the rock audience. But even here, the fact that so much of the music is drawn from the history of rock, rather than from its present, tells us not only about the primary audience which the ads address, but also about their inability to speak directly to the current generation of rock fans. But rock is also present as a commodity intrinsically linked to television. A recent ad campaign offers a video called 'Teen steam', starring the adolescent female lead of the prime-time sitcom, *Who's the Boss?* The product combines music video, work-out video and a chance 'to spend time' with the star and her friends 'in her room'. And yet another connection has been forged through the telephone: witness the rapidly increasing use of television to advertise '900' (limited toll) phone numbers through which fans can speak to their favourite rock stars (e.g., The Who), rappers and dance music performers. So successful have these campaigns been that Jazzy Jeff and Fresh Prince received 4 million calls in the first six months of 1988, raising the possibility that they would earn more money from the phone connection than from their album (although the music is clearly a necessary condition for the phone calls).

But rather than continuing to describe the relations between rock and television, out of which music video has emerged, I want to turn my attention to the changing relationship between sound and vision in rock cinema. Although interpreters of rock have always acknowledged the importance of filmic models like James Dean, they have rarely considered the continuing history of the relations between rock and film. In fact, I want to argue here that the contemporary youth-oriented film market is a crucial condition of

190

possibility of music video. It is no coincidence that MTV premiered in 1981, following an enormous explosion of youth films, films which exhibited an originality and appeal untapped by earlier films.

The relations between film and rock have a long and complex history. In the 1980s, that connection has become crucial in economic terms; film has become an important source of origination, distribution and profit. In 1984, all five of the best-selling pop singles came from movies. There were eight platinum soundtrack albums (including *Purple Rain*, *Eddie and the Cruisers*, *Flashdance*, *Footloose*, and *Saturday Night Fever*). *Saturday Night Fever*, released originally in 1977, had set the stage: it was not only the first film of the decade to focus on the life of contemporary youth, it also demonstrated the mutual benefits of the close relationship between film and soundtracks. *War Games* (1983) was the first film to use rock video to promote itself. This relationship, perfected in such films as *Flashdance* and *Footloose*, has become the norm and it has radically changed, not only the system by which films are exploited and promoted, but also the shape of the pop charts. And it has continued, even expanded through the decade, culminating in the phenomenal success of *Dirty Dancing*, which has sold well over 8 million albums, and has become one of the most popular videos of all time. Even films that have little to do with youth and rock culture find it necessary to take their soundtrack seriously: *Ghostbusters* created a hit theme-song, *Batman*'s soundtrack was written and performed by Prince, and even a film like *Wall Street* uses rock songs as background and narrative commentary.

But the relationship between rock music and youth films goes much deeper. By 1977, 57 per cent of all cinema tickets sold were purchased by those under 25. That figure has continued to grow. Of course, there are many reasons for the importance of cinema to youth audiences in the 1980s and 1990s, and their tastes are not confined to movies which directly represent youth culture. The teenage audience, for example, is the largest segment of the audience for contemporary horror films, and many of the decade's blockbusters (e.g., Spielberg's films, Stallone's films, *Batman*, etc.) depended upon heavy viewing by the under-25 market. Still, I think it is not coincidental that the 1980s have seen a veritable explosion of films directed towards youth which focus on the everyday lives of their audience.

ROCK CULTURE AND YOUTH MOVIES

Contemporary youth films, and their impact on rock culture, can be more clearly understood if we begin by briefly considering the youth films that were part of the emergence of rock culture. The so-called golden age of rock and 'teen films' – from the 1950s through the mid-1960s – was characterized by a small number of genres. First, and perhaps most importantly, there were films which functioned mainly to present images of rock performers and performances. The second-largest category involved films about the threat of teenage culture – juvenile delinquency, motorcycles and hot rods, or vice. The notion that films could and should represent the everyday lives of rock's fans seems to have had a minor place in the spectrum of 'teenpics'. Of course, there were films about 'mainstream' fans, but these often seemed less concerned with the actual experiences of youth than with specific activities (like the beach movies) or with narrative demands set outside the teen audience (e.g., *Gidget*, the films of Pat Boone, Frankie Avalon, etc.). Perhaps the great exception – and certainly the most powerful 1950s teen film – *Rebel Without a Cause* – was able to represent the feelings of its audience by thrusting its alienated hero into the middle of a delinquent subculture. The films produced in the decade between 1967 and 1977 were concerned mostly with the counterculture: hence, they often focused on the social and historical impact of the events of the decade, including the music (e.g., *Wild in the Streets*, *Privilege*, *Performance*). There were important exceptions to this inflection of the focus on youth and music: *Mean Streets* and *The Graduate* used the music to explore feelings of those not typically included in representations of youth and rock culture. Films such as *Bless the Beast and the Children* and *Joshua Then and Now* spoke more directly to the feelings and experiences of youth, however awkwardly.

The explosion of contemporary youth films provides one of the conditions of possibility for the emergence of music video. This involved not merely linking images with music but gradually shifting the location of the central representations and languages of youth culture. That is, even before MTV premiered in 1981, the cinema was already redefining the media economy of rock, with the ratio shifting from the primacy of musical (sound) images to that of visual images at the intersection of youth and rock cultures. It is not coincidental that the years 1978–80 provided the initial signs of the explosion of youth films, although many of the best movies from this period were not exactly box-office smashes (e.g., *Over the Edge*, *The Wanderers*). If the 1970s ignored youth culture, except retrospectively in its representations of the counterculture (*American Graffiti* in 1973 was a crucial exception, a foreshadowing of at least one trend yet to come), the three years between 1978 and 1980 provided a time for experimenting with all sorts of ways of attracting and representing the youth audience. There were an enormous number of performance films (e.g., *The Last Waltz*, *The Kids are Alright*, *Rust Never Sleeps*, *No Nukes*, *The Secret Policeman's Ball*, *Shell Shock Rock*, *The Decline of Western Civilization*) as well as films about rock (*Heavy Metal*, *The Idolmaker*, *Roadie*, *Can't Stop the Music*) and films about the history of rock, presaging the nostalgia revival (and the fascination with a certain kind of history) of the 1980s (*American Hot Wax*, *The Buddy Holly Story*, *The Blues Brothers*, *Grease*). And there were the first signs of an avant-garde underground (e.g., *Jubilee*, *Union City*).

But most importantly, there were a large number of films about fairly ordinary youth, set in the contemporary context. Here one has to mention the more successful films – *Fame*, *Flashdance*, *Animal House*, *Quadrophenia* (although technically set in the 1960s, it was treated as contemporary rather than historical). Perhaps even more important were a series of films which remained fairly marginal in terms of their box-office receipts. Some of them deserved their failure (*Times Square, Breaking Glass, I Wanna Hold Your Hand, Foxes*) while others were signs of the future of youth-oriented films: *Rock and Roll High School, The Wanderers*, Walter Hill's *The Warriors*, and *Over the Edge* (written by Tim Hunter). *The Wanderers*, while apparently nostalgic, explored the anxieties and friendships of urban adolescents. *The Warriors*, like *Rock and Roll High School*, used an almost surreal extremism to redirect attention from the signs of delinquency to the question of everyday survival. And finally, *Over the Edge*, certainly one of the greatest youth films of all times, explored the relations between postwar suburban living, and the alienation, boredom and frustration of middle-class youth. Perhaps more than any other film, it made clear the structural hostility between postwar youth and the parent–education alliance.

Each of these genres continued and multiplied in the 1980s: contemporary performance films (*Stop Making Sense*): films about rock'n'rock culture (*Sid and Nancy, Twist and Shout, Spinal Tap, Krush Groove, Purple Rain, Breakin', Beat Street*); nostalgia films (*The Big Chill, Diner, The Return of the Secaucus Seven, Dirty Dancing, Eddie and the Cruisers, Stand by Me, Breathless, Peggy Sue Got Married*). One of the most interesting developments has been the explosion of avant-garde films (some of which achieved reasonable commercial success), including *Smithereens, Brazil, Uforia, Liquid Sky, Blue Velvet, Repo Man, Brother From Another Planet, The Adventures of Buckaroo Bonzai, Down by Law, Stranger than Paradise, Robocop, Beetlejuice, Dead End Drive In*. (If Jack Nicholson was the icon of the 1970s in this genre, Dennis Hopper became the icon of the 1980s.

CINEMA AND THE REPRESENTATION OF YOUTH'S ALIENATION

But by far the most obvious explosion has involved films about youth's everyday lives, what have been called 'tits and zits' movies, although relatively few have been smash hits (*Back to the Future* is one of the exceptions). In fact, in order to talk about them, we have to make some internal differentiations. We might separate out those which represent an older fraction of youth (although whether their audience reflected this difference is doubtful): *St Elmo's Fire, After Hours, Something Wild, Bright Lights Big City, She's Having A Baby* and, to some extent, *Desperately Seeking Susan* and *Less than Zero*). What is left are what are frequently referred to as 'high school' movies, and there have been lots of them. There are literally hundreds of them besides those that I will refer to here; they are often shown on network and cable television. Some of the more successful ones were sombre and often touching re-creations of the alienation of youth: *River's Edge, The Outsiders*,

Rumblefish. But most located these feelings in a serio-comic context. A lot of them focused on one person's efforts to achieve some goal: *Girls Just Want to Have Fun*, *Top Gun*, *The Iron Eagle*, *Quicksilver*. In some, it is a question of survival, salvation and the battle between good and evil: *The Legend of Billie Jean*, *Footloose*, *Back to the Future*, *The Last Starfighter*, *Streets of Fire*, *Revenge of the Nerds*, *Porky's*, *Hiding Out*, *Heathers*, *The Karate Kid*. And in the largest group, the films focus on the needs and trials of contemporary life: *Fast Times at Ridgemont High*, *Risky Business*, *Pretty in Pink*, *Ferris Bueller's Day Off*, *Sixteen Candles*, *Valley Girl*, *Class of 1984*, *Meatballs*, *Wild Thing*, *Satisfaction*, *Seven Minutes in Heaven*.

In my experience, I have found that each generation of high-school students during the past decade has adopted a small number of these films as 'their own', as expressions of their own experiences. In each instance, a fair number of the students will have seen the films multiple times, and often they have a powerful identification, not with a single character but with the ambience of the film itself. Many of these films follow the genre conventions of other narratives: the hero seeking a particular goal, the hero fighting for justice, the hero attempting (sometimes unknowingly) to save another, the romance which cuts across incompatible cultures (usually defined by style which is sometimes, but not always, correlated with class). But in each instance, the terms of the narrative are translated into the everyday terms and concerns of youth.

I will, in the following discussion, focus on a few of these films. Some of the most successful examples of this genre do not follow typical narrative conventions; rather, they explore the everyday life of high-school students. In at least two of them – *Fast Times at Ridgemont High* and *The Breakfast Club* – we are given a map of the different clichés of youth's identity. While the former is unable to break those stereotypes because its narrative focus remains defined by the desire for romance and the demands of the genre of romance, both *The Breakfast Club* and *Ferris Bueller's Day Off* (both produced by John Hughes, the master of 1980s youth films) are about the characters' struggles to transcend such identities and find salvation in a common understanding of themselves as youth and of their alienation. (Hughes' films convey a powerful and very real sense of urgency, one that often strikes me as the visual equivalent of the music of Phil Spector). In these two films, romance is made subservient to the larger questions of youth's sense of identity, belongingness and purpose. If *Fast Times* dwells on the different styles of 'cool', *The Breakfast Club* is about breaking through those styles to uncover a shared affective relation to the world. Despite the imposed romantic ending, the film has already made it clear that these five kids – a delinquent, a jock, a preppie, a brain and a weirdo – want, above all, to escape their own imprisonment within these identities. But they cannot, or rather, in the end, they will not.

The Breakfast Club is a film about youth's sense of identity – their acceptance of their own responsibility, not only for their actions, but for their imprisonment. Each one conforms, knows it, hates it, struggles for a moment to escape it and reveal themselves, and then knowingly accepts their own conformity. They each suffer, in the school, and at home. Each in their own way is a small simulacrum of James Dean, a rebel without a cause and, in the 1980s, without a prayer. In the end, *The Breakfast Club* is a tragic statement of youth's continued desire to avoid becoming their parents – parents who beat them, ignore them, pressure them – to avoid growing up because when you do, 'your heart dies'. It is tragic because their ability to communicate with each other, to form a community of suffering and anger, is voluntarily rejected. They are all content to leave such moments of salvation and empowerment behind, to assume that they are unavoidably temporary and, even worse, tainted. That sense of alienation and empowerment is encapsulated at the beginning of the film, in Hughes' choice of the epigram (which is shattered like glass at the end of the opening credits) from David Bowie: 'And these children/ that you spit on/as they try to change their world/are immune to your consultations./They're quite aware of what they're going through.' It is this sense of awareness that lends an element of tragedy and empowerment to many of these contemporary films and that places them as both an ally and a competitor of rock.

Ferris Bueller's Day Off is both strikingly similar and frighteningly different: it too is 'a day in the life', and it too is framed by the oppressiveness of school. The family, however, remains more problematic, not the oppressor but the site of struggle (with a jealous sister) and manipulation (the film opens with Ferris giving the audience advice about how to manipulate parents). Unlike other films in the genre (with the exception of Walter Hill's), this one constantly breaks the naturalistic conventions of Hollywood realism. Moreover, it is a kind of adolescent version of Indiana Jones: Ferris constantly avoids being discovered only through the most impossible and fortuitous circumstances. Ferris himself is a kind of cool, popular, computer nerd. On the surface he appears to be not a troublemaker, but a rather superficial seeker of pleasure: the fact that he doesn't have a car constantly seems more important to him than issues or beliefs – and he constantly espouses a sort of conservative individualism: 'A person should not believe in isms, he should just believe in himself.' But this attitude, and Ferris's apparent commitment to fun, belies a number of deeper feelings. Ferris is condemned – and he accepts it as inevitable and even right – to a life which he seems not to welcome. As he repeatedly says, 'Life moves pretty fast. If you don't stop and look around once in a while, you can miss it' (echoing *Risky Business*'s 'Sometimes you've just got to say, "what the fuck" '). Like the characters in *The Breakfast Club*, Ferris seems to accept his imprisonment, and can only seek out temporary escapes, moments when the reality of life is manifested because of his own power, through his own actions. But even more importantly, it becomes clear in the end that this film belongs to the subgenre of 'salvation plots', for it is at least suggested that the entire day (during which Ferris, his girlfriend and

Cameron, his hypochondriac best friend, avoid school and attempt to have the most fun they can) has been staged for Cameron's benefit. It turns out that all of Cameron's problems are due to his oppressive family situation. Until he can assert his own right to exist against the 'sick' relationships into which his parents have placed him, he will be condemned to unhappiness, to reliving his own inadequacy. In the end, the film is triumphant when Cameron realizes that he must 'take a stand' against his parents: 'Right or wrong, I'm gonna defend it!' and assert his own right to exist. What follows – the absurdist race home – is anti-climactic, as the film itself acknowledges.

The entire genre of contemporary youth movies is often dismissed by critics, if not ignored. But these films are a key, not only to understanding the emergence and impact of music video, but also to understanding the changing place of 'youth' in contemporary social and political relations. For while these films do hearken back to earlier genres of teenpics, they are significantly different. And they refuse to privilege the earlier films or to treat them nostalgically. Rather, they are merely one among many self-conscious references to the media environment in which youth has been constructed, deconstructed and reconstructed. In the last analysis, the contemporary films bear little resemblance to the teenpics of the 1950s and early 1960s. For if the films themselves are self-consciously intertextual, their characters are often equally self-conscious, at least of their own ambiguous sense of, or contradictory search for, identity. In part, this reproduces in narrative form the fact of the multiple and competing definitions of youth available in the contemporary cultural environment: youth is alternately seen as something to be protected, victimized, celebrated, escaped and even sanctified.

If youth as a powerful ideological sign is something whose meaning is being struggled over in popular culture, then the signs of youth themselves have to be continuously reconstituted. In all of these films, there is an effort to define youth in some experiential terms which can transcend different styles, classes, desires and activities. That is, the boundaries of youth can no longer be taken for granted, traced out visually on the age or activities of individuals. Consequently, in these films, it not only seems irrelevant what it is that has to be accomplished (whether becoming the best bike-messenger, or saving one's best friend, or getting to dance on television), it often seems quite difficult to judge the age of the characters when they are not presented in high school. The Brat Pack, who have starred in many of them, are curiously capable of representing youth across a broad span of age groups, from high school to post-college. Youth is represented in terms of the experiential and affective consequences of inhabiting a certain place in the social order, of living everyday life according to someone else's maps. But youth is rarely presented as intrinsically subordinated or as isolated from the dominant culture. Youth's subordination is always active, never taken for granted or pushed into the background. Moreover, that subordination brings with it the very real sense that youth is a position of power and desire, that youth can empower itself, in its everyday life, to survive and transcend its social position. The contradictions and possibilities of contemporary youth's position seem to push every other consideration into the background; the films are often naïvely racist, sexist and homophobic, not in their everyday practices, but in the structural background within which they place themselves. In addition, the films are often puritanical, despite their superficial advocacy of the rock'n'roll lifestyle. Drugs, nudity and, to a lesser extent, concrete sexuality are virtually absent. (The most blatant exceptions are either treated more as comedies than youth movies – e.g., *Porky's* – or are rather dismal failures – e.g., *A Night in the Life of Jimmy Reardon*.) While this may be, in part, a reflection of the conservativism of the 1980s, it is within the terms of this new conservativism that contemporary youth must work out its own sense of frustration and alienation. For what is at stake transcends any single element of lifestyle or everyday life: lifestyle is not merely a question of pleasure or fun, and neither pleasure nor fun is ever sought simply for its own sake.

These films celebrate the extraordinary moments within the ordinary everyday life of youth. Or perhaps they are about the power to transform the ordinary into the extraordinary and the extraordinary into the ordinary. The narratively ordinary youth who define the major characters are always, somehow, represented as extraordinary. If the 1950s constructed youth as either carefree and innocent or inarticulate, contemporary films provide models of youth who are always exceptionally articulate and knowledgeable, who have a real need to talk and to prove their abilities, despite the fact that they can never trust talk or such vain efforts at self-justification. These films are about a certain kind of loneliness and uncertainty and the possibilities of identity and belonging. Individualism has become a sentence; condemned to seek their salvation, locked into the patterns (styles, tastes) of their own conformity. In the end, these films resemble their avant-garde cousins, not in formal or aesthetic terms, but in narrative and contextual terms. They represent the historically specific situatedness of contemporary youth, the doubly articulated alienation of history and youth; they are powerful affective statements uttered from particular places in our society, the places occupied by youth.

The last observation I want to make about these films is quite obvious: they all have a rock soundtrack. Sometimes rock defines the object of desire, the symbol of salvation and transcendence, but if one reads across the different films, there is no necessary or intrinsic worth assigned to the varied objects which serve this narrative function. And even when rock appears to be privileged (e.g., *Flashdance*), the real victory does not take place in the music but in the struggle to claim the music. The music, which may define the site of struggle, is at best the reward for a victory achieved elsewhere. More often, however, rock is incorporated into the narrative as part of the everyday lives of the characters (as is MTV in the later films). While it may be used (as in *The Breakfast Club*) as the empowering occasion for transgression, it may also be the soundtrack for other transgressive activities. In fact, more than anything else, rock is the soundtrack of the narrative representation of youth. Otherwise it has little privilege of its own.

Unlike the teenpics of earlier decades, in which either fun or resistance defined the taken-for-granted subtext, contemporary youth movies construct a dialectic between a certain sort of alienation and a struggle for empowerment. In so far as they are successful – and I have argued that they are – they compete with rock culture and even threaten to displace it as the voice of youth in the 1980s and 1990s. If rock seeks to empower its audiences by juxtaposing the transcending possibilities of everyday life against the social conditions of contemporary existence (so that everyday life is the site of the transcendence of history), these films rather cynically locate the very need for transcendence within the tortured boundaries of everyday life. If rock heroes exist ambiguously as people we relate to and people we aspire to, the star characters of these films refuse the responsibility of defining their audience's aspirations.

I am making what I suppose will be a rather unpopular claim: that these films construct a different relationship between rock and youth. For they speak about generations which have increasingly seen themselves visually represented, and that audience is broader than the high-school or college-age youth who populate their universes. Unlike the counterculture films of the 1960s and 1970s, these films refuse to accept any single definition of youth as the 'proper' locus and identity. And unlike the teenpics of the 1950s and 1960s, these films claim to speak *for* youth. The visual representation has – or at least struggles to – displaced the privileged place of rock, even as it may represent it. Rock is offered, not as the measure of the authenticity of youth, nor even as the soundtrack of youth's lives, but as the soundtrack of youth's media representations, commercial representations of youth's own struggles for salvation and identity. Here visual narratives displace or at least challenge rock music, for the soundtrack of such narratives cannot also be the soundtrack of our lives (at least within the terms of rock's own ideology).

AUTHENTICITY AND THE LIMITS OF ROCK'N'ROLL

I want to talk about the possible end of the formation of rock culture. I do not mean to suggest that the music of the 1980s is somehow intrinsically worse. Nor do I mean to suggest that there are objective musical criteria for rock which, for some reason, contemporary producers are unable to fulfil. In fact, I think the rock music of the 1980s is at least as good as any other period in postwar popular culture. Nor do I mean to argue that rock must necessarily politicize its fans – a task which contemporary rock seems decidedly unable to accomplish. I am not talking about rock as a musical form, or as a tool for political consciousness, but as a cultural formation. And as a cultural formation, rock involves much more than just music. It is ultimately dependent on the relationships which exist between the music, other cultural practices, the historical context, and the fans. It is for this reason that it is so difficult to define rock in musical terms, for what music counts as rock, at a particular time and place, for a particular group of fans, depends upon the way in which the music is made to (or is able to) function within the everyday lives of its fans.

Objectively, rock is a postwar musical culture, produced by a reconfigured music industry, for an audience, self-consciously defined (by the industry, the audience and other social institutions) by a system of generational and social differences. On this model, rock is music made explicitly for youth, although it remains unclear whether youth is defined by the ever-repeating appearance of younger generations or by the historical appearance of a specific generation of youth. In either case, the socio-cultural field divided by youth's difference is always also divided by structures of class, race and gender. Out of this diversity, a variety of rock cultures are constructed. And often, one of these cultures is taken as the central, dominant or 'proper' form of rock. But any attempt to define rock once and for all simply normalizes one group's articulation of it.

As a cultural formation, rock had a beginning and, it is reasonable to assume, it may have an end. It emerged at a specific historical moment, into and as a response to a specific historical context. There were identifiable conditions of possibility which enabled the rock culture to take shape and to occupy such an important place, not only in the cultural lives of its fans but increasingly in the cultural life of the society. I shall only address two of these conditions here.[3] First, the 'baby boom' created a very real population explosion, creating a youth generation which had enormous consequences for postwar society. Not only did the baby boom present economic possibilities, it also posed very real social problems. And by its very presence, it was implicated in the growing ideological contradictions of America's sense of its own youthfulness. Consequently, rock functioned as a statement of, and response to, the particular forms of alienation determined by the contradictory structures of empowerment and subordination into which the baby boom was placed. Second, the appearance of certain rather apocalyptic events, experiences and statements (from the boredom of the suburbs to the terror of the atomic bomb) increasingly presented the world as meaningless, history as irrational and the future as impossible. Whether these were merely the latest example of '*fin de siècle*' rhetoric is irrelevant for, in the postwar context, they had very real effects. They produced a crisis of sorts in youth's ability to connect the meanings and values which they inherited – the languages they had to speak and in which they had to live their lives – to the historically defined affective or volitional possibilities of survival and empowerment. Increasingly, gaps seemed to appear between the ideological possibilities of controlling one's life and the affective impossibility of intervening into the future. Everyday life seemed to be increasingly marked by

199

places where youth was unable to anchor its maps of what the world means in its maps of what can and should matter. Rock, then, articulated the intersection of this historical experience of 'postmodernity' with that of the alienation of youth.

If we want to understand the power of the music around which the various rock cultures were constructed, we have to locate the music within this historical context. The power of rock depended upon its ability to be articulated into this context at specific locations, with a very specific mode of functioning. Rock opened up the possibility of investing in the present without the necessity of a future which transcends it. Or perhaps more accurately, it offered salvation without transcendence. It defined those places where ideological and affective maps could be stitched together. By offering itself as something that mattered, as a site of investment in the face of the impossibility of any rational justification for investing, rock culture continuously constructed and reconstructed new mattering maps, maps which empowered fans in new ways. It articulated the need for investing in something (something has to matter) to the rationality of disinvestment. Rock then has to be seen as a tactical response to the changing context and place of youth in contemporary society. It offered a celebration of affective investment based on the historical impossibility of ideological investment.

Thus, rock refers to an affective investment in, and empowerment by, the cultural forms, images and practices which circulate with the music for different groups of fans, each defining its own taste culture (or apparatus). Rock is defined, for particular audiences at different times and places differently, by the affective alliances of sounds, images, practices and experiences within which fans find certain forms of empowerment. Rock culture can only be described as the historically changing, overlapping systems of competing and sympathetic apparatuses, or by its mode of functioning in everyday life.

What defines rock's difference – what made it an acceptable, even an important investment – is simply the fact that it matters.[4] It offers a kind of salvation which depends, in the last instance, on our obsession with it. It constructs a circular relation between the music and the fan: the fact that it matters makes it different; it gives rock an excess which can never be experienced or understood by those outside of the rock culture. And this excess in turn justifies the fan's investment in it. Rock refers, in this sense, to the excess which is granted to the music by virtue of our obsession with it. By virtue of the fact that it matters, rock is granted the excess which justifies its place. Thus it is not so much that rock's real difference matters, but rather the fact that it matters that defines its difference. Rock is empowering because it makes mattering matter again.

Consequently, the musical content and lyrical ideology of rock are always secondary to, or at least dependent upon, the fan's assumption of rock's excess, an excess produced by the ways rock is placed in the fan's everyday life.

The 'place' of rock defines possible mattering maps, maps which specify the different forms, sites and intensities of what can matter. It positions not only the elements of rock culture but other aspects of everyday life. It can determine how other things matter. Thus, for example, within rock's mattering maps, entertainment matters, but in a very different way. Or, to use a different sort of example, the fact that rock is usually located outside of the ideological institutions of the family and school (which are responsible for disciplining youth) does not guarantee rock's inherent opposition to these institutions. How rock occupies its place, how it is 'charged', cannot be separated from how it 'charges' or invigorates the fan's life. For rock works by offering the fan places where he or she can locate some sense of their own identity and power, where they can invest and empower themselves in specific ways. It is the investment in and of rock which determines other necessary and possible investments. It is in this sense that rock is enabling or empowering.

The question, then, of rock's death is a question about its changing conditions of possibility, and about its changing place – as a measure of the possibility of our investment in it. It is not merely a question of whether rock still matters, for lots of things matter in many different ways. The question is, does it matter that it matters? While I think that the historical conditions which enabled rock have changed significantly, I will focus on the question of rock's place, which is to say, on the functioning of rock's excess. But if this excess is not objectively contained in the music, how are we to measure its presence and its effects?

If the question of rock's excess escapes any normative definition of rock culture, it is nevertheless identifiable within the discourses and experiences constructed in and around the relationship between the rock fan and the music. Rock is, in part, always described by systems of tastes, and these systems are themselves organized around a particular ideology of excess, an ideology which distinguishes certain kinds of musical/cultural practices and certain kinds of fans (although the two dimensions do not always correspond). This ideology not only draws an absolute distinction between rock and 'mere' entertainment, it says that it is that difference that enables rock to matter. This ideological difference has taken many forms, which are not necessarily the same: the centre versus the margin, the mainstream versus the periphery, commercial versus independent, resistant versus co-opted. Moreover, the same distinction can be applied in very different ways to describe the same musics. In different rock apparatuses, the difference can be explained in different ways; for example, the line can be justified aesthetically or ideologically, or in terms of the social position of the audiences, or by the economics of its production, or through the measure of its popularity, or the statement of its politics. In all of these cases, the line serves, for the fan, to 'properly' distribute rock apparatuses: on the one side, entertainment; on the other, something more – an excess by virtue of which even mere fun can become a significant social statement. The excess links the social position and experience of musicians and fans with rock's ability to redefine the lines of social identity and difference. That is, the excess marks the rock fan's difference. Rock fans have always constructed a difference between authentic and co-opted rock. And it is this which is often interpreted as rock's inextricable tie to resistance, refusal, alienation, marginality, etc.

Additionally, this ideology has determined the structure of the various histories of rock, whether they are produced by fans or critics. At every moment in its history, rock fans have always identified some music which, along with their associated cultural apparatuses and audiences, are dismissed, not merely as bad or inferior rock but somehow as not really rock at all. Critics and fans have always argued that at certain moments, the dominant productions of rock had become 'establishment culture', that it has become dominated by economic interest, that it has lost its political edge, etc. Such histories read rock's ability to matter off the taste of the audience: i.e., that music can't possibly matter to anyone. The result is that the history of rock is always seen as a cyclical movement between high (authentic) and low (co-opted) points, although different fans will disagree over which moments constitute the high and the low points. Moreover, fans or critics who find themselves living in what they construct as a low point almost inevitably begin to predict the imminent 'death' of rock. It is less important, for my purposes, where the cycles are located than it is that such cycles are a constitutive part of the ideology of rock's excess. Concerns that rock has died or is dying are often the expression of the continuing power of this ideology.

Rock's excess is articulated as an ideology of authenticity.[5] But here we must be careful, for sometimes critics use the term to identify a single – and perhaps the dominant – form which authenticity takes in rock culture. But there are many forms of rock authenticity: one need only compare the various contemporary performers who might qualify as authentic rockers: Springsteen, U2, REM, Tracey Chapman, Sting, Prince, Public Enemy, Talking Heads, The Pet Shop Boys. Part of the problem is that authenticity refers to two separable dimensions: first, how and of what the music speaks (the problem of communication); second, to and for whom the music speaks (the problem of community). Nevertheless, I think it is possible to isolate three versions of this ideological distinction. The first, and most common, is usually linked to hard rock and folk rock. It assumes that authentic rock depends on its ability to articulate private but common desires, feelings and experiences into a shared public language. The consumption of rock constructs or expresses a 'community'. This romantic ideology displaces sexuality and makes desire matter by fantasizing a community predicated on images of urban mobility, delinquency and artistry. The second, often linked with dance and black music, locates authenticity in the construction of a rhythmic and sexual body. Often identifying sexual mobility and romance, it constructs a fantasy of the tortured individual struggling to transcend the conditions of their inadequacy. The third, often linked with the self-consciousness of art

202

(and manifested in art rock), is built on the explicit recognition and acknowledgement that the difference that rock constructs (and which in turn is assigned back to rock) is always constructed through the creativity and skill of the artist. Despite its rejection of the more common romantic version of authenticity, aesthetic authenticity still produces real and significant differences for its fans. As I shall argue, this form of authenticity has – in so-called postmodern pop – increasingly become a self-conscious parody of the ideology of authenticity, by making the artificiality of its construction less a matter of aesthetics and more a matter of image-marketing. The result is that style is celebrated over authenticity, or rather that authenticity is seen as just another style. But this transformation already required the changing media economy which privileges the self-reflexivity of sight over the (assumed) authenticity of sound.

My claim that the formation of rock culture may be ending is not meant as another statement of the difference, intrinsic to rock culture, between authentic rock and co-opted rock. I am not claiming that contemporary rock is co-opted, for that would merely relocate my argument within rock culture itself. I am claiming instead that the ideology of authenticity is increasingly irrelevant to contemporary taste, that the difference no longer makes a difference, that the history of rock is no longer convincingly constructed on the traditional cyclical map. And consequently, the way in which rock matters, its place in the fan's everyday life, is changing. I do not mean to assert that fans do not distinguish, within their own tastes, between authentic and co-opted rock, but rather that they do not invest the difference with any power of its own. While the music may still matter to them, it matters in a different way.[6] Thus, I am not claiming that whatever comes after rock culture will not have its own values and empowering possibilities, but merely that the difference between the contemporary situation and rock culture are significant enough to warrant our taking note of them. If the ideology of authenticity is becoming irrelevant, then the difference doesn't matter and we can, in very noticeable ways, become rather blasé about the configurations of rock taste. In fact, as many critics have pointed out recently, there is a very real 'crisis of taste' in rock culture, where, even for the fan, no single version of rock taste seems any truer than any other. This is manifested, not only in the increasing tolerance of rock fans, and in the increasing number of cross-genre musics, but also in the fact that it is impossible today to define any model of rock taste or culture which could serve as a definition of the centre, of the proper form of rock culture.

ROCK'S MEDIA ECONOMY AND THE END OF AUTHENTICITY

There are many reasons for the deconstruction of the ideology of authenticity: it certainly has been partly determined by the changing economic and technological practices of rock's production, distribution and consumption, by the changing historical context, by the ageing of the baby boomers and the resulting struggles around youth, and so on. If we are to understand the place of music video in this event, we must locate it within the larger visual context of contemporary rock culture. I want to identify two ways in which the new media economy of rock – in which the visual increasingly speaks for, or even in the place of the musical – is involved in displacing the ideology of authenticity, and with it the possibility of rock culture itself. First, the changing ratio between sight and sound in representing the alienations of everyday life challenges the very possibility of authenticity. Second, these visual formations have become important sites at which youth responds, in new and ever more ironic ways, to the increasing consciousness of the postmodern condition of everyday life. As the visual media have incorporated and foregrounded many of the postmodern aesthetic practices (often unselfconsciously part of rock culture), the possibility and even the value of authenticity is further called into question. For what these new visual formations of youth culture make clear is that authenticity is something that is always constructed. The result is that, increasingly, these visual youth formations (contemporary youth movies and music video) speak, in the place of rock and sometimes even against rock, of salvation without authenticity.

The authenticity of rock has always been measured by its sound and, most commonly, by its voice. Obviously, given the contexts in which rock was made available to the majority of fans, it is not surprising that its ideology would focus on sound. Moreover, rock's appeal to its black roots further secured the primacy of sound. The eye has always been suspect in rock culture; after all, visually, rock often borders on the inauthentic. Visual style, as conceived in rock culture, was usually conceived of as the stage for an outrageous inauthenticity. It was here – in its visual presentation – that rock often most explicitly manifested its resistance to the dominant culture, but also its sympathies with the business of entertainment. It might be objected that the importance of live performance argues against this view of authenticity. However, the importance of live performances lies precisely in the fact that it is only here that one can see the actual production of the sound, and the emotional work carried in the voice. It is not the visual appearance of rock that is offered in live performance but the concrete production of the music as sound. The demand for live performance has always expressed the desire for the visual mark (and proof) of authenticity.

There are perhaps deeper reasons for the close connection between sound and authenticity. We might, for example, consider the comparative phenomenology of the two media. Sound surrounds the listener who appears to be overtaken, against his or her will, by it. Vision is largely confined to a single vector and remains constantly under the control of the receiver as much as of the source. Vision is always organized in recognizable ways; it is immediately available for interpretation. But music, as Guattari (1984) describes it, is 'the most nonsignifying and de-territorializing of all' cultural forms. That is, music is the most convenient discourse for the constant effort to deconstruct the structures of meaning, will and emotion which society is constantly trying to impose upon the individual desire. And hence, it is the most powerful discourse for the construction of authenticity.

Similarly, psychoanalysis has always understood that there are significant differences between the psychic economies of sound and vision. Lacan (1978) emphasized their similarities, placing both on the side of 'desire' rather than 'demand' (i.e., as opposed to the oral and anal drives, neither the visual – or scopic, nor the aural – or invocatory drives have a specific object). But Freud (1966: 24) argued that the scopic drives were linked directly to language and the instincts, while the invocatory drives were tied to the relations between id, ego and superego. In fact, sound is directly tied to both the superego and the ego (the ego 'wears a cap of hearing'); yet it is also closer to the Unconscious. If the invocatory drives are directly related to the way in which the Unconscious is constructed by the paring-off of the ego and the superego from the id, then one can understand why sound would be the site of authenticity, for it is in sound that the very construction of identity takes place. This of course contradicts many contemporary arguments about the 'mirror stage' as the first moment in which the child begins to form a sense of its own ego through the sight of its own image and that of the mother. But it is not the image that is ultimately determining; it is rather the image as it is offered – isolated, identified and appropriated – by the sound of the mother's voice.

The new cultural formations of youth films and music video increasingly foreground the visual. It is not, however, a matter of attention but of priorities. One need not pay attention to the video screen; one's attention can still be determined by the song which calls one to the television. But increasingly, the visual images compete with the sounds as markers which tie the music to the experience and desires of the audience. And in this way, it becomes irrelevant, for example, that performers are lip-syncing their own songs, or that the performance is highly mediated through the technologies of visual and sonorial editing. In fact, the ability to manipulate the presentation becomes the very measure of affective power (e.g., The Pet Shop Boys).

The second result of the new media economy is that the newly emergent cultural formations have displaced the desire for authenticity into something else. But what is it that these new formations – in which the visual image displaces or at least competes with the privileging of the aural image – offer in its place? They have not given up the demand for a transcendence of and within everyday life, for the possibility of salvation. But they have instituted a new affective logic or, more accurately, they have increasingly foregrounded an element of the rock culture which had previously existed only in contradiction with the ideology of authenticity: namely a logic of authentic inauthenticity. It operated in the circular relationship of excess that located rock at the centre of the fan's mattering map: it is merely the fact that the music matters that makes it different (authentic) and it is this difference which justifies the fact that it matters. But the sonorial text of rock could never explicitly and reflexively code this logic. Increasingly, the media economy of the new cultural formations defines a tone which is determined by this logic.

All images, all realities, are affectively equal – equally serious, equally deserving and undeserving of being allowed to matter, of being made into the markers of one's own illusory authenticity, for all authenticity can only be illusory. The only possible claim to authenticity is derived from the knowledge and admission of your inauthenticity. If we think about the link between ideology and false consciousness, it depends upon a set of specific conditions: people are acting in certain ways which imply a certain condition of the world, but they do not actually realize this implication, nor agree with its conclusion. That is, people are doing something (e.g., acting as if there were a universal ideal measure of value – capital) but they don't know that they are doing it. The logic of authentic inauthenticity is the obverse of ideology: people know what they are doing but they do it anyway, even if they claim not to believe in the values implied by what they are consciously doing. 'I believe in the truth though I lie a lot' (The Human League).

Authentic inauthenticity says that authenticity is itself a construction, an image, which is no better and no worse than any other.[7] Authenticity is, in fact, no more authentic than any other self-consciously created identity, and it has no more to do with subjective realities or objective relationships than the choice that anyone makes, at any moment, to present themselves according to the dictates of some cultural cliché. This logic foregrounds an ironic nihilism which refuses to valorize any single image, identity, action or value as somehow intrinsically better than any other. But it goes even further, refusing to accept that there is any basis on which one can justify investing oneself into any such term – even an imaginary excess. There is no reason which would make one's decisions about what matters rational. It is not that nothing matters but that, in the end, it doesn't really matter what matters. Of course, something has to matter. You have to care about some things and not others; you have to make certain choices and not others. You have to construct particular images for yourself and adopt certain identities but, according to the logic of authentic inauthenticity, you must do so reflexively (not necessarily self-consciously, one can just as easily take it for granted) knowing that there is no way to justify the choice. The only authenticity is to know and even admit that you are not being authentic, to fake it without faking the fact that you are faking it.

In terms of the visual representation of rock culture within these new formations, it becomes increasingly important for performers and directors to incorporate signs of their ironic cynicism. Within the emerging languages of these formations, authenticity is no better than and no worse than the most ironically constructed images of inauthenticity. The notion of authenticity is constantly reduced to a signifier of the performer's place within the rock culture: that is, it increasingly serves to mark the generic investments of the performer, to affirm their commitment to particular apparatuses within the rock culture. Or else it serves to problematically reinscribe the codes of performance (e.g., direct-address) which have become little more than the signs of a decreasingly powerful appeal to authenticity.

If this description of the changing media economy and of the emergent cultural logic of the new media formations is correct, it does suggest that the dominant contexts within which popular music operates in the contemporary world can no longer be described as, or in the terms of, rock culture. Nostalgia for the rock culture is an inappropriate response. We cannot assume that all popular culture, or even all popular music, or even all youth-oriented popular music, works in precisely the same ways, on the same grounds, with the same effects. History is constantly being reconstructed, often by our own practices, and often behind our backs. The very specific relationships and effects of the rock culture gave it an enormous power for a short time (and for many fans, it still has some of that power). But that very specificity also condemns it to a finite flexibility. The musical practices which have been at the centre of rock culture are increasingly being appropriated by, re-articulated into, new cultural formations. As the relations to and contexts of the music change, the forms and places of its power change as well. We cannot simply dismiss these new formations; we must look instead at how they are working, and how they can be made to work.

NOTES

1 I would like to thank Andrew Goodwin for his valuable comments on an earlier draft.
2 The *Rolling Stone Illustrated History* has a single chapter on the topic. The annually published *Rock Yearbook* has nothing on film after 1983. In the 1981 edition, films ranging from *All That Jazz* and *Apocalypse Now*, to *Fame* and *Monty Python*, are listed with plot summaries. The editions for 1982 and 1983 follow a similar format, but films are collapsed into a single article with books. There are two books – one British (Dellar 1981) and one American (Ehrenstein and Reed 1982) – which basically list rock movies with short critical evaluations. It is often difficult to tell what criteria are used to determine inclusion, other than that the film has at least one rock song in its soundtrack. Recently, a study of 'teenpics' (Doherty 1988) in the 1950s has appeared but it offers little historical interpretation and dismisses films of the 1970s and 1980s as inadequate copies of the originals. Cagin and Dray (1984) talk about a number of significant films relating to the rock culture, but never deal with the emergence of youth movies. Two articles which one might have assumed would address the issues – Britton (1986) and Hoberman (1985) – virtually ignore youth culture movies.
3 Two other conditions of possibility are worth mentioning at least. First, the rapid growth of media culture and its extension throughout society and into everyday life depended on changing technological, economic and institutional relations (including a very specific organization of the music industry). Second, rock emerged into a rather unique social and political climate: the moment of the postwar consensus built around the corporatist or social democratic state. This consensus, which rearticulated the American ambivalence towards both

progressivism and conservativism, resulted in the unique postwar form of 'liberalism'. On the one hand, a commitment to extending economic prosperity and civil liberties to all citizens was justified by an imposed sense of unity (the 'end of ideology'). On the other hand, a paranoia directed externally to the threats of communism, totalitarianism and mass culture justified a strongly regressive and often repressive political and cultural ideology. The result was a very real ambivalence about emerging cultural forms, practices and values. This political context defined the parameters of the politics of rock culture, often enabling it to assume the liberal consensus and thus to reproduce many of the dominant forms of racism and sexism.

4   I do not mean to deny that textual gestures – music and lyrics – do not play a significant role in determining fans' tastes and the ways in which they are able to use specific musics. But this, it seems to me, does not account for the particularly powerful investment that fans make in their tastes.

5   The desire for authenticity has a long history, and in its most recent appearances is certainly tied to the rise of the middle class. Moreover, the image of authenticity in rock culture derives from a particular, historical imagination of black culture, and of the relationship between the blues and its black performers and fans.

6   For a different interpretation of these processes, see Goodwin (1988).

7   It is interesting to compare the various forms in which women performers have, in the past decade, regained visibility in the various rock apparatuses: e.g., the apparent but marketed authenticity of the Indigo Girls, the obvious inauthenticity of Madonna, the authenticity conferred via the college rock scene to Throwing Muses, etc. I also want to point to MTV as a very obvious site of this logic; it is not surprising, therefore, to find that MTV is increasingly going beyond music video to offer itself as a visual youth culture alternative to other channels.

REFERENCES

Britton, Andrew (1986) 'Blissing out: the politics of Reaganite entertainment', *Movie*, 31/32, 1–42.

Cagin, Seth and Phillip Dray (1984) *Hollywood Films of the Seventies: Sex, Drugs, Violence, Rock'n'Roll and Politics*, New York: Harper & Row.

Clark, Al (ed.) (1980–3) *The Rock Yearbooks, 1981–1984*, London: Virgin.

Dellar, Fred (1981) *NME Guide to Rock Cinema*, Middlesex: Hamlyn.

Doherty, Thomas (1988) *Teenagers and Teenpics: The Juvenilization of American Movies in the 1950s*, Boston: Unwin Hyman.

Ehrenstein, David and Bill Reed (1982) *Rock on Film*, New York: Delilah.

Freud, Sigmund (1966) *Standard Edition of the Complete Psychological Works*, vol. 19, London: Hogarth.

Gaines, Jane (1991) *Contested Culture: the Image, the Voice and the Law*, Chapel Hill: University of North Carolina.

Goodwin, Andrew (1988) 'Sample and hold: pop music in the digital age of reproduction', *Critical Quarterly*, 30 (3), 34–49.

Grossberg, L. (1988) 'You still have to "fight for your right to party": music television as billboard of postmodern difference', *Popular Music*, 7, 315–32.

Guattari, Felix (1984) *Molecular Revolution: Psychiatry and Politics* (trans. Rosemary Sheed), New York: Penguin.

Hoberman, J. (1985) 'Ten years that shook the world', *American Film*, June, 34–59.

Lacan, Jacques (1978) *The Four Fundamental Concepts of Psycho-analysis* (trans. Alan Sheridan), New York: W. W. Norton.

Miller, Jim (ed.) (1980) *The Rolling Stone Illustrated History of Rock & Roll*, New York: Random House/Rolling Stone Press.

Robbins, Ira A. (ed.) (1985) *The Rolling Stone Review 1985*, New York: Rolling Stone Press and Charles Scribner's Sons.

NAME INDEX

FILM, TV PROGRAMME
AND VIDEO INDEX